ART OF DARKNESS

Sara K. Schreider Copy

OTHER BOOKS BY SARA K. SCHNEIDER

CONCERT SONG AS SEEN:
KINESTHETIC ASPECTS OF MUSICAL INTERPRETATION
(PENDRAGON PRESS)

VITAL MUMMIES: PERFORMANCE DESIGN FOR THE
SHOW-WINDOW MANNEQUIN
(YALE UNIVERSITY PRESS)

ART OF DARKNESS

Ingenious Performances by Undercover Operators,
Con Men, and Others

Sara K. Schneider

Cuneiform Books
Chicago, Illinois

Cuneiform Books
P.O. Box 412456
Chicago, IL 60641
www.cuneiformbooks.com

Printed in the United States of America

Schneider, Sara K.
    Art of Darkness: Ingenuity in Performances by Undercover
    Operators, Con Men, and Others.
    4 6 8 10 9 7 5 3 1
    Includes bibliographic references and index.
    ISBN-13 978-0-9793093-0-4 (paper: alk. paper);
    ISBN-13 978-09793093-1-1 (cloth: alk. paper)

In memory of the playful Marjorie M. K. Schneider

Things are disguised. Actions are disguised. Reasons are disguised. Results are disguised. Objectives are disguised. Maneuvers are disguised. Everywhere you look in connection with deception—be it performer, apparatus, movements or what not—one encounters disguise in some form.

—Dariel Fitzkee (1945)

CONTENTS

ART OF DARKNESS

INTRODUCTION

Born Originals, how comes it to pass that we die Copies?

—Edward Young, 18th century

"Not *Not*" Identities

Louise Fitzhugh's children's book *Harriet the Spy* tells the adventures of a young girl born to inattentive upper-crust parents on New York's Upper East Side. Enjoying the benign oversight of her nanny, sixth-grader Harriet spends her after-school hours on her "spy route." Her flashlight, notebook, pencil case, and canteen hooked onto her belt, she shimmies up to her neighbors' high-rise windows and skylights and makes careful notations on their activities. Harriet's pied subjects include a reclusive wealthy divorcée who spends most of the day in bed on the telephone; an Italian-grocery family; and a man who shares his apartment, despite all Health Department efforts, with 26 cats.

Harriet is spy, anthropologist, and story-weaver, and she was my childhood heroine. In identifying with Harriet, I wore a trench coat around the house and leaned up against walls, peering around corners and being a generally vigilant kid. I was delighted when I needed my first pair of glasses—very investigative! Harriet's were black-rimmed, though hers had no lenses.

For Harriet, things go terribly wrong when her classmates seize her notebook and her frank opinion of each of them is made known: her paperwork does her in. However, Fitzhugh's book is not just a morality tale about the danger of keeping secrets (well, of leaving a visible trail of them); it's also about the delights of observing and analyzing others' behavior in a unilateral way—being omniscient and invisible, even if temporarily. Harriet doesn't merely record what she sees: she goes searching for problems, questions, perplexities, and then works them out in her notebook.

In my *Harriet* days, I wanted to see the act of spying as monocu-
larly powerful: others acted, I recorded and analyzed. Now I see
that in her own story Harriet, just like other detectives, spies, and
undercover workers, had entered a web of activity in which many
other players were also striving for omniscience and invisibility.

Through the *Harriet the Spy* years, I pictured myself grown up
as a man in a gunmetal-grey business suit, carrying a mean briefcase. This was during the 1960s and 1970s—when women who
entered the workplace did so in some senses as "men," emulating
their successful male predecessors and role models. Born to a family that had already produced three boys in short succession half a
generation before I came along, I wanted very much to catch up
with my high school-age brothers, to be where the action seemed
to be. The only apparent alternative was to remain their baby-
sister toy, singing "Hello, Dolly" dutifully into a reel-to-reel tape
player or posing atop the bathroom counter so they could tease
my hair up into a troll hairdo. At the age of five I told my parents
not to assume I would want to play with another girl just because
she happened to share my biological age. Such external signs of
commonality as age seemed arbitrary and unconvincing to me as I
sought to establish rapport with others in the world.

Training me to sing the scores of their favorite Broadway musi-
cals was my big brothers' game. Mine was to "pass"—in my imagination, anyway—as one of them, older and self-consciously ungirly.
When there was the chance to pick out new furniture for my bedroom, I selected for my bachelor pad-style "mod" modular
furniture pieces, in sun yellow and parrot green. (It was, after all,
the '70s.) The arrangement made me feel I wasn't still living under
my parents' thumb or my brothers' whimsy (even though I didn't
get the separate entrance I wanted).

Like my age and gender, the racial identity I inherited sometimes seemed a strange, and not necessarily natural, choice. Once
in college on the East Coast, I took the train to New York City to
see a passionate performance by the Alvin Ailey American Dance
Theater. A contemporary jazz and modern dance company pro-
moting black dancers, this company floored me, a longtime ballet
student, with the power of those who danced with a personal conviction I'd never before seen; they seemed to dance not someone
else's steps or technique, but their very selves.

Returning to school, I tried to balance respectfulness and camp as I took on a black persona, "Luana" ("Magnolia" to my friends) that gave me a sense of groundedness in my own reality that I couldn't yet find in my experience of myself as a white woman. I'd quip edgily, "I'm tired of being judged by the color of my skin!"—meaning, tired of being taken for white (for example) just because I look so and, on the outside at least, am white. But now the tongue-in-cheek plaint stands in for a whole host of personal identifiers that, along with my age, race, gender, and birth order, have seemed arbitrary at best.

It's possible I didn't become a woman—or maybe even a girl—till I was 30. At this point, I think I'm finally white.

You could say it's a triumph to grow at last into one's color, age, or gender—if your idea of authenticity is reconciling your inner sensibilities under all conditions to your outward "body categories." Except that playing in public doesn't work like that. Even now, I am Jewish when it suits me, not particularly identified by religion or ethnicity when I can get away with it.

Even when they don't specifically intend to deceive another, many people frequently experience some disjuncture between how they appear and how they experience themselves. Elders frequently remark that they feel themselves to be an age that is a fraction of their body-years. A professional peer group can seem more real than one's "own" age or ethnic groups. I think of a fair young acupuncturist and chiropractor I went to see who told me he thought of himself as a wizened old Chinese man, despite his English schoolboy looks. The body dysmorphic disorder of anorexics and bulimics, who pathologically misrepresent in their own minds the size of their bodies, is perhaps merely an extension of the experience of those of us who continually bump into furniture, misremembering our hips as being the same width as when we were adolescents.

I'd been searching for the subtleties of identity, given that, even well into adulthood, I readily experienced cross-category identifications—on some level, I was not *not* a gay man, or a substantial black woman, or a host of other ways of being. And so, oozing between my somewhat categorical rejections of my given qualities was my sense that there had to be a way of thinking about identity that transcended gender polarization and other, largely physical, identifiers. Even in the 1990s, diversity trainings focused on these "hard," or given, categories, helping different populations working together for the first time to do so with respect. Yet it still felt as though we hadn't made public the real diversity. Through one's internal processes and through the unique relational dynamics between any two human beings, one can *become* a different person, even slip into the skin of another.

The real identity game is neither about the individual body nor the solo self. Rather, it is socially constructed, embedded in the interplay between my perceptions and yours of what I *might* be, between the shape of the nest you make for my identity project and the one I make for yours. Identity play, this book argues, takes place not in the *self*, but in the *scene*.

Elementary Collusion

Western culture has long dallied with the identity player—the spy, the undercover cop, the federally relocated witness, among others—which has had all to do with the dramatic potential these players have for getting into close scrapes, as their identities are questioned, challenged, and defended. The key factors are that these identity players' audiences are there—and active. The enormously popular genre of detective fiction and the vast universe of movie and television programs whose heroes are identity artists survive because the relationship between an identity worker and those he plays off of is inevitably a hot one.

On both sides of the law, identity artists operate in the material and face-to-face universes, altering their physical appearances, their documents, and their stories to capture what—or whom—they want. Most of the identity encounters in this book depend on face-to-face, mutually reinforcing games of wit, based solely on the matches possible between talking, performing criminal deceivers and their marks, and between those same deceivers and the law enforcers who perform strikingly similar deceptions on *them*.

As a society, we readily make room for the roleplays of children. We believe, for children to grow up to become productive members of society, they must engage wholeheartedly in identity play early in life, trying on various social roles. Indeed, one of the most profitable toy categories for young American girls is "dress-up." We also expect adolescents to try things on, to experiment, even sometimes with risky behaviors. By adolescence, what we call roleplay has a clearly social dimension, as we acknowledge how peer pressure and other forms of influence etch a boundary around the self.

By adulthood—we're led to believe—the roleplay should be over and, in many cases, at the level of the costume play and the overt behavior testing, it is largely curtailed. But an identity play more subtle than this is part and parcel of adult life in the free-market economy, where we devise credible identities—with our audience's help—to get jobs, friends, political office, and other desirable objects. In addition to asserting identity's interactive construction, then, this book assumes that identity play—far from being merely the work of childhood—remains a pervasive activity of adult social life in both work and play.[1]

Such interactions never occur in a vacuum; they take root in the structures and contexts of their time and place. Frank Abagnale, the virtuosic identity artist and check-passer of the 1960s and author of the memoir *Catch Me If You Can*, was able to ply his scam because of the banking practices of his time. The success of his schemes hinged on the length of time it took for checks to clear. However, the inter- and intrapersonal ingenuity of the performer—with an active audience—is what takes our breath away.

For a long time to come, the United States will try to make sense of what it means to have harbored terrorists unwittingly and treated them hospitably. There are many dimensions to this, and many more yet to uncover. The predominant early national coping method was to search out those who (evil) would harm us (good). A subtler and arguably more accurate formulation of the horror we have experienced acknowledges our complicity in it. However unsuspectingly, we nevertheless contributed to sabotaging one of the archetypal relationships of society, that between host and guest. A weird blend of fascination and horror overtakes us when we see that professional deceivers enter our worlds as guests—of our trust, our homes, our workplaces, our civil processes—and ply their trade from within. The host role, a sacred obligation in virtually all cultures, proves an unwise one to have played.

Knowing that dangerous others can pass among us fuels our fascination with others' secrets. The throughline of Western drama—as it unravels in stage plays, movie plots, and the docu-drama of everyday life that gossip and TV news capture so well—is very often about how a single, concealed character flaw can un-ravel an entire life. An ambitious and talented lawyer's drinking appears swank at first, allowing her to build relationships with exciting men, employers, and clients, but eventually it causes her to lose everything. The excavation of a prominent politician's sex-ual habits derails the campaign for which he's prepared his entire career.

Far from waiting for the newspapers to carry the headlines of public figures' secrets, we go searching for them, in many of our friendly first-time conversations in social gatherings of all kinds. Here's where we see that, far from disappearing from our own lives, identity work only becomes more interactive and subtle with increasing age. We game, we make deals, we strategize quietly dur-ing fights with intimates, we—in the intimate language of my Elope, my three-syllabled Labrador Retriever—sniff each other's tail ends.

A person in search of information about a potentially threaten-ing conversation partner plays a diffident game. She may open her eyes wide, act as though this were the first question she's asked all evening, so of course she's not forming any kind of composite portrait of who her conversation partner is. She knows at some level not to cock her head to the side. She files each bit of data and catalogs and sorts it on her own time, leaving no signs of what she's doing.

But the person she's inquiring about is playing a complemen-tary game. This interlocutor's act is that he doesn't sense his inter-rogator is systematically forming an impression of *him* while acting as though there were no system or story there for anyone to get about herself.

The pervasiveness of these scenes means all of us could con-sider ourselves members of the intelligence community, even in situations in which we're supposed to be friendly with each other—after all, I'm on a date (it's supposed to be pleasant), or I may hire this lawyer, or this guy does the same kind of work I do and therefore (theoretically) shares my values.

In my own identity-intelligence play in childhood and early adulthood, I was in some sense trying to have it both ways—to relate to all possible identities equally and to escape whatever identities others might say were more properly "mine." You could say I was trying for the dual prerogative sought by the master disguise artist and the undercover operative: omniscience and invisibility. It's no accident, I suppose, that I opted academically to work in the field of performance studies, which was heavily anthropological in its methods and cross-cultural in its subject matter interests; nor that I later entered the consulting world; nor that I was interested in studying undercover work, con games, and the phenomenon of passing undetected in a group to which one does not ordinarily belong. Traditionally, anthropologists have entered cultures as "professional outsiders," valuable because they can perceive patterns and behaviors that operate at a tacit level for members of the culture. Like many anthropologists, consultants usually come from outside. They are hired guns, prized not because they are any smarter than the people who already work in an organization, but precisely because of their outside perspective. By contrast, undercover operators can be thought of as "professional insiders," making their livings making others believe they're one of them.

The late twentieth century, the focus of street-level performances in this book, was a period in which personal identity and individuality were valuable currencies and thus particularly subject to fakery. However, there have been many historical periods in which this has been the case. Public fascination with professional identity fakers achieved special prominence in the eighteenth century. Count Alessandro di Cagliostro, once known merely as Giuseppe Balsamo, became one of the great impostors of his day with his claim that he was actually a man 1,800 years old; he gained work experience for his impostorship not only in other forms of crime, such as forgery, theft, procuring prostitutes, and counterfeiting, but also as a fortune teller and magician. Baroque culture gave birth to a new generation of turners of tricks (*faiseurs de tours*), who performed visual illusions that baffled spectators through their deft use of "novelty, variety, and rapid succession."[2]

Everyday people's needs to ferret out the real and useful from the sham took the plane on which virtuosity would have been mapped and tilted it. By the early nineteenth century, as an outgrowth of earlier sentiment against "charlatanism, delusive machinery, and 'technological speech,'" significant anti-virtuosic sentiment could be discerned, as well as a desire to subject virtuosic displays to rational examination.[3] Paradoxically, this made the nineteenth century a kind of art forgers' "golden age," because of market conditions, the rise of the cult surrounding the individual artist, the century-strong revival of Gothic style, and because "the rudimentary nature of expert criticism made it more economic to make fraudulent imitations than to search for authentic objects." Within the Romantic aesthetic, demonstrating that a work was the genuine production of a famous hand became more important than any sort of fidelity to a particular subject matter. The growing popular fascination with individual genius also fed the market for forgeries.[4]

This book may explode any remaining notion you hang onto that you are not at some level a member of the intelligence community, discerning who's "for real" and who's presenting a self for personal gain. In the chapters that follow, we look at the virtuoso techniques and interactions of identity players who are fugitives from the law, con artists, and above all undercover operatives—not because they are doing anything that is essentially different from what any of us does in everyday life, but because their self-awareness about their techniques can bring our own to consciousness. Like us, these virtuosi of identity seduce others into cozy mental worlds of their own making; they're just especially skilled at creating an appetite in their audience for more. Like theirs, your own most powerful fantasies take human form, and go out looking for company.

Based on my own extensive interviews of undercover operatives, observation of undercover field training, and research in the literature of deceptions, the progression of chapters takes us from the birth of a trick operating identity through its life cycle toward either a necessary or an untimely retirement. Chapter One, "Craft and Artifice: The Undercover Cover Story," looks at how undercover operators construct their trick identities through the scripting and safeguarding of their cover stories. Chapter Two, "Being

Good at Being Bad: Going Undercover," scrutinizes the casting, training, and performance techniques of the undercover operator, an expert and yet almost entirely street-trained actor. Chapter Three, "The Artifacts of Identity," establishes how the foundation of public identity is customarily built up with fake ID—the sandy bedrock that permits amateurs to practice medicine, smugglers to escape detection, and underage kids to buy liquor. Chapter Four, "The Crafty Expedient: Scenarios for Passing Trick Identities," shows how con scenarios—and, by extension, storefront operations and other undercover scenarios—are constructed. It looks at the heart of collusion, by which identity artist and mark bend their personae toward and around each other. This chapter offers insights into the scenario structures that serve the "good" and the "bad" guys alike, nearly matched identity players on opposing sides of the law. Chapter Five, "Muddied Identities," explores deceptions in which it becomes hard even for the players—undercovers and their informants—to ascertain in which of the look-alike tents deception and fact have set up camp, to determine who "us" and "them" are. The "Identity Breakdown" of Chapter Six peers into perhaps the most dramatic scene of undercover work, in which the bad guy threatens and potentially unmasks the undercover's adopted identity, or an undercover purposely stages the retirement of an identity before it can be "blown." While the chapters on identity documents and con games are based largely on secondary sources, the chapters that deal with identity play in undercover work also draw on material from interviews I conducted and undercover training sessions I observed and in which, for certain exercises, I participated.

Investigating professionals' techniques of secrecy and deception sounds like an oxymoron. And, it's true, members of the law-enforcement power structure were not exactly eager to talk at first. Agencies' entire tactical palette can be compromised by an apt description and analysis of their practices: after all, bad guys read, too. Individual undercovers do better without public attention, too. When a bad guy recognizes him, it can cut a narc's viability in the field short—literally. Even having his way of putting things appear recognizably in a book about undercover techniques can "waste" a narc for future assignments.

Federal, local, and private agencies, as well as individual operatives, did talk to me anyway, even giving me access to their undercover training. To protect themselves and their colleagues, what they shared with me often had to do with their arsenal of established practices rather than with the leading edge of their current and proposed techniques. In order to protect those still working in the field, I've quoted most undercover operators and trainers I've interviewed without attribution. Experts on undercover work not requiring anonymity—those no longer operating in the field or having already published their stories—are credited explicitly.

My informants came my way by one of two methods: referral by others in the field, generally affiliated with either United States or Canadian federal law enforcement, or local and state officers whom I observed in their undercover training. In 1995 and 1996, I attended two weeklong undercover training courses for law-enforcement officers. A training run by the Professional Law Enforcement (PLE) Group, a private Dayton, Ohio-based agency, consisted almost entirely of young officers who were being trained to infiltrate corporate and high school settings and believably take on job or student roles within them while investigating suspected drug and other problems.

The other undercover training, held in the American Southeast, focused on state and local police officers. The class of twenty or so men and two women represented a cross-section of street-experience levels, ranging from those with significant on-the-street and undercover experience, down to "baby narcs," just starting out, even down to a real newbie who referred to himself as a "narc fetus." Participants called me "Doc," and—perhaps because their undercover-movie experience had given them the notion that the only "doctor" who would be hanging out with undercovers must be a clinician—made glancing little confessions about their personalities during breaks. They included me as a participant in field roleplaying exercises—and gave me a hand when my skill at developing and enacting believable pretexts lagged miserably behind theirs.

Once I was at the trainings, participants were only too eager to talk about their work. Undercovers as a whole are a garrulous lot—that's what they're self-selected to be. Police culture, to begin with, is strongly individualistic and competitive. Officers routinely share stories about their exploits and compete with each other for honors and recognition. Good-natured but pointed put-downs were common in the everyday banter I heard among undercover trainees. Officers earn social rewards for how skillfully they devise an improvisation that saves face or propels them a major step forward in their investigation, how close they venture to an act that might lead to the breakdown of their identity without actually going that far, or how close they dance to the edge in their roleplays.

Undercover operators are by definition masterful presenters of concocted selves. Therefore, the trouble isn't getting them to talk: it's wrestling with the question of how much of what they say about themselves can be believed! In police culture, officers get good social mileage out of creating stories about what they may or may not have done. Confirming what they say is virtually impossible, as undercover work is necessarily covert and performed with few witnesses. The witnesses that are available—the bad guys— might arguably provide less reliable reports than the undercovers themselves. Even video and audiotape fail to capture the essential subtleties of what an undercover says and does, and what it means in context.

Interviewing undercover operators presents an additional challenge: often on the offensive as information-gatherers, they much prefer to ask the questions, not to answer them—and they're certainly not used to answering them "straight."[5] One "skanky," all-too-cool rebel trainee evoked all kinds of negative reactions from his classmates, ranging from disbelief to contempt. From behind his dark sunglasses, he denied ever using the drugs he was commissioned to fight: "I don't touch the shit ... I never did. I moved here from Sweden when I was 18, and I hadn't had any experience with drugs up until I was 18." When I asked him if the Sweden reference was part of his cover story, he replied that he doesn't mention it if he doesn't have to, but that he's prepared to back it up with fluent Swedish, as well as with a "Sweden" tattoo on his left arm. The textbook quality of his persona, as well as of his methods of creating a cover story, made it hard for me, as well as for some of his peers, to believe just about anything he said.

At last I came to the—arguably convenient—conclusion that, given the likelihood that my undercover informants had virtually unfalsifiable license to embellish or distort the stories they told of their work, I could treat what they said as reflective to varying degrees of both their practice and of the popular mythologies surrounding undercover work, particularly as many of them reported being attracted to the profession by a perception (largely fueled by television images) of its glamour. This book is thus as much about the myths cloaking undercover work as it is about the "actual" practices: real undercovers draw on both.

Early on, building rapport in the undercover training group came as a challenge to me. These were largely men who had grown up valuing street smarts as the badge of advancement in their profession. What a far cry from the academic life I was then leading, as a professor of performance studies, where you advance in your field by amassing degrees, positions, and publications founded on a tower of abstractions. I was female, highly educated in private institutions, with precious little practical intelligence, and—as I was soon to demonstrate—limited dissembling skills. I was purporting to write about *their* experience, in a field in which I have had no physical experience of my own, other than—and here I was leaning hard on the assumption that this would be relevant to them—having been a performer and a trainer of other performers.

On the first day, as participants introduced themselves according to how much undercover experience they had had, I cast about for what I was going to say about myself that would be meaningful to these fellows. I was a classically trained dancer, I told them, a ballet dancer, which meant that I took the choreography others made up, from within a standard lexicon, and reproduced it faithfully. I didn't make up my own steps based on the needs of the moment. My admiration for undercovers' gifts for improvising under the most stressful conditions possible had drawn me here.

I was quickly very sorry that I'd said anything about my dance experience. Being a dancer in the academy in the politically correct 1990s and being a "dancer" in cop culture were two divergent activities going by the same name. I know now that there were reciprocity implications that would play themselves out in jokes about my doing some form of dance other than ballet for the guys, since I had gotten the chance to see *them* "perform."

This book is the performance they've been waiting—a long time!—for.

1

CRAFT & ARTIFICE:

THE UNDERCOVER COVER STORY

Undercover means living on the edge, the extreme edge. At the level of optimum performance, like a surgeon. The only difference is, if a surgeon makes a mistake, the patient dies.

—Michael Levine

Under cover, law-enforcement workers infiltrate, investigate, and build cases against those engaged in illegal traffic in drugs, sex, art, immigrants, weapons, exotic animals, and counterfeited currencies, as well as those involved in organized crime and terrorist activity. Undercover operatives have also been used to exert local social control over fraud and illegal commerce, such as political corruption, the sale of liquor to minors, white-collar crime, and the rigging of odometers and meat scales. The Royal Canadian Mounted Police has had great success deploying undercover officers to investigate homicides. In well-publicized deep-cover operations during the late 1960s and 1970s, the United States government sponsored infiltrations of groups of political activists and subversives, such as the Ku Klux Klan and the Symbionese Liberation Army. In private industry, undercover workers have kept abreast of trafficking, industrial espionage, theft and embezzlement, and, during times of heavy layoffs, of internal unrest and threat of violence.[1]

Television images of undercover identity workers have presented souped-up images of invulnerability through advanced technology, exceeding physical gifts, and a glamour little reflective of the actual work. In the 1950s radio drama *I Was a Communist for the FBI,* the main character's nobility of character shines through the sacrifice he makes to ensure the security of his country. Hero Matt Cretic undergoes a total lifestyle change in order to be fully accepted as a member of the Communist Party. In the segment entitled "Undercover Man," Matt Cretic goes all the way, letting on that he's a Communist even to his rejecting mother and brother; actually, it is his FBI affiliation that is under cover even to his family. In "Little Boy Blue Turned Red," it is only when Cretic thinks he is about to die that he prepares a confession to his mother to explain to her that he had actually been a true American patriot all along.

In actuality, undercover work bears only scant resemblance with how it is portrayed in artistic productions. The covert nature of the work has of course inhibited ready reality checks on portrayals in television, film, or novels. A certain amount of public mystification can also aid law-enforcement's cause as, to succeed, undercover techniques must always be a few steps ahead of the public image of them. As soon as they are known to the bad guys—who watch TV, too!—the techniques must once again evolve.

Stepping back from the twentieth-century media popularization of undercover work, we see that European nation-states have actually defended their political, military, and economic interests by covert means since the sixteenth century, the United States since at least the mid-nineteenth. Eugène-François Vidocq, the great French virtuoso identity fugitive and the seminal undercover operator of the late eighteenth and early nineteenth centuries, professionalized and sensationalized the role of the covert operator who trafficked adroitly within the criminal world in order to build his cases.

Born in 1775, the "wild boar's" early life was none too cautious—he stole from his baker-father's cash box to finance running away from home. He later joined the circus for a time, then played both sides of the army in the revolutionary war—defecting from one to go to the other. In 1812, Vidocq was "turned over" from criminal and prison spy to become Paris' first Chef de la Brigade de Sûreté. From his start as a master fugitive and picaresque disguise artist, Vidocq became the inspiration for a host of literary detective figures. As an undercover, Vidocq employed many of the same techniques that had kept him alive while he was running from rather than defending the law. Law enforcement forms its own categories—and crime circumvents them.

As both master criminal and undercover detective, Vidocq embodied the double ingenuity of the system, documented and embellished in his four-volume *Memoirs*. He revolutionized law enforcement by employing criminals to catch criminals. His practice of using criminals to fight criminals influenced the subsequent history of covert policing, particularly in its infiltration and detection methods. When Scotland Yard was started in 1842, its sergeants were to mingle with the very criminals they sought to capture.

Modern undercovers are associated with the rise of a uniformed police force, notably in early nineteenth-century Britain: "With a uniformed police force, there was a moral separation of police from criminals and a visual separation of police from everyone else. It was thought that citizens would be more likely to come to the aid of an officer in uniform if requested."[2] Following Europe's example, during the second half of the nineteenth century, the newly formed American police departments systematically forged relationships with criminals:

> Deceit and trickery were seen as necessary to respond to the con artists, pickpockets, counterfeiters, safe-crackers, and ideologically inspired conspirators who were appearing in increasing numbers. New forms of criminality appeared, and greater enforcement priority was given to types of crime for which evidence is not easily gathered by other means—counterfeiting and other monetary violations, fraud and narcotics. The planned and conspiratorial nature of these lend themselves to secret means of discovery.[3]

The American government hired private agencies such as Pinkerton's and created the Secret Service in 1865, and individual detectives readily crossed the public-private divide, working for both types of agencies. In the first decades of the twentieth century, the growth of significant immigrant populations made it necessary to cast undercovers with an eye toward their ethnicity: infiltrators had to be able to pass in the target culture. Specialized vice departments also developed during this period, with individual units using undercover techniques to collect evidence of gambling and illegal manufacture and trade of alcohol and narcotics—not to mention to infiltrate pro-labor groups and political radicals. Though it has had a tumultuous history with undercover work, the FBI searched out and covertly investigated suspected domestic Communist and fascist groups.

Throughout the history of undercover detection in the West, undercover roles and practices have been conflated with criminal ones, raising meaty ethical and dramaturgical issues.[4] The first popular treatments, in a host of nineteenth-century novels, capitalized on the inherent dramatic complexities and paradoxes of identity work. Vidocq's notorious figure inspired much nineteenth-century literary activity, including, perhaps most notably, Victor Hugo's *Les Misérables*; work by Honoré de Balzac, Eugène Sue, Edgar Allen Poe, and Alexandre Dumas also owe direct influence to that archetypal undercover's *Memoirs* and reputation.

At the time that Vidocq was rising to prominence, French and British police were viewed with great suspicion; French police in particular were known for corruption and for their activities as political spies. Vidocq's *Memoirs*, published in 1828–29, evoke a new era, one that continues to this day, in which the detective becomes a glamorized and heroic figure. The Vidocq of the *Memoirs* could be termed a crime connoisseur. For, even as he tried to hunt them down, Vidocq expressed his deep admiration for fellow criminals who continued to skirt the edge of danger, demonstrating increasing levels of skill in their profession. At the same time, he displayed a nostalgia (combined with shameless self-congratulation) for his own most dastardly acts of roguery.

A popular television topic, undercover work was presented for the range of bells and whistles that it appeared to offer. For example, an "Undercover Man" is the subject of a 1963 television special on counterfeiting entitled *Money for Burning*. The sponsor, Bell & Howell, a manufacturer of cameras, xerography machines, and other devices for enhanced visibility and surveillance, seems unusually apt for this presentation of the "Undercover Man's" surveillance technique. As the then-Deputy of the Secret Service put it, "Counterfeit money is hastily made, generally on the run. ... You have today fine cameras, fine, fast reproducing machines, which eliminates the skill that was needed to counterfeit in the old days." Undercover Man Dick Roth, who "[fights] bad money," is also profiled as a "machine" of sorts. Footage showing his preparation for his work emphasizes his physical prowess: namely, his agility and his skills performing judo and sharp shooting.

Undercover work is by its very "nature deceptive; it is the adoption of a false persona for the purpose of gathering admissible evidence against suspected criminals whose covertness seldom provides obvious evidence."[5] Aware of some of the ethical concerns raised by covert investigative techniques, agencies determine when they believe the potential gains outweigh such considerations. Usually, this is in cases in which covert means are the only feasible way of observing undesirable behavior.

Before the rapid escalation of undercover work in the 1970s and '80s, many undercover infiltrations were used not to "make" a case nor to build evidence in an investigation, but rather more open-endedly, to slowly and somewhat freely gather intelligence about undesirables. When Sal Vizzini began working undercover for the FBI in the 1950s, individuals took their roles rather far. Undercovers made up their own rules and lived and died by them. When Vizzini prepared to go undercover, as Major Michael Cerra, for the FBI against "Lucky" Luciano, the message he got from his contact in Rome was:

> We want information that connects Luciano with the narcotics traffic between Italy and the U.S. We'll sacrifice cases, and even individuals, to learn everything there is to know about Luciano.

> We realize Luciano's prominence and power will make all this very difficult and our prospects not very promising. However, we think it's important enough to commit at least a full year to it.

And, quipped Vizzini to himself, "Not to mention, if necessary, 'Major Michael Cerra.'"[6] Supervisors of this generation appeared to give relatively little consideration to the permissibility of sacrificing individual agents to an investigation.

Following J. Edgar Hoover's wishes, the FBI stayed out of heavy involvement in undercover investigation of crime until after his death in 1972. Hence, smaller, local agencies provided the lead in undercover practices. A rise in attention to white-collar crime and joint operations with the Washington, D.C. Police Department got the FBI more interested in undercover practices. FBI covert operations increased from about 30 during 1973 to nearly 400 ten years later.[7] Between 1977 and 1984, FBI expenditures on undercover operations increased from one-half million to 12.5 million.[8]

Up through the early 1970s, the typical FBI undercover operation had been relatively short; a "buy-bust" would last only a day or two. The buy-bust involved the purchase of stolen property while in role and a more-or-less immediate arrest of the seller. Joseph Yablonsky was the Boston-based agent most closely associated with the buy-bust technique. During the 1960s, Yablonsky "regularly took to the street for a few days, posing as a hustler, con man, pimp, or fence in order to gain the confidence of whomever he was hoping to arrest." Arrests would occur soon after the criminal behavior exhibited itself.[9]

The FBI's move into deep-cover operations changed the role-plays, the timeline, and the teamwork. A fencing operation

> was to work like this: we were to open an office and give the impression of operating a business while other agents and deputies spread the word to their contacts on the streets that we were in the market for any kind of illegal deal that would turn a quick buck. In essence, we were simply to sit back and wait for the crooks to come to us.

Success in fencing operations spread quickly to other areas, and the FBI began to approach deep cover with great energy and range:

> Undercover agents in Baltimore had begun posing as dockworkers, looking into suspected corruption and fraud in local labor unions. In New York, agents were driving eighteen-wheelers in an attempt to break a truck hijacking ring. A Miami agent, posing as a Middle Eastern sheikh, was working himself into the inner circles of ABSCAM, and in New Haven the FBI had finally managed to infiltrate the Mafia when one of its agents landed a job as a chauffeur for a high-ranking mob figure.[10]

In this longer, deeper form of undercover identity play, the arrest could be suspended until all possible crooks could be made part of a grand "round-up." At a well-publicized event, the FBI's Bob Lill and his team threw a huge "thank-you" party for the fencing operation's patrons. The "party" quickly became a round-up. Lill's men had hand-picked the atmosphere music for irony—the score for the 1973 movie *The Sting*.

Jumping into deep cover work with both feet meant that the FBI encountered relatively quickly a wide range of the potential problems associated with the work. Agents suffered psychologically from being separated from their families, abusing alcohol and drugs, being threatened, "going bad," being isolated, and just from playing the (often unsavory) role.[11] Undercovers in the field made many decisions on their own, and little distinction was made between their needs in role and their needs as workers, as shown, for example, by FBI undercovers' paying their undercover expenses directly out of their per diems. As Joe Pistone (a.k.a. "Donnie Brasco") recalls,

> At that time all an undercover agent got was a per diem for expenses. Out of that you had to pay for hotel and meals. It was never enough. Often when I was with bad-guys, I picked up a check, and often it came out of my own money. I called home a lot, and for security reasons I didn't want any phone numbers on my hotel bill, so I always called collect. I didn't get reimbursed for my home phone bill, so I ended up eating that, which was a big sum over the long haul. Sometimes I had to ask my wife to wire me money because I had run out of cash. Naturally, my wife wasn't happy about seeing our money used in this way. In the end I used a total of about $3,000 of my own money in this operation.[12]

By the mid-1980s, a typical deep cover assignment lasted not a day, but a year. In penetration assignments, the FBI focused on subtle and gradual infiltrations of political systems and organized crime rings. Multiple-agency assignments required cooperation between agents at different levels of law enforcement. Supervisory and surveillance support were provided more systematically and were viewed as helping to protect the life and psychological well-being of the agent.

Much has changed since the strongly escalating period of undercover work of the 1970s and 1980s. Increasingly, undercovers work in complex, coordinated teams rather than as "cowboys." They use undercover tactics not only to investigate lower-status but also white-collar criminals and networks of activity as well as individual crimes. These changes impact the difficulty of maintaining the integrity of a trick identity over a longer time, and with more co-actors, each of whom has increasingly complex duplicities embedded in his role.[13]

Undercover work has required increasing levels of risk over the past few decades. In the days of dressing "skanky" and staying on just this side of actually using the drugs, if an agent got "narced," or accused of being an undercover cop, the dealer would simply refuse to do business with him, and the agent lost only the time invested in developing the case.

Beginning with the rise of crack-cocaine in the early 1980s, however, and the upward lurch in violent behavior it brought with it, undercover narcotics agents who perform implausibly run a high risk of dying. As one trainer put it in a session I observed, "They will kill you in a heartbeat for nothing—just to say they killed you." With increasing gang involvement in drug trafficking, safety became the overriding imperative: any artistic choices agents make in planning their undercover roles and scenarios must make just living through the performance primary. Training for undercover performance in this volatile environment thus emphasizes sealing up an undercover identity not simply to safeguard the likelihood of a buy, but to protect the agent's very life.

Undercover identity work can be arrayed according to the extent of the roleplay and how much and what types of deception are involved. First and simplest are those situations "where it is advantageous for the officer to use his real name and the fact that he is a police officer, changing only the fact that he is honest."[14] Decoy work is slightly more complex; here, the officer makes himself visible and accessible as he portrays a stereotypical crime victim. More complex yet is light cover, as is used for street-level buy-bust operations; this requires a more fully developed trick identity and skill in improvisation.

Arguably the form that has received most media treatment is deep cover, defined at one point by the Drug Enforcement Administration as "an undercover assignment in which the operative completely abandons the protection of his official identity and adopts a new one as a criminal, isolating himself in the dominion and complete control of his target."[15] However, an undercover trainer maintains that, contrary to media and researcher fascinations, deep cover is actually much less challenging than "lighter" roleplays, which demand that the undercover be able to switch roles readily. In an interview, he chided me,

> You keep bringing up deep cover and long-term. That's not the skill: that's the easy stuff. Because if you give a guy an identity that he's gotta do long term, and that's all he's doing twenty-four hours a day, seven days week; that's an easy job. The hard job is the guy who's gotta adapt and change nearly every day, the kind of guy who on Monday has to go to a benefit party that's tie and tails, and he's gotta get in with people who are millionaires, and the next day he's gotta be a biker, and the day after that he's gotta work a gay bar, and the day after that he's a college student. Because here's a guy who's changing identities and being successful five times in five working days. There's guys who do that every single day of their life.

Chris Mathers, formerly of the Royal Canadian Mounted Police, agrees that the acting work that offers the greatest test of an undercover's skills is not deep cover, but street-level buys. The outstanding perspicacity and detecting experience of the bad guys working the streets challenge even the most experienced roleplayers.

Deep cover is also the form that has most fascinated psychologists, who have studied why undercovers "go bad," "cross over," or become more fully identified with the criminal side than with law enforcement; it has also compelled sociologists, who have explored the ethical and tactical dimensions of undercover work; and authors of popular films, television, and literature. Deep cover is inherently dramatic; it is the street-stage adaptation of a highly developed fictional text, the cover story.

Cover Story: Talking to Save One's Life

A good cover story is a life net: like Scheherazade, undercover agents talk for their lives. In an interview, an undercover trainer suggested to me that police as an entire occupational category "are the best liars in the world. That's why we say, undercover officers usually get promoted real fast. They're so used to bullshitting people that they can walk into an interview board and completely bullshit them. ... All it is is you know the right things to say and how to say them." He elaborated,

> Cops lie twenty-four hours a day, seven days a week. Every single call that a cop goes on, he's gotta lie to people. He has to make them believe either that he's the baddest guy out, the most sympathetic guy out, the most compassionate guy out ... either to give them this perception so that they relax in his presence or to get the truth out of them.

It's a far different thing to work for a hypersuspicious criminal audience, which demands veracity, than for a paying audience for traditional theatre, which as a rule willingly suspends its disbelief. As Jerry VanCook blithely put it, "There is one major difference ... between doing Shakespeare in the park and working undercover: the audience that doesn't find your portrayal of Othello convincing may show their disapproval by throwing tomatoes at the stage—the bad guys you haven't convinced tend to throw bullets."

Of the trilogy that comprise identity—what one "has," what one "knows," and what one "is"—the latter takes probably the greatest smarts. It is the basis of contemporary undercover training, which focuses not on disguise make-up nor even how to simulate drug use while on a case, but how to talk the talk in a way that won't get a person killed. In the building and in the consistent and plausible performance of a cover story, one sees the most virtuosic exhibitions: the ability to create and sustain a total world.

Particularly in the 1990s, that world centered on language. A successful undercover performance started from a deep knowledge of jargon that included an understanding of its immediate cultural relevance. A good undercover had to make explicit all kinds of tacit cultural knowledge, such as the childhood songs and schooling experiences of his generational and geographic cohort, or shared historical occurrences. He had to know the attitudes of those against whom he wished to camouflage, as well as how those attitudes would be expressed. He had to be ready to perform all the little points of knowledge and experience one possesses purely from being brought up or living in a country ... [one will be expected] to be familiar with a nursery rhyme, a proverb, or a song; to know the names of some famous sportsmen or film stars; to show an awareness of the common attitudes of the community which reflect, amongst other things, class and regional differences, whether related to food and wine, religion and customs—all this is entailed in the attempt at blending into the background.[16]

A good cover story seamlessly blends elements of one's own biography with fresh elements that play directly into the case one is trying to build. Like magician Dariel Fitzkee, the undercover "cleverly, skillfully and dexterously mixes the true with the false." Nowhere is this truer in identity work than in the development of the cover story for undercover narcotics agents working in the last third of the twentieth century. As he prepared to enter a target's world, the undercover scripted the backstory, or complete background details, of the play he was about to enter as a new character. Neither the identity nor the scenario design—which are closely related—could leave openings for suspicion. Instead, they must give the illusion of air tightness through the set of constructive and evasive techniques undercovers collectively refer to as "backstopping."

Two properties govern every aspect of undercovers' narratives: plausibility and coherence.[17] The undercover operator's manipulation of identities, motives, instigations, and stagings is like a magician's handling of objects, objectives, and circumstances:

There is hardly a trick in magic that does not somewhere during its performance require something to be disguised as dissimilar to what it truly is. It disguises a condition, as in the secretly empty or secretly occupied hand. It disguises a manipulation, a movement or an operation, such as with the card houlette or the production box. It covers special preparation, special requirements, special restrictions. It overcomes difficult obstacles. It changes the spectator's sense of significant situations and suspicious handicaps. It disguises the secret presence or absence of something. It disguises purposes, reasons and clues which might be suspicious.[18]

In the undercover's preparation of a cover story, one backstops for the evasions and sidesteppings one is likely to need to perform.

Jose Pistone chose jewel thievery as his criminal specialty, as

> I needed a specialty that allowed me to work alone and without violence. I couldn't be a stickup man or a bank robber or a hijacker or anything like that. We had an okay from the department to get involved in certain marginal activities, but you had to avoid violence. As a jewel thief, I could say I worked alone. I could come and go as I wanted, and come up with scores that everybody didn't have to know about because I committed my "crimes" in private.

> For a jewel thief and a burglar, it was not unusual for a guy to work alone. And since if you pull off the job correctly you don't confront your victims, there is a minimal chance for violence. That specialty gave me an out whenever anybody would want me to pull a violent job.[19]

Traces of identity need to be plausible enough not to be checked and sealed tightly enough to leave no aroma if they are.

Coherence is built in with the undercover acronym "K.I.S.S.," or "Keep It Simple, Stupid." As one experienced undercover trainer frequently intoned to his students, "Failing to plan is planning to fail." The less that needs to be kept coherent, especially once one is in the moment of performance, the better. But little things must be attended to; the cover story should be ready to address any disparity between the undercover persona and every physical sign he presents, down to the vehicle he drives.

Preparing to drive an undercover vehicle is like preparing a fake provenance, or set of documents for a forged art work that establishes the direct line of transmission from one trustworthy hand to another. It can be as materially detailed as going to an auto salvage dealer and buying discarded license plates from a car that is of the same make and model as the car one plans to drive, researching who was the last owner of the vehicle, and working one's purchase of the car from that owner into the cover story.[20]

Like a fugitive, the undercover needs a name, an occupation, and a geographic history. Many sources recommend that the undercover change his last name, but retain his first as the basis of the new identity. Then, if an old friend sees him and calls out his real name, his natural, instantaneous head turn will not be out of keeping with his role. Retaining one's initials can be a safeguard against mistakenly signing the "wrong" ones while under.[21]

The right choice of name can help make sense of evasions or of strange behavioral or bodily signs that the undercover knows he will be presenting. One undercover operator used a Muslim name and neatly sidestepped demands that he engage in drug use with sellers to establish his credibility, since it was well known that Muslims don't believe in using drugs: hey, he was just a distributor. Another undercover used the tattooed initial so evident on his arm as the first letter of his undercover name. The body, he knew, also has to substantiate any claims made. Don't say you're a bricklayer if you don't have calluses on your hands; don't say you're a competitive body-builder if you have hair on your legs. Con artist Cecil Brown Smith made a good living (to the tune of £6 a week in 1904) posing as a paralyzed beggar, until a London detective observed him enjoying a dinner of oysters and ale and then bounding aboard a train headed for the suburbs.[22]

A vital part of the identity is being able to furnish the right *other* names, those of contacts held in common with the target. Handing a bad guy a contact's name—so long as it's the right name —is the best way to open the door of a relationship under a false identity. Once he had made contact with a big dealer, Vizzini "used Tutter over and over as a reference. It was a magic name, an open sesame, that helped lead me to smaller fry in the Istanbul underworld."[23]

One's work knowledge is never faked, and in fact becomes equated with the identity itself. As an undercover trainer put it to me, "Whatever you've done in the past *is* your identity." Through a close friend, one undercover had grown quite familiar with the funeral business, and chose to play a role as a worker in a funeral parlor owned by his "father." Another undercover, a devout Catholic, undertook a supporting undercover role as a priest. An undercover student who applied this technique directly to a class simulation exercise decided to build his undercover identity on his existing knowledge of the grocery business, a choice that also fit in tidily with the target's cover business in meat-packing.

Bill Taylor, who headed the private undercover investigation company The PLE Group, took as his first undercover occupation the running of a cigar shop that was actually his own business. The complete assumption of a work role when working undercover—rather than just referring to it in conversation—provides the "reason for being there" with the bad guys.

Undercover work identities need to be multi-layered, in part because the bad guys' are. Often, a bad guy has a business that is performed as a cover for those he knows to be in law enforcement; the cover business hides his behind-the-scenes criminal work. Even with a law-enforcement trunk identity, the undercover may be one level up even on the bad guy, since he too has a legal cover occupation and one or more illegal occupations that explain why he seeks concourse with the bad guys. VanCook's persona, Mick Jordan,

> might be a drug dealer one day, a gun runner the next, and a burglar the day after that, but he had the most fun when he got to play hit man. ... Mick had been arrested for everything from possession of marijuana to manslaughter. He'd done a little county jail time but had no felony convictions. ... That he'd always beaten the rap insinuated that Mick had a certain animal intelligence that I wanted him to possess.[24]

The layering of cover identities may be necessary to maintain a cover at all. For a Beirut gun trafficking assignment, Vizzini determined that the best cover was a "cover within a cover": in this case, dealing with the reasonable possibility of high-level intelligence and counterintelligence from his own government, Vizzini drew on his already-developed role, Mike Warner. Even his own agency believed that he was going to Beirut to cover for another agent for them.[25]

Vizzini kept in stock several different, separately developed identities, and studied his cast of characters anytime a new assignment came up. His cover could then be selected for maximum adaptability to the range of international situations in which an American could plausibly appear. In Marseilles, Vizzini presented to his contact the full range of possibilities:

I told him I had several which seemed to fit the situation; he could take his pick. I had forged Italian seaman's papers under the name of Pasquale Lombardi. I also had a United States Merchant Mariner's document issued by the Coast Guard. It was made out to Joseph Angelo Vento and had a "Z" number, which meant that the papers were in order and the bearer was cleared to sail. ...

We decided on the Vento cover. I would be a purser waiting to rejoin my ship, the S. S. *Mormacsea*, scheduled to dock in Marseilles about two weeks hence. This kind of cover seemed most suitable for the assignment. For one thing, merchant seamen transported most of the heroin which was illegally getting into the United States, at the going rate of $500 a kilo, and pursers had more standing on shipboard than stewards or other functionaries.

We agreed that I would be a big spender with a mysterious source of money. I would check into the best hotel in town.[26]

Vizzini's ability to maintain several identities in reserve enabled him to keep the option of leaving the country under another of his cover identities.

The popular image of the undercover identity that is birthed afresh for each operation is actually regarded by many working operatives as inefficient and impractical. In a training course I attended, students were encouraged to create identities that would be versatile and long-lived. They were not expected to fill out a new identity for every operation, but rather to grow a single new trunk identity that would be supple enough to last them for a few years and whose branches or offshoots would deal with the needs of different situations. Within a given trunk identity, the undercover name ideally has a number of plausible variants that can be used in different undercover operations—simultaneously, if need be. One of the instructors had had long-term success with a long, foreign-sounding last name that could be shortened in various ways to create memorable nicknames.

Likewise, the chosen occupation does best if it permits its owner to play roles at a range of different social classes to encompass all the types of assignments one may come up against. It's a good idea here not to let oneself get too heavily pinned down and to be sure of having the knowledge base to support claims of occupation.

An experienced undercover explains how it's done:

> I use one identity, one cover story every time. ... All I do is change the costume or change the coloration.
>
> *Like Barbie & Ken?*
>
> Bingo! I'm always the same guy, no matter what I'm playing.

In all his incarnations, the undercover's trunk identity was involved with the selling of hot dogs, yet had to have the flexibility to

> be the owner of a business, drive a very fancy car, be the top dog. Yet if I have to get down and dirty and buy crack, I can also say that I'm a counter man and all I do is slap together hot dogs and sell them over the counter at $4.50 an hour. And I know the business. I know my business. I know a little bit about the restaurant business, because one of my best friends is a retired policeman ... who actually owns a couple of hot dog stands.

That the undercover had worked as a butcher during college gave him the confidence and the real knowledge on which to base this particular occupational stance for his undercover persona.

Of course, his assertion that he works for "Tony's Beef and Dogs" always had to be backed up. He needed a business card with a real phone number on it and someone who would answer the phone on the other end appropriately: in this case, his old friend would simply reply that he was in the field and would ring him back. If any of the other employees answered the phone and took a request for the undercover, they were all instructed to just hand the phone to the owner, who could make the appropriate reply.[27]

The longevity of this undercover's trunk identity is telling: the cop got more than fifteen years' mileage out of it, with all of its variations. Naturally, the undercover persona had many of the same dimensions as the undercover officer himself: same height, weight, and birth date. He also happened to enjoy many of the same vices—fine cigars and wines—"because I want to do things that I enjoy and that I have knowledge of." (The undercover did research the class identities of those against whom he planned to play the role and varied the brand preferences of what he smoked and drank to fit in with those he was trying to infiltrate.) He maintained, because it's just too difficult—and treacherous—to remember separate identities, undercover officers and their agencies tend to hang onto these flexible trunk identities as long as they can.

In addition to the occupational identity, the cover story needs a rich avocational background. Here again, the player pulls from his own personal interests and areas of knowledge. The ability to carry on a conversation, to show the regular-guyness of one's character, can help steel an undercover through some of the early tests of identity he'll face. One is more likely to be suspected of being a cop if seen as unwilling to kick back and enjoy the kind of idle banter that establishes which people, places, and activities the bad guy and the newcomer have in common. It is perhaps worse if the undercover appears indifferent to the bad guy, particularly if he reports to have made the contact in the first place on the recommendation of a mutual friend. Having the same hobbies as the cops themselves, undercover personas can be pretty interesting guys: an undercover instructor's dominant undercover identity, like the instructor himself, was a history buff, widely read on the Civil War. In this sense, the undercover operator is simultaneously not himself and not *not* himself.

After the name and occupational identity, a geographic history must be built up. Here again, the places with which the operative is actually very familiar make the best choices. Some sources consider it a rapport-building bonus if he can use a place that is also part of the bad guy's history; others recommend building a story around the places one knows well that are unlikely to be checked out by the bad guy.

Pistone found it easy to keep the geographic part of his cover for Donnie Brasco from catching up with him. To help him backstop his early childhood history, the FBI's research department had conveniently turned up an orphanage that had burned down

> We came up with the idea that I would be an orphan. Without a family it's harder for people to check up on you. If you had a family, you would have to involve other

agents to speak up for you as family members. If you're an orphan, the only thing they can check on is if you lived in a neighborhood or if you have any knowledge of the particular neighborhood. I had knowledge of areas in Florida and California because I had done some work there.

We knew from our research people about an orphanage in Pittsburgh that had burned down, and there were no records left of the children raised there. That was perfect for me. One of the agents had lived in Pittsburgh, and I had grown up in Pennsylvania.[28]

James J. Ness, a "policeman-cum-professor-cum-policeman," shifted his geographic identity to be a believable fit when he went undercover:

The Cairo area is primarily rural and agricultural and I did not know enough about agriculture to pass as a farmer; besides, most farmers were known locals. However, since I raise Quarter horses I do know about horses so my cover was an itinerant horse trainer from Murphysboro, Illinois, working for a firm in Indiana. Murphysboro is far enough from Cairo to keep curious people from going through the trouble of checking, yet it is close enough to be considered a local.

Occupation and geographic data were the basis of Ness's undercover identity.[29]

That geographic history can quickly become dicey; perhaps this is one of the reasons the bad guys tend to require it as they probe the identities performed for them. The undercover needs to be quite canny as he strikes a balance between building up the kind of detail that lends credibility and plausibility and making sure he drops no information that can later be shown to be false.

It's quite a fine line. An experienced undercover would never say that he had gone to a local high school, where the bad guy could easily get hold of the relevant yearbooks and not find a corroborating picture in any of them. Likewise, biographical elements should not have him virtually certain to have crossed paths earlier in life with one of the bad guys that he'd never met before:

... If, for example, the agent claims to be from a certain city, and to have attended a certain school, it would be compromising to have a member of the group confront him and announce that he lived in the same place, went to the same school, and didn't remember him.[30]

Undercovers employ a variety of means to help them commit the details of their stories to memory. Like many teachers of stage actors, VanCook advises that the best way to create a character who is as "deep, well-rounded, and complex" as oneself is to write out a detailed biography for him.[31] The biography may include experiences and probably includes areas of expertise the undercover actually had, but casts them in the light of the character:

> The first undercover identity I ever created was Mickey Jordan. "Mick" was born in Ozark, Missouri, a little town about eight miles south of Springfield and my college roommate's hometown. I'd spent enough time there to know the area quite well, and after writing what turned out to be a 300-page biography of Mick's life, I knew him, too. I knew what kind of grades he'd made in high school, that he'd played defensive tackle on the high school football team, and that he'd been a drummer in a highly unsuccessful rock-and-roll band that did little more than practice in the lead guitar player's garage and disrupt the neighborhood every Sunday afternoon. More importantly, I knew how to talk about being a defensive tackle and a bad drummer, since Jerry VanCook had done these things as well as Mickey Jordan.[32]

The undercover should "write out the complete history, every item of it and every word of it several times, and then memorize it. He must learn each significant detail of the fictitious identity so that he can reply to it as may be necessary and then have an associate drill him on every aspect."[33] Thorough, deep memorization ensures coherence in the story, as well as the undercover's ready access to answers to any questions or challenges as anyone who had come naturally and truthfully to the role.

Together with an experienced partner at his agency, one agent writes out everything that he knows about the role. He keeps the document at the center of his desk and reads it through each day. For him, even a weekend's worth of reading and thinking are sufficient rehearsal for the kinds of roles he creates: "You see that

[page] often enough, you talk like that person long enough ... and you actually have to step out of it when you get home." He be-lieves that there is no other way to "practice"; you just have to get out and perform it.

The richest part of planning a fictive undercover identity is cu-riously interactive, existing in a realm that somehow combines the undercover's actual physical and personality qualities and his own hobbies with invented ones, then regroups all of them as a com-plement to the bad guy's profile and the psychological needs the undercover has ascribed to him. This relational, complementarian aspect of the undercover role stems both from the undercover's understanding of his own identity and from those characteristics law enforcement views as significant in the profile of a particular target or bad guy—for example, his propensity toward violence, how quickly and on what basis he forms friendships, and his safety threshold. The undercover will also want to have back-ground information on the target's family, relatives, and associates, and to know about his character or temperament, vices, hobbies, occupation, criminal specialty and modus operandi.[34] The point of gathering and working off this detailed information on the target is to anticipate and create performance conditions under which he—like the successful con artist—can control much, if not most, of what happens.

The most important part of the relational history is the pretext that permits the paths of the bad guy and of the character the un-dercover plays to cross. Particularly crucial is some kind of match between the bad guy's personal history and that of the undercover officer's fictional identity. In constructing an identity essentially out of the projective identifications of his target, the undercover can implicate his deepest desires and wishes, carving out a short-cut to an intense and productive history together. The undercover who appears as the fulfillment of the target's unconscious wishes stands a strong chance of succeeding in his mission, especially if he can manage the target's conscious and subconscious attention. Vizzini's ability to infiltrate the Sicilian Mafia hinged in part on his own Sicilian heritage but also importantly on his American identity as Major Michael A. Cerra, United States Air Force, which was calculated to provide the expatriate Lucky Luciano with the connection to the United States that he was known to long for. Although Luciano had been deported from the United States to Italy, he remained active in organized crime and had a certain homesickness. Each feature of the undercover identity had its place in the plan for evoking particular responses from the target, for tugging on quite specific heartstrings:

> The Bureau was counting on my experience, plus my Sicilian background, to pull me through. The plan was to masquerade as a lonely Air Force pilot, maybe not fussy about turning a fast buck on the side; a man who in the line of duty would travel extensively on Air Force business ferrying military planes between the U.S. and Europe, and be accepted by Luciano, who was well known for his longing for the States and things American.[35]

One undercover instructor tells a memorable tale of a cover story by an inexperienced narc—himself, just starting out. He had decided that he would present himself as the owner of a sprinkler systems concern, and made up a name on the spot, "Sprinkler Heads of Florida." The dealer quickly became suspicious and asked the narc to show him his advertisement in the telephone book. Shuffling anxiously for an answer, the narc replied that it was his brother's business and his brother didn't advertise in the St. Petersburg phone book, just in Tampa's. Unfortunately, the dealer happened to have a Tampa phone book on hand.

The narc shifted again. He said that his brother didn't advertise through print at all, after all, but by word of mouth.

No deal.

As this undercover developed his technique, he learned a great deal about developing a plausible cover story in advance from a more experienced narc for whom he served as back-up. This performer presented himself as a caterer to a major drug trafficker whose daughter happened to be planning a wedding. When the bad guy started asking for advice about where he should hold the wedding, the narc was ready with props and research. He took out a pad and pen and asked detailed questions: How many guests did he want to have? How much did he want to spend per head? Would he want the caterer to hire the band, or did he prefer to hire the band himself? Within forty-five minutes, the trafficker had taken the narc into his bedroom and shown him his pilot logs and manifests for his buying trips to Colombia and Bolivia. Within a week, he had fronted him nine kilos of marijuana, while accepting payment for only one. The story was presented as an exceptional example of a narc's establishing trust by appealing to the bad guy's needs and motives; the fact that he was able to fit so smoothly into the bad guy's world made shorthand of the process of building trust.[36] Thus, the best cover story is one that balances a keen appraisal of the self with an assessment of the needs of a given context. As Buckwalter writes, "The secret of undercover operations is the private investigator's ability to live a cover identity convincingly in acceptable association with those whom he has been assigned to investigate."[37]

The diffusion of a cop's constructed undercover identity makes the best sense once one recognizes that bad guys are people with full lives, too, as one undercover reminds his students: "I always tell the guys, crooks have friends. They have places that they go, they have wives, they have kids, crooks do things outside of the life of being a crook. I mean, they're always thinking about being a crook, but they still have to go to the grocery store."

A magician must always assume that "his spectators are fully his mental equals—perhaps, even, his superiors." Inevitably, it's vital for a cop's safety for him to assume that any sort of research he can run on a bad guy can also be run on him, so he must backstop with internally consistent data on any legal, financial, or historical claims he makes. And "the depth of the cover required will depend on the thoroughness of the investigation the opposition is likely to make." The undercover must anticipate how the bad guys, or investigators they hire, would actually research the veracity of statements by, for example, looking at vessel and vehicle files, post office records, video and pizza delivery databases, medical information databases, and fish and game licenses. Since many criminals have access to the National Crime Information Center database, he would be well advised also to back up any criminal history he claims with an entry there. The undercover may even need to plead guilty to a charge and spend a certain amount of time in jail establishing contacts with other prisoners to give weight to the contacts he claims.[38]

The development of an undercover identity involves anticipating the strategic perceptions, moves, and conclusions that the bad guy might produce. There's also a recursive element in such development: you need to have a sense of what the bad guy would want you to believe about himself, should he have succeeded in penetrating your identity. This way, you can be on guard about how he represents himself to you, should he not know—that you know—that he knows.

2

BEING GOOD AT BEING BAD:

GOING UNDERCOVER

I feel that [a] reform is now in progress. ... I think that the "new" magic will be founded entirely upon psychological principles.

—Dariel Fitzkee

I n the 1968 series premiere of *Mod Squad*, entitled "Teeth of the Barracuda," the character of Captain Adam Greer is the only member of the conservative Los Angeles Police Department who recognizes that "times change and the cop had better change with them": that is, the Department had better start using covert intelligence-gathering techniques. He tries to convince the Chief that the three "kids" he wants to work undercover for him "can get into a thousand places we can't." Pete, the Beverly Hills surfer, Linc, who comes from a poor black family, and Julie, a "kid on probation" who happens to look great in a bikini, seem to the Captain to be the last people one would suspect to be cops. The opening sequence—in which the kids ride daredevil on motor scooters, clamber to the tops of vans, rabble rouse, and, when they're hauled off to headquarters, shout, "It's a bum trip, citizens!"—turns out to be a training session staged by the Captain.

Back at the office, he chews them out for overdoing their act. He's pissed: he chose them because they would fit into the very groups he wanted infiltrated; now their own concept of acting is making them too highly visible: "You know how these kids act, you've *been* there. Now the whole idea was to meld in with them, not stand out. You *stand out!* You might as well wear your badges, tell 'em you're cops."

The ability to act the role—while concealing that it is a role—is essential to undercover performance. When it freely chooses to go to a play, a theatre audience conventionally suspends disbelief, accepting the actor as the character she portrays. By contrast, audiences for identity performances at the fringe of legality will not knowingly accept the convention of performance. As Michael Levine puts it,

> If actors who flopped on Broadway were taken out and shot in Shubert Alley, they'd still have it easy compared with the undercover. Actors have the luxury of immersing themselves in their roles for audiences who pay to see their act—people who expect and want to be convinced. They're on the actor's side, rooting for him. But an undercover works with his audience a foot from his face. An audience looking for something wrong in his performance. For any hint that he's not the real thing. An audience that suspects he's a narc when they meet. One slip, one error of judgment, and his audience won't just take a walk at intermission. They'll probably blow his fucking brains out.[1]

Undercovers play live for a very limited audience, most of whom ideally never recognize all the frames that contain the performance, that electronic goldfish bowl into which they are placed when their performances are caught by hidden audio wires and video cameras. Even as undercover performances are captured by a variety of surveillance instruments, any signs of such recording media can, if discovered, threaten the performer's livelihood—in many senses of the word.

Casting the Role

The undercover operator lies both about his identity and about the context in which he, by putting his "skin in the game," implicates both himself and his criminal target. Not everyone's skin is for the job. Indeed, criminals may be specially attracted to undercover work: The "desire for power over others is twenty times stronger in a criminal than that of a normal person. A surprising number of ... criminals want to be cops."[2]

Police officers may be motivated to seek out undercover work by very practical reasons. They may be attracted by the independence of the undercover role, as one undercover operator wisecracked, "Otherwise, we'd get an honest job!" According to Michigan State Police psychologist Gary Kaufman,

> The majority of people who go into undercover work *absolutely love it*. They enjoy the risk; I mean, it's such a contrast to typical police work. They enjoy the team-management approach, as opposed to chain-of-command kinds of things. And everything they work on is a felony, a major crime, rather than being out there chasing taillights and writing traffic tickets and helping people change tires.

The work may appear to offer a way to get away from troubled relationships with family members or work supervisors, to learn a business or profession, or to stockpile per diems in an expensive city. In some agencies, the prospect of promotion in uniformed work is held out as bait for undertaking an undercover assignment. However, some experienced undercover operators believe that new undercovers should regard any promises of a happy transition to uniformed work with suspicion. Working undercover may mark a cop as permanently dangerous to those more comfortable with conventional policing. Levine warned an undercover class, "Don't plan on a career working undercover. It's a better way to make enemies than win awards. Everybody who knows what you do, from your supervisor on up, will mistrust you. No matter how much they may applaud you on the surface, to them you're like a beautifully colored but very poisonous snake."[3] Even within undercover work, cops may have a short career.

To some extent, social availability—or the willingness to act available—determines who can choose undercover work. A married person or a parent is likely to encounter great difficulty working undercover while trying to maintain normalcy in his family life. Because a spouse and children cannot be expected to assume undercover identities along with the worker, the undercover operator must often leave home for the assignment. In addition,

> He can't receive mail, as the conflict in names would give him away. He can't save letters, or write to his relatives and friends, because if his home is ever searched, the paper would give him away. ... The telephone is one way of keeping in contact, but this means he must place his calls from a public phone, to avoid tell-tale traces on his bill. It also minimizes the risk of a wiretap disclosing his identity.[4]

Married undercover operators' divorce rate is significantly higher even than the alarming rate of cops as a whole.

Other cops are drawn to undercover work by the chance to make policing proactive rather than reactive, "to beat the bad guys at their own game." For Royal Canadian Mounted Police former undercover Murray Simms, the work offered "logistical" opportunities in the field, the chance to hatch out and act upon multiple levels of strategy in the moment.

The work has powerful intrinsic attractions that keep certain performers coming back: the excitement, the chance to work on felonies and, as one undercover operator put it, "the team camaraderie that kind of places things in a bitter triangle phenomenon." When everyone on an undercover team is wearing a pager, and a player is suddenly called away by the operation from his child's birthday party, his team's action may feel more immediately compelling to him than his family life.

For RCMP former undercover Chris Mathers, undercover work is "the sexiest thing in the police. And in the mid-1970s, that was the coolest thing that there was." Bill Taylor of Professional Law Enforcement Group, a practice dedicated to corporate undercover investigations, found the excitement of working undercover addictive, as he told me:

> I tell you, it's worse than sex. It gets in your blood. ... It's the last frontier for a police officer; it's you conning the con man. ... You've literally penetrated their whole world, and been able to convince them that you're somebody that you're not. It's kind of like walking out there in the street in the old days of Texas, and it's you and him.

For Taylor, undercover identity work was a seduction: As a successful undercover, you have "wooed, conned someone out of their life ... You are literally seducing them out of their livelihood." Levine taught his novices, "Working undercover is the ultimate form of seduction. Even the terminology is sexual. 'I *did* the guy,' you'll hear an undercover say. First is the winning of confidence. Then the penetration. But in this seduction it's his *life* you're after."

Mathers hypothesizes that one chooses a particular line of work for one reason—the glamour, the working conditions, the excitement—yet may want to stay in it for quite other reasons. Long-term undercover agents, he believes, stay in, as he did, as they find they're good at it. And the work itself can end up being tremendously reinforcing for those who enjoy risk-taking. While police work as a whole reinforces those who "Homestead," enjoying the routine of managing the day-to-day aspects of law enforcement, another breed of cops, "Explorers," will do anything to avoid boredom. Undercover operations offer the thrill that Explorers would not otherwise find in police work.[5] Mathers himself was spurred on by the artistic and dangerous aspects of the job, by

> the whole play itself, the whole psychological game that's being played—actually, the art! ... You always want to know, can I do it? Can I perpetrate this particular thing? Or, here's a bunch of dangerous people. I'm going in there. Can I do it without them knowing that I'm scared to death?

One rarely finds a female undercover cast in solo work; female officers' safety, particularly given a threat of rape, is frequently offered as a reason. Some male officers may also perceive a female partner as a threat to their own safety, as Larry Wansley notes:

> I should admit, I was very biased against women in law enforcement. ... We had only two female officers ... One became adamant about her right to work the streets, to the point of threatening litigation, and was eventually assigned to patrol. In her first week she found herself in a position where she could do nothing but stand by and watch as members of a gang attacked her partner.[6]

When they are on the undercover scene at all, instead of operating solo, women tend to be treated as part of the backstopping of the male character's trick identity; they substantiate his reality in the eyes of the bad guy. Typically, they play the role of the girl-friend, though they may also play a prostitute or the male's secretary. Sam Skeete used another officer to help build his trick "image": "We had a female black police officer in the squad, Alicia Parker; now we're gonna have her go with me [to the bar] as my girlfriend, be good for my image and we'd have another cop there. She's very impressive—used to be a model." James J. Ness asked his wife, who was not a cop but "had a degree in criminal justice and was also looking for a summer project," to help him substantiate his undercover role: "I felt I needed a partner, and that a female would add credence to my being in Cairo [Illinois]. ... People appear not to suspect a male/female team as readily as two male partners."[7]

Female agents were also used in late twentieth-century under-cover work to water down the danger level of a situation:

> Pat Livingston, a Miami agent who was working under-cover in [the] nationwide pornography sting operation ... MiPorn, may have been the all-time champion at invent-ing methods of staying out of harm's way. Insisting that a woman companion was a better weapon than any hand-gun the Bureau issued, he rarely met with dealers without the company of a trusted female—usually an agent or member of some local law enforcement agency—posing as his girlfriend.[8]

Wansley believes his employment of a female colleague in the role of his girlfriend helped him avoid both violent acts and sexual of-fers in the field.

Whereas women are more likely than men to successfully evade demands that they use drugs in front of the bad guy to prove their veracity, presenting themselves as prostitutes runs them the risk of having to follow through with sexual acts. When Wansley would bring in a female officer, he would let her know he expected her to "dumb down" for the role:

I outlined the role I was playing and explained to her what her assignment would be. I made no secret of my concern that she might be anxious to get too deeply involved in the action. "All I need," I said, "is someone to act the part of my girlfriend. Nothing more. Look pretty and speak when spoken to. It's that simple. Don't go off on any free-lance investigations or act too interested if someone starts talking business. In fact, if something like that happens it would be a good time to go powder your nose or something.

Casting a female foil is of course also a form of misdirection, dependent on the bad guy's expectation that the locus of action will not be in a female player. In the misogynistic world in which much crime is committed, having someone "insignificant" there can prove quite useful to intelligence-gathering: anyone would confess to a fool.

As institutions became clearer about what qualities worked for undercover operatives, they also began to specify their own character requirements. Early on, general intelligence was regarded as a principal criterion for success in undercover. A set of 1976 guidelines for undercover operations in Phoenix enumerated the qualities of character one should have to do well in this field of policing:

Undercover work does not require any special type of individual so far as appearance or personality is concerned. Anyone can operate undercover if he is intelligent, resourceful, and possesses the requisite qualities of initiative, energy, and courage. ... The undercover narcotics officer should have self-confidence, good judgment, mental alertness, good memory for names, faces, [and] information, and knowledge of underworld operations.[9]

The ability to assess the unspoken conditions and rules of a new environment and to behave in accordance with them was viewed as invaluable:

A chameleon is a member of the lizard family that has the ability to change the color of its skin to blend in with its surroundings, which makes it much less readily detectable. Good operatives have this chameleon adaptability,

> to blend into their UC environment—to change the color
> of their lives, so to speak, and to appear as a natural part
> of their new environment.[10]

In identifying new undercover workers likely to succeed on the job, one trainer looks for visual as well as verbal versatility: "I want a guy who can put on a suit, and go into the classiest of restaurants, and pass like a millionaire, and I also want a guy who can dress down and walk into a biker bar and look like a biker or a skinhead or a racist or something like that." Being willing to play the straight man to the bad guy's performances is also key, as undercovers provide the moves that will show their scene partner's intentions, actions, and style off clearly.[11]

High-achieving undercover workers (like their characters) tend to be good talkers who start and carry on conversations with new people with ease and some grace: in the words of one cop, "bull-shitters." Sal Vizzini, for example, found it easy to work at a San Juan blackjack table in one of his undercover roles, since the job "required nothing more from me than a fast patter and an ability to add."[12] The ability to keep language coming, almost regardless of its content, helps to convince others of the propriety of a presented role."[13]

Vizzini credits his "ear for languages," and his resulting knowledge of Sicilian, Italian, Japanese, Cantonese, Spanish, and Turkish, as invaluable components of his success as an undercover agent. Eugène-François Vidocq was acclaimed in his many guises, in part because of his mastery of jargon. His ready memory for criminal argot led to his publication of *Les Voleurs*, a lexicon of underground terminology, and his facility with both the verbal and the physical signs of the immediate homosexual culture came quickly and handily to the fore.[14]

In a mid-1990s undercover training course, students were deemed capable of giving body to a claimed identity if they could "talk the talk" of a particular expertise, and function believably when the bad guy in their simulations quizzed them on any history or qualifications they claimed. Thus, they drew quite heavily on their own resumes, and selected roles that would allow them to demonstrate convincingly that they were who they said they were merely by *talking about it*.

Given the gift for gab that most undercovers have, knowing when to hold back is a more rarely thought-of skill, though it may be the one that saves. Working with a heavy-hitting Mafia man, Vizzini had to remind himself "above all to shut up. One of the hardest cons is saying nothing at all. It works best with the tough cases, cases like Giuseppe Mancuso. Besides, not volunteering information is an old Sicilian tradition. So I stayed traditional." The operator advises, "If you want to stay cool, or give the impression of staying cool, the less you say the better. You don't overexplain. When they try to put you on the defense, you turn it around and put them on the defense."[15]

Initially rejected in the 1970s for undercover work by the Royal Canadian Mounted Police on account of an "overaggressiveness" they identified in him, Mathers told me he took on undercover jobs informally—and even started teaching undercover techniques. It was only considerably later that he was given a "headquarters number," the identification that gave him the status of an official member of the undercover force. Mathers found that what the evaluators had deemed aggressive was exactly what ended up working for him in the field; he believes that the bad guys perceived him as aggressive, too, but the result was that they backed down when he wanted them to.

Federal Bureau of Investigation guidelines require some "knowledge of the criminal element," the ability to perform "the same know-how, ideas, background, language and slang as that displayed by the criminal." Vidocq had credited his own investigative virtuosity in fair measure to his criminal skills: "Being the most adroit of spies, was the result of having been the most expert of robbers."[16] Taylor hired those who were "mavericks," self-directed and willing to try something to pique their own ego needs; he estimated that only one out of 150 cops would make a good undercover operative. As Levine admonished a group of novices, "You've got to *love* the idea of flirting with death. In the middle of everything, you got to *enjoy* knowing that your life depends on your ability to *outthink* the danger. To be calm. Manipulative. You understand what I'm saying? Unless the idea of death makes you feel more alive, stay out of undercover. It's not for you." Donald Goddard also emphasized the attraction of working close to the edge of death:

The true warrior, when confronted with a choice of life or
death, will always choose the way of death. That doesn't
mean he wants to kill or *be* killed. It simply means he
won't choose the safe way *because* it's safe. And I've never
done that. I've never played safe. Family and child, it
didn't matter. I already knew you come in alone and go
out alone. Nothing is permanent. I was, and I am, prepared to live my life the way the cards are dealt. I felt that
as strongly then as I do now, only then I didn't think
about it. Now I do. Now I understand it better. But then,
it was just a hunger to be where the action was.[17]

A loner identity is closely connected with the preparedness to
give all to the risks of the work. In Southeast Asia, Vizzini considered himself "to be on my own, of course, if anything backfired.
Nobody would lift a finger to help me. But I had to take the
chance." Joe Pistone described the life of the undercover as more
alone than truly being by yourself, as "you're with badguys continually, pretending to be one of them, cultivating them, laughing
at their jokes, keeping feelings and opinions and fears to yourself,
just like your true identity."[18]

However, the very risk-taking that served Vizzini well might just
as easily have been his own or another undercover agent's undo-
ing. One side of the paradox is that it takes a kind of "cowboy" to
succeed as an undercover: the Washington, D.C. Metropolitan
Police once identified the ability to operate under minimal supervision as a positive sign. Naturally, the cowboy characteristic has a
double edge: independence needs to be balanced by good judgment and a willingness to submit to the overall needs of an
investigation, as assessed by a supervisor. Indeed, once agencies
began to recognize the psychological and legal dangers of being
that autonomous in a seductive, illegal world, they sought operators who could successfully blend independent thinking with
frequent contact with and reliance upon a supervisor.

Undercovers who are shy, self-doubting, or heavily encumbered
by questions and rules, unable to think flexibly under rapidly
evolving circumstances, would be deemed unlikely to succeed.
These identity artists have to be able to keep the overall operation
and the risks of any present gambit in perspective, as Michael
Levine warns:

If something smells bad, if that little warning bell goes off in the back of your mind, *walk away*. Leave it right there. Fuck it. There's so much dope on the street you don't have to risk everything you got in the world just for *that* little bit. Get another informer. Cut another deal. Make another case.[19]

The Undercover as Director

Cops direct others' behavior even in everyday street policing. When, for example, they detain suspects in a building search, they call out commands for the physical postures they want the suspect to adopt and the movements by which he should arrive at them. Undercover officers direct the acting of their suspects no less forcefully, albeit covertly, over long, interactive scenes in which they co-star. The "script" is the production of verbal and physical signs that will "make" the case without overblowing it—that will prove the suspect intends of his own free will to sell contraband for money.

In undercover performances, identity workers must find balance between the charismatic behavior that could strike a rapport with the bad guys, and an understated, or "natural," performance style that would help keep them safe. An undercover's resourcefulness should be matched by his unobtrusiveness. The ideal undercover is gifted at "roping," or steering a suspect to reveal pertinent information without his ever knowing that he's doing it. Sociologist Erving Goffman would characterize this as performing a "covert interview" with the intention of maneuvering the subject toward an "unwitting move."[20]

An undercover field training exercise in which I participated was designed to cultivate skill at roping. It demanded that participants gain, from a simple, "cold" meeting with an innocent, same-sex shopper at a mall his name, address, educational background, work history, family information, and the make, model, and license number of his vehicle. One student commented on the ease with which he had engaged another man in line to buy Mexican fast food. The cop's Midwestern accent had caught the other man's attention—and "the guy will never know he was had because we talked about so many other things." With its requirement for the simultaneous deployment of performance and investigational skills, roping is one of the means by which the undercover manipulates the frame of performance while remaining covertly outside it.

Undercovers were instructed always to control the location of the scene in order to help it go their way:

> If you or the informer can influence the choice of location for the meet, make it a public place, like a restaurant or bar. Or out in the open, on a street corner or in a park. Surveillance can do a better job, then. It can protect the undercover better and corroborate the deal better. And if somebody's wearing a wire, there's less chance of them finding it.

An undercover instructor presented to our class as "cardinal" principles subtle but powerful ways of remaining in physical control: If you use the informant's car because it's the one the bad guy expects, *you* drive. Otherwise, you're the informant's hostage. Obviously, you never let the bad guy drive. Never let a bad guy sit behind you. Never do a deal in the bad guy's car.

When the undercover controls the location, he better ensures the occasion is preserved electronically, as well as keeps back-up with him more successfully. His willingness to change locations should, if possible, be based on his ability to carry surveillance personnel and equipment along:

> If you gotta move, a good undercover can always slow things down so he doesn't lose his surveillance. "Hey, what's the rush? Lemme finish my coffee." Or, "Jesus, hold on a minute. I left my fucking lighter back in the room." That kinda thing. If you keep on your toes and stay loose, you can run the whole deal the way you want to from start to finish.[21]

Video and audio recording become the immediate audience to a criminal performance, as undercovers ensure the essential visibility and audibility of their performers. They alter their own positions so that the bad guy can be fairly identified by hidden surveillance video recording, or encourage him to speak loudly enough to be picked up by hidden wires. In FBI undercover training, a major goal is to teach students to teach the bad guy how to play for the camera.[22]

According to Jerry VanCook, as stage director the undercover must balance being in role with maintaining the objectivity required to remember details and to make accurate reports:

> Too much emphasis on either can be destructive to your case and possibly to you. If you get too far into your character (subjectivity), you will have problems later when you try to recall the details of the case. But too much objectivity can cause a superficial performance, which will destroy your credibility and create doubt in the eyes of the bad guys.[23]

When undercover officers ply their roles, they unite investigation and imagination, and wrap together their abilities as both artist and connoisseur of identities. Yet the job, as Levine has described it, is really three- rather than twofold: in addition to performing the role and conducting the investigation, the undercover has his reputation, his credibility to preserve for his appearance in court.[24] An undercover must be careful that the gestures he performs in order to build credibility with the bad guy don't end up compromising that very credibility in court or with uniformed police. At some level, the undercover operator performs the difference between himself and the bad guy and must take care to balance perfectly his challenging roles as actor and visionary for the scene. One undercover thought it would be well within character to urinate against a wall, which didn't help his court testimony. Similarly, while playing an undercover role Vizzini was picked up by local police because of financial practices that had helped establish him to a criminal audience as one of them: "Except for walking-around money, I kept my funds in post-office money orders and hinted to guys I dealt with that they were forgeries picked up at a discount. It helped my image with the criminal element."[25]

The balance is clearly a sensitive one. Pistone describes the little dance he and his partner had to do to get close to the bad guys while keeping themselves out of trouble:

> Rossi and I were continually working on potential drug deals. That is, we worked to line them up and then tap-

> danced to keep them from happening. We had to en-
> courage drug sources by promoting our contacts and out-
> lets, how much we could move through "our" people. We
> had to keep Sonny and Lefty interested by promoting the
> capabilities of our drug sources. But we couldn't let any
> big deals happen. Nor could we have any busts that would
> compromise our operation. So the trick was to contact
> sellers, drag information out of them, keep them on the
> hook, and keep Sonny and Lefty excited—all while keep-
> ing the two sides apart.[26]

In a sense, the mandate to keep clean—or clean-*looking*—mediates
between the actor and director hats: by making sure that the undercover governs the choices he makes in role according to the
needs of the investigation, he makes canny investigatory decisions
in role, and helps conserve the credibility of the persona that testi-
fies in court. Three distinct role responsibilities, all for the most
part improvised, is a lot to handle. It can be helpful to imagine
someone else performing the directorial role: Levine specifically
thought of the "detached intelligence" that made the decisions for
him while he was in role as the "Producer/Director."[27]

When acting as their own scenario director, undercovers typically maneuver the dialogue so that the bad guy will summarize
his intentions and his actions for hidden surveillance audio recording; they keep the bad guy talking till he incriminates himself
since, as Mathers explains, "People [can] put themselves in jail by
opening their mouths, and that's what we get paid to do: is make
them open their big trap." However, when a cop disarms himself
of his official, uniformed role, he loses the tacit right to steer the
flow of information. If he wants the bad guy to open up, he must
earn his trust. And police culture in general doesn't teach or reinforce reciprocal disclosures. Thus, the steering of conversational
flow must be performed very carefully, or else it can be the pin-
prick on the cop's carefully sealed cover.

In playing Donnie Brasco, Pistone made sure his trickster persona clearly appeared indifferent to information that an investigator would have found relevant. Simultaneously, he sharpened
his own ability to take everything in and process it:

> I wanted to get known as a guy who didn't ask too many
> questions, didn't appear to be too curious. With the guys

we were after, it was tough to break in. A wrong move—even if you're on the fringes of things—will turn them off. While I was having a couple of drinks or dinner, I was always interested in what was going on in the place. I was always observing, listening, remembering, while still trying to put across the impression that I was oblivious to who was in there.

Like a dissimulating magician, Pistone misdirected attention about his true conversational aims by treating significant topics as having no particular value:

Occasionally I would change the subject or wander away from the table purposely, right in the middle of a discussion about something criminal that might be of interest to the government—precisely to suggest that I wasn't particularly interested. Then I would hope that the talk would come around that way again or that I could lead it back, get at it later or in another way. It was a necessary gambit for the long term.[28]

Pistone had learned the essential lesson of misdirection, as a magician does. Then, when he had specific issues to raise, he lay the groundwork very carefully: "For everything I did, every operation with Lefty, I first laid a foundation, introduced the matter in casual conversation, and dropped it. Brought it up again, dropped it. Then finally brought it up and made it stick."[29] The directorial consciousness remained strategic, in charge of the long-term role-play.

Role Features

Undercovers necessarily share some of the attributes of the characters they play. However, credit is due undercovers' real acting prowess, as there are also important differences between the qualities of the successful undercover and those of his typical character. For example, during the 1970s FBI guidelines specified that the undercover must be coolheaded, to "avoid exposing his cover with some rash act, emotional explosion, undisciplined outburst, or heated argument." He had to be especially good at controlling any display of fear, anger, disgust, and surprise.[30] By contrast, the undercover's *character* had to have the heart for the power plays and gamesmanship that characterize the tenser moments of business dealings in the drug world. Wansley noted that

> a great deal of game-playing goes on during any first meeting between two parties, each of whom is attempting to determine just how crooked the other might be. Generally, it becomes a ritualistic contest to see who will admit first that he's less than a law-abiding citizen. ...

> You avoid specifics and talk in guarded innuendos, dancing slowly toward that moment when one or the other finally admits his love of the ill-gained dollar.[31]

In an undercover training course, two would-be agents practiced asserting verbal control over each other. Using words as their show of weapons, they jabbed and thrusted at each other while trying to parry the other's attempt to control the conditions of a drug deal. What they argued over sounded at first like school-bully stuff: Who would hand over his wallet to the other first? Who would get to ask the other the leading questions? Above all, whose call would it be at each turn to control the interaction? In this course, the ability to win (or at least play) these mind games was prerequisite to gaining ground toward an incriminating drug buy.

A dialogue from the experience of New York Police Department Detective Sam Skeete shows the value of the operator's playing the requisite mind game while never letting the dealer outstrip him. The dealer opens with:

> "How much you want to start with?"

> I had five hundred dollars in buy money. I said, I want five hundred worth of cocaine.

> "All right, no problem. Give me the five hundred."

> Wait a minute—you have the drugs?

> "No. Give me the five hundred and come back later. I'll have the stuff for you."

> Well, I don't do business like that.

"Who do you think you are?" He took this indignant attitude. "C'mere, lemme talk to you." He told the
informant, "You wait here." He pulled me in a small
room, he says, "Look, lemme tell you something—"

He takes out a wad of hundred dollar bills about two
inches thick. Real hundred dollar bills. "You think I need
your five hundred?" It was really like being in a movie.

I can understand you don't need my money, I said—but
business is business. You wouldn't give me the drugs and
have me come back tomorrow and pay you, right?

"I'm beginning to like you."

Well, you know—maybe we can work it out. Laid back.

He put his arm around me. "I think we can do something."[32]

During our training, instructors emphasized the undercover
should not focus on his own performance, but rather on the other
guy's presentation of any signs of stress or erupting violence, and
on any evidence of interests, weaknesses, or proclivities that can
be penetrated or exploited to build a case. One instructor strongly
advocated adopting an aggressive questioning technique. His ra-
tionale was, if you continue to overload the other guy consistently
and heavily enough, all he'll have energy to do is to act and speak
honestly.[33]

An undercover student who became a chief player in one of
the evening field exercises found that this kind of aggressive
stance even helped him survive the stress of his first roleplay:
Heart pounding, mouth dry, he was still conscious of how hard he
was going to find it to look the bad guy in the eye while feeding
him lies, so he made a special effort to stare him down. The novice's "win" in the stare-down gave him additional confidence in
his ability to support the fictitious identity and pretext he had
prepared. The greater freedom he gained from concern about his
audience's opinion of him, the farther he progressed in his undercover training.

Building certain character features right into a trick identity
can make it easier for the law-enforcement officer to cover for the
necessary idiosyncrasies of his work. Pistone intentionally created

Donnie Brasco as an unreliable character, making the undercover's periodic disappearances part of the character pattern:

> From the time I began in California, I stayed in virtual
> daily touch with Lefty. [But] he didn't know how to reach
> me directly. I said I was always moving around. While
> Lefty was schooling me, I was also schooling him about
> me. I wanted him to get used to the fact that I was unpre-
> dictable. I would be vague about what I was doing, where
> I was. When I needed to cover myself, he would already
> be used to my style.[34]

Similarly, professional impostor Frank Abagnale found, when he
was suddenly called upon to replace an absent pediatrician, that
building absentmindedness into his character helped him (quick
on his feet but without any medical training) remain believable in
his role:

> I was aware from the moment I accepted [the request to
> fill in] that there was only one way I could carry out my
> monumental bluff. If I was going to fake out seven in-
> terns, forty nurses and literally dozens of support
> personnel, I was going to have to give the impression that
> I was something of a buffoon of the medical profession.
>
> I decided I'd have to project the image of a happy-go-
> lucky, easygoing, always-joking rascal who couldn't care
> less whether the rules learned in medical school were kept
> or not.[35]

Only the character of someone who had consciously determined
to transcend the norms of his profession could stave off accusa-
tions of not knowing *enough*. Absentmindedness, like Pistone's
evasiveness, filled in for what Abagnale really did not know. Likewise, a magician who acts absentminded can perform an action
essential to a trick, making the character feature a form of misdirection.[36]

Inattentiveness is also a serviceable character feature. Pistone
used his love for reading to advantage in creating a character that
could gather information unobtrusively:

> I am an avid reader. In this job especially, I was an avid
> newspaper reader. I read whatever newspapers I could get

my hands on. The guys would say, "Give Donnie the newspapers and he sits in a corner and he's happy all day."

But I wasn't always reading just to read. It was a good cover. While I was reading the *New York Post* or *The New York Times* or the *Daily News* from cover to cover, I was listening to their conversations.[37]

Jerry VanCook detailed four basic undercover character types, each of which has its peculiar Achilles' heel. The "tough-guy career criminal" has a high-school education at best, and acts as though he expects to spend his life bouncing in and out of prison. The danger is that, with his "bad-ass attitude," an undercover electing this type of role should expect to be challenged at some point to a test of toughness. A "Good Times Charlie" will do whatever offers short-term fun and profit. While the character's strengths are that he appears "too goofy to be a cop" and is unlikely to threaten other criminals, his "apparent passivity makes him a likely target for a rip-off." He might be a "Burned-Out Hippie," who "may spell V-I-C-T-I-M to a younger criminal who was raised on a diet of heavy metal or hate rock." Finally, the "White-Collar Con Man" is subject principally to legal and political traps, such as bribery or the enactment of a personal vendetta.[38]

Aside from these four types, for VanCook the greatest challenge and "the most fun you can have with your clothes on" is the role of hit man, in which one anticipates others' homicidal intentions by stepping into the role of the person who for a price will complete the murder. Many of the ordinary people who would hire a hit man have only seen one in movies. This frees the undercover to play the stereotype to the hilt:

> You're waiting ... at a local Burger King wearing your favorite safari jacket. Your hair falls to your shoulders, your beard is unkempt, you're doing that crazy little twitch you do with one eye, and you look like the burned-out, Vietnam-era, U.S. Marine Corps sniper-turned-hippie that is part of your identity when you go undercover as a hit man.

> Don walks in. You wave him over, and he sits down. You can growl, talk in a low, menacing voice, exaggerate the

tick, eat broken glass, or put cigarette butts out in the palm of your hand, but you don't have to do any of this. Nothing you do is going to change the way Don already feels about you, because what Don sees across the table from him is not a real-life hit man, but the manifestation of a Hollywood image he's been watching on the big screen since he was a kid.[39]

In any case, the features of the role rest on a solid knowledge of what the audience for the role will be expecting to see.

Certain legal and practical restrictions circumscribe aspects of the roleplay. In the interest of safety, in the 1970s, the Phoenix Police Department guidelines advised against oversexualizing one's role: "Do not associate with or show too much interest in subject's wife, girlfriend." The Peoria Police Department stressed, "AN UNDERCOVER OFFICER SHOULD NOT COME ON LIKE HE IS A USER OF DRUGS, but rather that he is interested only for monetary gain." The undercover who avoids playacting the role of a drug user can sidestep challenges that he do drugs together with dealers (which is expressly forbidden), or that he simulate using drugs (a technique to be used only in an emergency). Aside from the agency regulations, coming on as "a dealer only" also prevents a budding actor from having to do technically detailed physiological performances, whose contours his audience probably knows much better than he.

Peoria Police Department guidelines called for a distinctively minimalistic "naturalness." The dominant attitude of the undercover should be nonchalance, and he should take care not to "overplay [his or her] part." As a means of maintaining control over the suspect and to avoid presenting information he would later have to corroborate, the undercover should also avoid excessive exposition—not "make too many explanations," "give information," or "talk too much or bluff more than necessary." While withholding in these ways, the undercover also offers something that will attract the suspect, such as friendship, the "ability to purchase contraband," or readiness to "assist in criminal activity."

Goffman writes, for us to accept a performance as "natural," "we demand ... that [the performer] not be too good at acting, especially during occasions of talk." Paradoxically, however, certain situations may demand elaborate emotional displays to establish a persona's reality.[40] The two principal characters of the 1991 film *Rush* provide a balance between the low-key naturalism typically expected of the undercover cop and the charismatic behavior he must be ready to exhibit in order to "fit in" with the bad-guy drug dealers: Jennifer Jason Leigh's intent observation from within her girl-next-door character is counterbalanced by Jason Patric's testos-teronic intensity.

Naturalness is also commanded by the proper aging of a char-acter. Vizzini was wise in thinking to have his cover role, Air Force Major Mike Cerra, advance in his career over the course of a long-term investigation of a target:

> Since the last time I'd seen Charlie Lucky [Luciano], Ma-jor Mike Cerra had been promoted—he was now Lieu-tenant Colonel Cerra. This had been done to impress Lu-ciano and keep the cover looking legitimate. It also gave me a new reason for contacting him. When I wrote and told him about my new rank he was delighted. "We'll celebrate next time you're in town," he wrote back.[41]

By having Mike Cerra evolve in real time, Vizzini safeguarded the identity's viability.

As professional deceivers, magicians must psychologically en-dow their stage props as they would wish the audience to perceive them, using their own belief in them to arouse the audience's confidence. Referring to a trick using a nested die and shell, Fitz-kee cautions,

> This thinking of [the nested die and shell] in terms of how it is desired to have the spectators understand them is essential, I believe. Unless you force yourself to believe them to be but a single die, even though you know them to be otherwise, your own psychological responses will not conform to the desired impression. Somewhere, un-less you too believe, your words, your attitude—even unknown to you—may, and probably will, betray you.

Thus, it is unthinkable that a magician would "refer to [a trick die] as an 'ordinary' die, if it actually were ordinary. One naturally stresses that a thing is ordinary only when there is reason to sus-pect that it isn't."[42] Conversely, using objects with an aura of total belief, along with mastery of the performative apparatus of belief, can generate the necessary acceptance level on the part of the audience. Stage actors also "endow" objects with the qualities they wish the audience to believe they had—carrying a suitcase that is actually empty as if it were fully packed, sipping at an empty mug as if it contained piping cocoa.

Harry Houdini's virtuosity as an illusionist was magnified by his reliance on the simplest materials possible. For Fitzkee, a performer's virtuosity is demonstrated as he places increasingly fantastic demands on apparently ordinary objects. He asks rhetorically, "Tell me, do you believe it is possible to walk through a brick wall? Do you think it is possible to walk through a wall made of specially built and obviously specially painted panels? Which would seem the more difficult to accomplish?" Fitzkee's operating principle is that "no frankly magical device is nearly as deceptive as a device which looks like some ordinary thing familiar to the spectator."

Crucial to the audience's interpretation of the identity and function of objects is how the performer instills belief in them, stage by stage. Fitzkee writes approvingly of the process work of a fellow magician, who methodically completes all the technical stages that will encourage his audience to believe in his objects:

> When Frakson simulates the plucking of a cigarette or a coin from the air, the mere revelation of the cigarette or the coin is not sufficient. No. First, he sees the object. Then he indicates where it is, with an expression of happiness that it is there. Then he goes through the physical simulation of reaching for it. When it is revealed, he eyes it, with some astonishment that it was actually there. Then he expresses joy that he succeeded in getting it. And, having gotten it, he looks for more. Everything he says and does conveys the idea that the cigarettes are invisibly floating about in the air.[43]

Acting with a belief in the purported identity, status, and function of the objects—performing "psychological simulation"—convinces the audience.

Building Rapport and Fitting In

Most famously executed in con games, face-to-face performances quite typically involve the solicitation of the audience's
confidence. Just as in developing con games, the acting of an undercover role is a rapport-building activity, designed to gain the
confidence of suspects, to create trust and an easy relationship
within which business may be conducted. Earning the suspect's
confidence becomes especially important with high-level infiltrations, for example, of political systems or of organized crime
networks, where suspects may be well insulated and careful to
limit those with whom they communicate. Gifted undercovers
are, Mathers told me, "nice people—likable. ... If [bad guys] are
going to confess to you that they just murdered their mother-in-
law, they're not going to do it if they hate you."

The building of confidence in a target has everything to do
with how the undercover makes judicious self-disclosures that can
indicate the potential of a bond with him, one that can deepen
and allow the creation of new experiences together. When investigating a theft ring, the undercover operator can

> tell his target that he was once fired from a job for steal-
> ing. He can go on by saying that he felt he was justified in
> stealing from his company because the wages were so low
> that he felt he "had it coming to him." This fits in per-
> fectly with the "unwritten law" [about its being okay to
> steal from The Man], and may provoke a response from
> the target. At least, it will show a degree of trust the agent
> places in his target by revealing this damaging informa-
> tion, which presumably is not on his employment
> application.[44]

Over time, an operator knows that rapport has been established
by how willingly the subject follows him, leaving his own turf and
following the undercover to his:

> You are actually entering the other person's world. Once
> you establish rapport, you can do the leading. That is,
> once you match or mirror the other party you can gradu-
> ally switch gears and the other person should follow you.
> This can also be used as a test to see if you have estab-
> lished the human communication link of rapport in the

first place. That is, if you start to switch into another mode of communication and your subject isn't following you, stop. You have not established rapport.

Establishing himself as a member of the same club as a subject enables an undercover to signal that they can bend certain rules together. While in general banking workers are prohibited from releasing account numbers, they may do so with a person who identifies himself as a colleague in the banking industry who demonstrates awareness of this rule.[45]

Paradoxically, the prior establishing of rapport and trust are essential foundations for being able to build a case against the target. Vizzini recounts the story of watching hungrily as his target played with a fistful of big bills. Dying to record their serial numbers, the pretext the undercover came up with to do so hinged on his target's affection for him, as well as on his playing on the bad guy's somewhat paranoid worldview:

> "You know," I reminded him, "that I'm going into the hospital for a checkup on my neck tomorrow, Charlie. How about giving me one or two of your bills for a bunch of my small ones? It'll make it easier for me to keep track of my money."
>
> He agreed and I gave him five twenties and a handful of lire for two hundreds.
>
> He looked close at me as we made the exchange. "That's a good idea, Mike. You're smart not to trust anybody."[46]

An affinity or collusion between an undercover and a bad guy can often be developed by identifying each other as allies against an external enemy. A narc in training succeeded in connecting with the bad guy by enjoining him in the joint "ragging" of a waitress.

The strategy of becoming the fulfillment of the target's fantasy was illustrated in the previous chapter, in the case of the undercover who appeared to the criminal father of the bride as a can-handle-anything caterer. Similarly, Vizzini's willingness to play into the American spy fantasies of the Turkish National Police officer with whom he was partnering helped build rapport:

"Signor Vizzini, do you mind if Ali Eren calls you Mike?" I spoke no Turkish at all at the time. Ali Eren spoke nothing but Turkish. ... Until I could handle his language, the only thing I ever heard him say in English was "Tank you very much." He said it all the time, whether we were shooting at opium peddlers or boiling tea over a campfire out in the hills. He was really proud of those words, although I don't think he knew what they meant.

"Why does Ali want to call me Mike?" I'd asked Labernas.

"Because you remind him of Mike Hammer, the American detective."

He showed me a copy of a Mickey Spillane paperback, printed in Turkish, and pointed out that Mike Hammer carried his gun in the small of his back, as I sometimes did.

"Sure," I said. "He can call me Mike if I can call him Ali Baba."

So Mike became my name with them and I even took out a cable address under the name of Mykham. I had never read a Mike Hammer story in my life.[47]

Attempting to establish commonality too facilely can backfire. An undercover in training recounted the story of a frightful mistake: thinking he would win points with the bad guy for being as suspicious and paranoid as he assumed his target was, he glanced out of the restaurant window at a white Ford Taurus. He expressed concern that it might be a surveillance car from the social work agency; he was behind on his child-support payments, and was expecting to be tailed. This particular tactic, which might have brought murmurs of sympathy from other men at a casual dinner, only angered the bad guy, who held as a strong value the financial support of children. This incident ended up providing a lesson for the undercover class as a whole: in developing an undercover identity that does things as rich as talk about personal matters and interests, one must do ample advance research to ensure that one is well aware of the likeliest topics to touch off the bad guy's ire. It makes sense to tell heterosexual-bonding gay jokes only if one is absolutely certain his bad guy is homophobic.

Even given the emphasis in contemporary undercover training on improvisational skill, over and against costuming and appearance, many undercover assignments are actually "cast" according to specific physical types. In some agencies, computer files support a kind of in-house casting service. To meet the exigencies of a specific assignment, they keep track of race and age, in addition to such skills as driving a bulldozer. In 1985, the FBI had "a cadre of people in our undercover bank of personnel ... that we can draw on to play certain roles."[48] Vizzini felt he was only able to have a chance at penetrating the Sicilian Mafia because he actually is of Sicilian descent:

> An outsider can't crack that family sense, and you can't fake being a Sicilian. Al Capone tried it and got a scar on his face.

> The best con artist in the world would stand out like an albino Watusi if he tried. Put me in a pitch-dark room with twenty men who have no accent and after a few minutes of conversation I can tell you who is Sicilian. Or put me in a lighted room with no conversation, and if the men are moving around, I'll do the same thing. Any true Sicilian can.[49]

Since a major realm for undercover infiltrations and investigations into drug trafficking is high schools, experienced undercovers with youthful appearances can be in high demand. These undercovers typically appear in their new classrooms as high school students whose families have recently relocated.[50] Like other students, they study (or not), take tests, turn in homework. Undercovers who were good in algebra the first time may need to perform in trick identities at a lower level in order to be accepted by the target group, once again distinguishing what they as performers know from what the characters they play do.

Roleplays in high schools and workplaces, where students and workers may be suspected of selling drugs or stealing, demand that the undercover demonstrate, in addition to the social skills of the role he represents, appropriate institutional performances. Just like endowing props in magic, in order to get a trick identity accepted one must first establish its legitimacy and then build the suspect's confidence in it. One establishes legitimacy by "going through channels," by gaining an introduction from a person the suspect respects, or by entering the work or social world of the suspect by widely accepted practices:

> There should be no attempt to sidestep the usual hiring or initiation procedures. [The undercover's] introduction to employment or an organization must have all the earmarks of being on the up-and-up. The first task of the [undercover] is to become identified with his new associates in the usual manner.

The undercover must demonstrate appropriate patience in developing rapport with his new comrades. He must follow any unspoken social conventions; indeed, undercovers who attempt to infiltrate high schools have great difficulty gaining sufficient social acceptance when they are not permitted by their departments to spend time with students after school or to attend weekend parties or sporting events. To the degree possible, the undercover must act the way other members of the group he is infiltrating do; any appearance of what Bruce A. Jacobs terms "transactional over-aggressiveness," or trying to move too quickly into making buys, will instantly reveal him to be an undercover. Confidence-building is linked with personal patience: "The key to such confidence building is to carry his share of the load, be friendly, and become well liked. Any conscious effort to win confidence or to be liked by his fellows must be truly unobtrusive. It is under the guise of "regular employee" or "regular member" that the [undercover] becomes a "regular fellow." It is actually dangerous for an undercover to attempt to infiltrate a work setting through any other means than a straightforward interview: even in the unlikely case that the personnel officer understands why the undercover really wants the job, it is crucial, for the benefit of all other staff who will be watching, to follow the normal procedure.[51] And, because it is likely that only one person in a job setting knows the undercover is not simply a regular worker, the operator can get fired if he does not demonstrate sufficient output or progress in his ostensible work.

In an institutional performance, the corporate values of reliability and regularity may supplant the character qualities of evasiveness and unpredictability that would otherwise succeed in protecting a cover. The undercover operator must not miss work unduly and draw suspicion to himself: "If it is necessary to be absent from time to time, the [operator] should vary the time of day when he is gone. He must not establish a suspicious routine that in any way departs from the accepted norm of his fellow workers or associates." In addition, "an experienced operative avoids loafing on the job or taking advantage of his undercover position to ease his work load. He follows company rules and does his share." He must also spend money in ways and at rates that are reflective of the local culture. Emotional displays, especially of undue aggression, must be avoided. [52]

Additional players can enhance the plausibility of the undercover operator infiltrating a work setting, either by also discreetly hiring themselves in apparently regular work roles later, or by sending in a decoy agent "who makes himself conspicuous by asking indiscreet questions, by listening in on conversations, looking in drawers and toolboxes, and trying to get too friendly too soon." This agent is free to leave once the real agent has gotten "in" with the target crowd. [53]

Finally, an undercover who infiltrates a work group needs also to be wary of aligning himself too neatly with those in power. When Vizzini worked undercover as a blackjack dealer in San Juan, he received so many compliments from the boss that his coworkers hazed him by stealing his uniform. He recognized he would have to play their game to be reincorporated into the group. Similar to anthropologists' tales of how they pulled pranks, acts of violence, or destruction of property in order to gain social acceptance with the cultures they came to study is Vizzini's tale of how he sprayed his fellow blackjack dealers' uniform jackets with orange soda as a ritual of reinclusion. [54]

Learning and Transmission

Every moment you spend undercover, you're just a hair from dead. The only reason I'm alive today is dumb luck, bad marksmanship and something I can tell you about but can't teach you.

—Michael Levine

Because of its covert nature, few would-be undercover opera-tors have had real contact with any practitioners. Thus, it is televi-sion and film images, as well as newspaper accounts and popular fiction, that impress upon newcomers compelling images of these jobs much more than do operators already working in the field. As media that rely on the seductiveness of the appearances they create, television and film have used undercover law enforcement, double-agentry, impostorship, and impersonation as stock-in-trade subject matter.

Trick identity lends itself neatly to dramatic treatment. In a "well-made play," a revelation to other characters of information (already known to the audience) permits thematic closure. The inherently dramatic power of revelation is reinforced when the subject of such revelation is identity itself.

Before he began working with the Royal Canadian Mounted Police, Mathers already had a well-formed picture from film and television of what undercover work and its lifestyle would be like:

> Oh, yeah, and I think it would be a complete lie to say that you don't. The crooks do! I've seen the young po-licemen display behavior that is reminiscent of something they might have seen in film—and that's being very kind. And when it's young guys, most of the time you just let it go; they're just growing up.

Mathers and other experienced undercovers joke about the "baby steps" they have watched novice undercovers take as they learned to adjust their television images to the realities of the work. Even baby narcs' costuming notions came straight from popular media: "We used to have a saying with the young guys, 'If it's black and it has Velcro on it, these young kids will buy it.'"

At the technical level, the performances of emotion that are conventionally accepted as "real" on film or television have little to do with how emotion may be believably expressed and ac-cepted, a gap that can have tremendous impact on new undercovers' safety. From his years of experience on *Candid Cam-era* and *Candid Microphone*, Allen Funt noted the difference between "candid" and "canned" emotion:

> I have seen cold anger expressed with nothing more than a limp smile. I have watched a man get the surprise of his life without the slightest visible change of attitude. We have photographed joy that looked like dismay, sorrow that resembled gaiety, and terror that could easily have passed for genuine.[55]

Because of this discrepancy between emotion in real life and as it is represented in the media, early undercover performances can court dangers. One of these is the mimicking of media portrayals in situations where the local behavior departs from the media image. Another is the undercover's failing to recognize a bad guy's own attachment to such media imagery, since the good and the bad guys have grown up on similar images:

> When a criminal goes to the theater and watches Arnold Schwarzenegger's facial expressions and body language, he remembers those mannerisms at a subconscious level. He associates the lowering of an eyebrow with bad guys getting the hell beat out of them, and when he hears Arnold say, "I'll be back," he knows the hero will be shooting when he returns. Even though some criminals have dealt with real cops since their first juvenile bust, they have still seen more cops on TV and in the movies, and the differences they perceive between Hollywood and real life are not as distinct as one might like to think.[56]

Key in either case is determining what appears to be "real" or "natural" to the audience for one's performance.

Even veteran undercovers may still warm to the old television images. One undercover instructor tuned in to *NYPD Blue*. Another recalled warmly a *Miami Vice* episode in which Sonny Crockett (played by Don Johnson), is asked, "Sonny, you ever forget who you are?" to which he responds darkly, "Darling, sometimes I *remember* who I am." The undercover swelled, "I *love* that line!" Nevertheless, he would warn novice undercovers that they needed to be wary of the "John Wayne syndrome" and keep in check the power media imagery hold over them when they work. He cautions, "Ego puts more coppers into the grave than anything else."

Because media images have contributed so much to the recruit-
ment of new undercovers, much must be unlearned in their actual
training. The need for training was recognized by the mid-1970s,
but it took some time for roleplaying technique to be articulated
within a practical curriculum. What training there was focused on
helping students manipulate the paraphernalia of undercover
work—surveillance electronics, drug simulation props, or even the
most current street jargon. Thus, even in the late 1970s in the
United States, little planning or training went into the roleplaying
aspects of undercover operations and relatively little support cov-
erage was supplied. Undercovers learned on the job and by
making mistakes. Mathers initially went on his own devices "and
from what I could steal from anybody else that I met—crooks,
other UCs—anything that I saw, heard, read that I figured I could
mold into something that would have an effect."

The performances of other undercovers and of confidential
informants—held by many undercovers to be superior roleplayers—
were one new performer's school. An undercover trainer admitted, "I'm a parasite: I'll just sit down, take as much information as
I can from an individual, use what's beneficial to me, and throw
out the rest." Vizzini believed in the catch-as-catch-can, on-the-job
method of proving oneself, as opposed to submitting to classroom
training and tests: "Dope peddlers in the hills of Turkey, and in
New York City, don't read books. They're predators, and they
learned by doing. When you go undercover you become one of
them."

FBI regulations forbade agents helping or even watching people use drugs. However, without any personal experience, and
knowing he would have to play a junkie role believably, Vizzini
supplied his informant with money to buy heroin, stole his works
from him, and then maneuvered him into shooting up—and afterward spiraling down—as he watched. Vizzini "sat fascinated,
watching this shaky man perform his murderous procedures with
the artistry of a watchmaker."[57] He also discovered that, if his informant depended on fixes at three- or four-hour intervals, there
would be two useful hours between fixes during which he could
siphon information that would further the investigation.

By the 1980s, many of the legal, ethical, and health demands
of undercover work had been identified, and undercovers had to

learn ways to be more careful while still getting close to the bad guy. More or less formally, undercovers were taught how to simulate drug use.[58] Drug simulation techniques involved a form of sleight-of-hand—or of-mouth—and were good examples of misdirection. Marijuana joints would be put to a cop's lips but not inhaled. Alternatively, the cop could keep "a standard tobacco cigarette going at the same time, the smoke from which will help to conceal his ruse with the marijuana or hashish." Pills could be passed in front of the mouth without being dropped in, then inconspicuously stored in a pocket. A mirror was a magical prop in snorting a line of cocaine.[59] During the worst years of the AIDS epidemic, however, any type of intravenous drug use simulation was completely discouraged.

The American training emphasis on plausible talk emerged in part from the ethical, legal, and practical problems of using simulation to establish a trick identity's authenticity. As concerns for preserving the credibility of the cop in court grew, undercover training in the early 1990s stressed the somewhat tidier skill of mastering street argot for drug names and practices. In one course, as many of the students joked informally of now needing to have an ear pierced, of growing longer hair or beards, or of dressing in "skanky" clothing, the instructor assured them that "Your brain is the most powerful weapon." Warning of a period in the history of the New York Police Department in which cops began killing their own undercovers because they couldn't tell them apart from the bad guys, one instructor stressed that it was not a disaster to differentiate oneself from the bad guy to some degree visually. Students should therefore dispense with any sort of "*Miami Vice* Syndrome," downplay the importance of their appearances for being accepted, and develop their abilities to "talk your way in and talk your way out."

Overall, the more recent training style has emphasized the cultivation of mental skills, though actual techniques have ranged from Neuro-Linguistic Programming, to the assumption of a particular mindset by listening to war stories of veteran undercovers, to the training of the ability to calculate one-upmanship opportunities in the moment. At one agency's training, the key skills developed were negotiating and planning. The job of working undercover was characterized as determining the best "deal" of gaining criminal evidence, while gambling with existing conditions and reasonably assessing risks.

The Royal Canadian Mounted Police experimented with training undercovers in self-hypnosis to help them get into character. More consistently, undercover trainees learned, as do stage actors, to use sense and emotional memory, to develop the physical realities of their roles. They might practice having a rock in a shoe to help produce a limp, or recall an emotional situation in their own pasts to help produce an appropriate emotional reaction in an undercover scene.

FBI training belied its commitment to "osmosis learning." Agents who had made it through especially risky times would come in and tell their war stories, and were regarded as having more to contribute than so-called "egghead" instructors. Supplementing classroom and structured field training, those who live to tell their stories have become the most valued teachers of undercover technique, since, as one trainer put it, "There are no experts in this field, just people with more or less experience."

In the war story, cop culture builds its own lasting images of undercover work. However, brag accounts, experts caution, are fashioned according to the teller's needs, and many raconteurs readily introduce ego distortions. Thus, the war story can be both one of the most powerful and one of the most misleading sources of representations of the undercover role.

Roleplaying exercises, in which the student practices developing and performing a role under more or less controlled conditions, were introduced into American undercover training during World War II, when the U. S. Department of Defense's Office of Strategic Services trained military spies by means of the realistic scenario or the "work sample exercise."[60] The FBI's first undercover training in 1975 lasted only three days. By 1983, Bob Lill had added roleplaying to the curriculum, and expanded the format to two weeks. Experienced undercover agents resurrected actual scenarios they had faced in the field and portrayed bad guys opposite the students. Even early on, training made use of videotaping and critique. Recognizing in the early 1990s that going under involves a form of acting, the Michigan State Police expressly laid out its recommendation that this aspect of undercover work be taught through roleplay and scenario, rather than through classroom lecture or discussion.

When in 1981 Taylor founded the Professional Law Enforcement Group, he looked to the training he had known at the FBI and the DEA, as well as at the Michigan State Police and the California Department of Justice. As head of his own organization, he scheduled roleplaying for approximately 24 of a 130-hour undercover drug enforcement training course. PLE instructors would videotape the roleplaying sessions, then critique the performances of trainees before their peers.

Rather than using the more controlled set-ups typical of American training centers, in the early 1990s the Royal Canadian Mounted Police trained its undercovers through live-action roleplays on the streets of major cities. Despite the very real risks, RCMP trainees would wear wires and do actual drug deals while trying to survive on the streets for 36 hours without money or identification. Unseen evaluators awarded points for the ingenuity by which they lived by their wits. As it taught and tested resourcefulness, this exercise allowed evaluators to identify students who experienced too much anxiety or too little improvisational ability to succeed well in the undercover role. Since then, a focus on organized crime and higher profile criminals limited this style of training aimed at catching drug dealers.

In the U.S., undercover training is considered much more extensive at the federal level than at either state or local levels. At all levels, undercover training has a certain amount of centralization, both geographically and by discipline. It is not uncommon for agencies to send their people to a centralized training center to learn undercover techniques, and to find personnel from several different kinds of agencies at training. Undercover training normally centers on drug enforcement, even though clandestine investigation techniques may be used for a panoply of criminal exchanges. This is because drugs provide the pretext for talking with people on the street; further, much of the illegal traffic in such areas as art forgeries, firearms, and even immigration also involves drug traffic.

Lill believes each case necessitates its own inventions: "You wouldn't recognize anything from one operation into the next." By contrast, Mathers likens the recycling of bits of dialogue or behavior that have succeeded in the past to the use of stock footage in film.[61] In Mathers' estimation, undercover roleplaying is "*very* improvisational," and particular licks are good enough to re-use where appropriate: "You just keep the things that are good. 'That worked the last time, so I'll use it again.' ... It's a trade, like being a plumber: you know what works, so you use it." Mathers found in his mother's advice the best acting manual:

> One thing my mom told me when I was a kid, and I always go back to it, People think of you what you think of you. And I used that on the crooks. If I think I'm a bigtime mobster, so do they. They don't know what the hell, they've never met a mobster! [They think,] "I guess that's what a gangster's all about!"

In preparation for his undercover professional role as a blackjack dealer and to pass a Puerto Rican licensing test, Vizzini practiced topping off the chips "alone before the mirror ... hour after hour, watching myself, looking for a clumsy or amateurish move. My legs got so tired they ached."[62] Perhaps because he had to camouflage a built-up body that had spent long hours at the gym, RCMP undercover Murray Simms told me how heavily he would rely on physical means to get into character, which involved taking on "a different posture, a different walk, a different disposition." For him, twenty to thirty seconds would bring him in. First, he changed his walk, then the posture. Drawing the feet inward helped them to shuffle and drag. Next, he brought the shoulders and the head down, and began to peer out of the tops of his eyes.

The posture felt "lazy" to him. He didn't swing his arms as he ordinarily might, and he kept his hands in his pockets. The patter connected with his role came out of his sense of his costume, which, to conceal the power of his upper body, typically consisted of oversized pants and shirts, hi-top runners, and a full-length jacket.[63] Two signs would let this performer know he was ready to go: first, he could place his attention outside himself; second, he could recognize that he looked like everyone around him. The power of the altered exterior to convince one of a changed identity Newman names as a key part of shifting identity: "You should be able to clearly see the difference between the old you and the new you. As time goes on the old you should seem more and more like a stranger to you. A key factor in this is your physical appearance."[64]

The Undercover Performer

The one audience that never misses the undercover's performances is his own watchful consciousness. And the greater his performance skill, the more his watching self warms to his identity tricks. Not the least of the motivations for continuing in undercover work are the rewards of performing well, and of having the opportunity to playact roles unavailable in one's home identity.

Some undercovers have opportunities to "play up" in their roles, to take on trick identities that are higher in the social class hierarchy than their own experience. And, having adapted to the role, many of them find it difficult to abandon their newly developed, sometimes expensive tastes. Mathers found he was "a lot *more* comfortable driving a Mercedes," and enjoyed eating in the fine restaurants he frequented in his high-status identity.[65]

Other undercovers appreciate not having to live up to their own social class, and find a kind of relief in slumming via the medium of their trick identity. As one trainee put it one evening after the day's classes:

> You get to be whoever you want. If you want to be the guy who drives the nice car, has all the money, lots of flash, you can do that if you want to. I'm not really a scummy person, but I'd rather have a pair of jeans with a hole in it and no shirt laying in a lawn chair drinking beer than be out playing volleyball on the beach, I'm just that kind of person. I like motorcycles. I like strip joints, not strip joints for the women, but the kind of people that go there, I associate with the kind of life that they lead.[66]

Whether they move up or down socially by taking on a trick identity, undercovers find an intrinsic reward in the roleplay that draws them further in.

It is not surprising that, in many cases, undercovers form a strong attachment to their roles. Stage actors sometimes experience an almost filial bond with favorite characters to which they have given body. It is perhaps even more likely that, having developed a character largely out of their own vital statistics, history, personal experiences, and interests, undercovers quickly come to feel attached to the role. Vizzini reminisces, "The one I liked most was Pasquale Lombardi. He got to be almost my other self." Notably, Lombardi (like many of the characters Vidocq impersonated) had been a real criminal who happened to have similar physical descriptors as the undercover who took over his persona.[67] Assuming the role of the vanquished is a special kind of identity conquest, where identity performance constitutes a specific act of power. When the vanquished person's right to a particular public role is totally emptied as he is put away, the remaining identity is available for inhabitation by another—perhaps most richly by its conqueror.

One undercover reported the role felt more "his" than his own identity; for this loner, at least, the trick identity emerged out of real social interaction. One of the most profoundly moving experiences of his undercover career, signaling his acceptance by his target, was being tagged with a nickname: "Somehow, the nickname is 'real' and the name on the driver's license is a fake. The name on the driver's license ... I [just] made this up. ... [But] I was the one who did whatever it was that generated [the nickname]." A trick identity may also feel real to its performer because re-use is expected. Character exits are specifically orchestrated to permit re-entry if necessary; and there may be cases in which the resurrection of a specific role is the best available choice.[68]

A DEA agent once said of the undercover role, "You gotta live it, you gotta love it, you gotta leave it." As an undercover operator exits a trick identity, he must wash himself wholly clean of any residue of the role. This is no easy process; even Eliza Doolittle in George Bernard Shaw's *Pygmalion* could not simply go back to being a street urchin after she had been trained to pass as a highborn lady. For the undercover operator, this process is doubly difficult because he is not only actor and director but also scriptwriter, the very inventor of his character. Failing to allow time to get out of character before accompanying his wife to her parents' house for Thanksgiving dinner, after his in-laws' minister gave the prayer, Van Cook said, still in the role of "Mick Jordan," "Now, will somebody please pass the motherfuckin' turkey. I'm hungry."[69]

The resistance of some undercovers to completing the transition out of their trick identities may stem not so much from shifting back to a primary or different reality as from letting go of the occupational perks that go along with the work. As Kaufman puts it, "There's a very significant loss and grief process that goes along with going back into uniform. That's where the stress comes from." It is generally with deep cover that reality-shifting problems occur, "and I think that the reality-shifting problems are supervision problems."

It *is* hard to turn off the qualities that cause one to succeed in undercover work, and it's not clear how compelling, in many cases, the motivation is to do so. Levine's ex-wife Liana reflected,

> Michael's life was a constant challenge to him. Every situation he was in, every person he met, had to be mastered in one way or another, and where women were concerned, that usually meant in a sexual way. And it wasn't enough to rise to a challenge now and again. He had to do it every day. Twice a day. Which is the perfect motivation, I suppose, for a cop, but absolute hell on one's personal life.[70]

Undercover Pistone knew that the "wiseguy attitude" would remain with him, whether he was in or out of role:

> Most people back down from a confrontation in public, but in the wiseguy world, you don't back down. Not from waiters or salesmen or anybody. Instead of saying "forget about it" to yourself, you take the offensive right away. It's not bullying, at least in a physical sense.

> But my brother will see me act this way, and he'll say, "Joe, you're not out with the wiseguys." My answer is, "Why should you be intimidated by somebody when you know you're right?"[71]

By the 1980s, many supervisors recognized that regular psychological upkeep would be necessary to maintain undercovers' ability to distinguish themselves from their roles. In addition, changes in operating procedures made appropriate separations easier to make. Agencies found they could help operators keep the trick role separate from a home identity by ensuring that there be a separate physical space associated with it; having an apartment at which the undercover could live and conduct business while in role went a long way toward keeping his private life clean and un-encumbered.[72] At the RCMP, Mathers modeled the behavior of calling home frequently. The FBI required its agents to find con-crete ways to distance themselves from the physicality, mannerisms, and manners that were associated with their trick roles.

The Michigan State Police instituted a regular "transition meet-ing" for the undercover, his undercover supervisor, and his uniform supervisor. Typically held at the end of two to three years of undercover work in anticipation of the move back to conven-tional policing, this meeting has been used to summarize the un-dercover's achievements in role, to determine which of the new skills gained could be applied to meet the expectations of the uni-form supervisor, and to discuss significant changes that have occurred in uniform work since the officer has been under. In addition, a transitioning undercover went through a weeklong debriefing session, in which a group of transitioning undercover operators described and debriefed their experiences with the help of experienced "transitioned" officers.[73]

Royal Canadian Mounted Police undercovers visited a psy-chologist at least every six months in the 1990s in order to iden-tify any developing identity problems, touch base in their home identity, and de-stigmatize psychological treatment in case of a later emergence of serious issues. Before an undercover undertook a deep cover role, the RCMP interviewed him about his personal activities, so that he wouldn't lose track of those things that could reinforce him in his home identity—even as, with success in the trick role, he would be heavily reinforced to stay under. As a means of re-engaging them within the street-cop frame, supervi-sors might shame or mock undercovers whom they thought potentially in danger of going too far in their roles, or who were already roleplaying outside of appropriate arenas.

A certain amount of the distress associated with the transition out of the role comes with the player's recognition of parts of his life he may have ignored during his time under. Studies of the personal problems of police officers as a whole consistently show marital troubles heading the list; undercover officers even more consistently report marital difficulties. A significant number of undercover cops return to their primary reality to find that it has shifted in irreversible ways. As Levine framed it, "I never knew a good undercover with a happy home life. Or, look at it another way, if a guy's not happy at home then very likely he's good on the job."[74] In one study, at the start of an operation, two-thirds of undercover cops recognized their taking on undercover work would represent a significant strain on their marriages, while only one-third of their spouses anticipated a problem. Six months into the operation, the proportions were reversed: two-thirds of the spouses had seen the havoc that long absences, evasiveness, and overinvolvement in the role could make of family life, while many undercovers had lost their ability to perceive this, suggesting the high level of denial about impact on family life that forms the core of the undercover experience.

For some undercovers, it's getting into role that feels like jumping hurdles. An undercover wishing to carry a gun has probably not made the full commitment to playing a trick identity. Initially, one Christian undercover had difficulty reconciling some of the language he had to use with his sense of morality. Eventually, he came to the sense that he could speak those words because he believed in the ultimate end of enforcing the law, and in the necessity of fully mirroring a culture that uses foul language in order to do so.

Another undercover's sense of an appropriate worldly hierarchy made his transition into work in narcotics arduous. Prior police work had instilled in him a firm sense that what cops and citizens did was in the service of what was good and right, and what criminals did furthered wrong:

> I was working my tail off to get these people in jail—and in Narcs, you work your tail off to get them back out of jail, to turn them into informants, to have them assist you to put people in jail. Plus I hated the criminal element so much, I found it hard to get to the place where I could associate with them. I found it really difficult to socialize with them, to hang with them—you know, all of the qualities that you have to have in order to work undercover effectively.

Even working with informants was vexing: "I was kind of prejudiced. You've committed a crime, you're a scumbag, you should be labeled for life." He left narcotics work for two years, during which "I grew out of that. I mean, everybody makes mistakes, they really do." Now back in narcotics work, his new ability to see more than one side of an issue has never compromised his facility in moving psychologically out of a case. After arrest, people he had apparently befriended would express their sense of betrayal. He recalled one dealer who dissolved into tears as he was taken away, calling out, "You're my friend! You're my friend. How could you do this to me?" He replied without hesitation, "I was never your friend, you scumbag."

More typical, perhaps, was Vidocq's ability to maintain, or at least perform, some sympathy for the victim of his lies, while holding fast inwardly to his official identity. In role, Vidocq represents to the mother of a criminal that her son is planning to escape to her:

> Madame Noel was happy in the expectation of seeing her son, and shed tears of tenderness at the very thoughts of it. I will own that I was affected, and for a moment wavered if for once I would not betray my duties as a police agent; but when I reflected again on the crimes committed by the Noel family, and considered what was due to the interests of society, I remained firm and determined in my resolution to go through with my enterprise at all risks.[75]

An undercover can never fully retire. He always continues to live with the knowledge that, if he is recognized by bad guys he helped put away, his life remains in danger. He avoids being photographed. An undercover is the "one actor who never wants [his] picture in the paper."[76] In the 1963 special *Money for Burning* Secret Service agent Dick Roth warned, "You realize to photograph me may destroy my usefulness to the Service." And in his memoir of his undercover exploits, a self-glamorizing Vizzini emphasizes how dangerous the act of writing is. He opens:

> I could end up dead by writing this book. I'm not being melodramatic. Against all the rules of undercover work,

> I'm "putting myself in the window." I'm putting myself
> on display. I'm revealing my true identity. Many agents
> have been killed because their identity was revealed. ...
> This book is meant to give some insight into the world of
> undercover. It puts nobody in the window but myself.

The cover story is one way that, as identity artists, undercover operators fake what they say about who they are. However, the persona that traffics in the world is not comprised merely of what one says about oneself. In addition to identifying a person by what he knows and what he is, the undercover persona is also comprised of the costumes, props, and scenarios that the identity artist stages for his audience's consumption. [77] The next chapter details how material artifacts contribute to the staging of a passable identity, focusing particularly on the physical disguise techniques and the production of paper-based identity documents in the late twentieth-century, before the incursion of electronic identity theft. To a large extent, the techniques of creating and presenting such material artifacts are shared by identity artists on both sides of the law: indeed, it takes one to know one.

3

THE ARTIFACTS OF IDENTITY

A forgery is a document which not only tells a lie, but tells a lie about itself.

—C. S. Kenny

Today a person finds himself accepted more on the basis of his documentation than his personality. Paperwork is everything.

—John Sample, *Methods of Disguise*

I t came just in time, this appealing job offer: master impostor Frank Abagnale's pediatrician identity was reaching the end of its life expectancy. All he'd have to do was present a Harvard Law School transcript, and he'd as good as have a job with the state attorney general's office.

The master craftsman went to work. Abagnale had never so much as seen a college transcript—much less graduated high school—but the woman he was sleeping with had one. Heckling got him just what he wanted: the girlfriend, who had been a business major at Ohio University, dug out her transcript to demonstrate to him that she had in fact gone to college. Abagnale reports, he quickly

> committed the structure of the transcript to memory, absorbing it as a sponge absorbs water, before handing it back. "Okay, you're not only sexy, you're also brainy," I said in mock apology.
>
> I went shopping the next day at a graphic arts supply house, a stationery store and an office-supply firm, picking up some

> legal-sized bond paper, some layout material, some press-on
> letters in several different type faces, some artist's pens and
> pencils, an X-Acto knife, some glue and a right-angle ruler,
> some gold seals and a notary's press.[1]

The letter-perfect transcript—which Abagnale meticulously pasted up
and then xeroxed—got him hired as a lawyer. He passed the state bar
exam by his third try. The transcript simply acted as the ticket for
Abagnale to perform to his own abilities.

Fake Identities: Paper People

Identity change is no longer this simple. Complete medical, financial, and legal histories can be recorded and stored on the surface of
universal identity cards, or implanted just below the skin of their
owners, changing significantly the rules of the identity game. In this
world, a bit of computer programming and medical knowledge can
enable identity borrowings, ruptures, and erasures.

For most of history's identity fugitives even up to the present day,
however, special techniques for creating or for kidnapping and traveling on the visas of others' identities have been neither particularly
technological nor surgical. Rather, they have hinged on the ability of
the identity artist to lock wits with those he wishes to evade or fool.
In recent generations, identity tricksters have engaged directly with
governmental agencies and their strategies of detection. They have
successfully plied the very categories of identity that such agencies
have established to identify criminals. The drama of identity creation
and detection pits protagonist and antagonist against one another in
a game of high-stakes marksmanship and ingenuity.

Paper ID is the first mode of trafficking the self in the public, specifically, in the legal, commercial, and—for others like Abagnale—the
professional arenas. It is one in which we have perhaps all taken part.
Gary T. Marx challenges his readers to look themselves squarely in
the mirror:

> Is your vita a perfect reflection of your biography? Are there
> any salient omissions or embellishments? Have you ever used

a ticket or enjoyed a benefit that belonged to someone else and was not to be transferred? Have you ever used an alias (even if for nothing more serious than making a reservation you were not sure you would be able to keep)? Do you know of any cases where a student took an exam for someone else? Did you (or your children) have fake IDs permitting you to buy liquor, although underage? ... What would happen if the IRS were to do an in-depth audit of your taxes, looking especially at deductions and unreported income?[2]

Although documents help to link "particular flesh-and-blood individual[s]" with "their past characteristics, misdeeds and accomplishments," the personal mobility that is an accepted feature of contemporary American life has made it possible to start again, as if from scratch: "The complexity, size and anonymity of our society make it fairly easy to leave the scene of one's previous misbehaviors. Only documentation can link those who do so to their pasts."[3] This is easiest for those living outside the pervasively computerized credit system, and buying with cash. Paper ID is the medium by which selves get permission to act in the world—though sometimes permission is just taken, and forgiveness asked later.

Like the costume arranged just so on the shoreline, paper ID provides a conventional set of signs of a state of being one may never have occupied. They indicate where one wishes and will be permitted to go: a bar for an underage drinker, a professional position for an eighth-grade dropout, a whitewashed legal record for a fugitive from prior misdeeds.

Professional impersonations hinge on the presentation and acceptance of fraudulent credentials: an M.D., a J.D, a Ph.D. in nuclear physics. The untrammeled passage of untrained persons into the professional ranks makes significant crimes possible, perhaps the most heinous the murders committed under the guise and aegis of health care. Given the potential rewards, it is certainly little surprise that unqualified practitioners, particularly those with criminal intent or mental illness, make sad but efficient work of the people whose lives and fates are entrusted to them. As an all-too-typical example of its era, in 1984, Ebrahim Sadeghy got himself established as the personal physician of Myrtle Reid, an elderly Californian with heart problems. As he convinced her to stop taking her medication, Sadeghy also gained certain other influences over Mrs. Reid:

> About a month after Dr. Sadeghy arrived at the Reids, Myrtle "decided" that she and Rodney should adopt Dr. Ebrahim Sadeghy as their son. ... In an adoption petition, Sadeghy swore under penalty of perjury that he had known the Reids for six years, had resided with them for six months, and had "provided them with love, companionship, and all assistance expected of a natural child."

Mrs. Reid made Sadeghy a joint signer on her checking account, and executed a new will, leaving him her estate. After she happened to die the same night she had turned over access in her stocks and bonds to him, Sadeghy was charged with murder.[4]

While cases of medical and spiritual frauds, usually performed in connection with sizable monetary rewards, are certainly common, more astonishing and provocative are cases in which holders of fraudulent credentials distinguish themselves in professional performances for which they have received little or no formal training—and in which the external rewards can at best be only a secondary motivation. In the 1970s, Roberto Coppola was so convincing as a priest, that he was able, while still a teenager, to perform numerous weddings and masses without obstacle. Likewise, though he never finished high school, Ferdinand Waldo Demara was able to pass as, among other things, a Ph.D. in psychology who taught at the university level; a cancer researcher; and a markedly forward-thinking guidance counselor in a maximum-security prison in Texas. Demara's most extraordinary "feat of impersonation"

> took place during the Korean War when he served as a lieutenant-surgeon in the Canadian navy. Boning up on medical texts, he pulled teeth, removed tonsils and amputated limbs. His crowning achievement under severe battle conditions was removing a bullet from within a fraction of an inch of a South Korean soldier's heart. Those assisting him in the harrowing operation gave a lusty cheer when he successfully completed the procedure. Although totally unqualified for his medical service, Demara never lost a patient, and doubtless saved several lives.[5]

Demara's case was spectacular but by no means isolated. For example, distinguishing himself as a San Francisco neonatalist, "Doctor" Barry Allan Vinocur received national attention in 1978 for the part he played in the discovery of a cure for a rare and fatal infant disease. George E. Allen headed an inmate medical program of the Tennessee Department of Corrections for 13 months undetected, supervising a staff of 70, including six M.D.'s.[6] Cases such as these suggest that the professional credential can be useful not because it refers to training and certification honestly earned, but because, like Abagnale's business-major's transcript, it presents working papers for future tasks. Used in this way, the fraudulent professsional credential highlights the situational bases of and the performance demands on identity.

Tasks completed successfully under such covers can avail a high degree of satisfaction: there's both the thrill of getting away with it and the gesture of triumph against members of closed or previously rejecting professional societies. In addition to the estimable financial and potential revenge rewards, posing as a doctor, an anesthesiaologist, or a dentist clearly presents a high degree of risk and challenge. Would-be identity changers who seek less high-status trick identities may undertake their own risks: to evade justice, bad debts, or a vengeful lover. The identity-change manual *Scram: Relocating Under a New Identity* maintains it's no less natural than longing for a vacation to want to experience life under a new identity. A change of name alone can also represent an opportunity to sever oneself from the criminal history, attachments, and lifeways that have constituted a prior identity—to "undergo a dedeviantization process," as one develops a new, mainstream identity.[7]

A 1976 report by the U. S. Department of Justice report found that five major classes of people employed fake ID criminally: drug smugglers; illegal immigrants; white-collar criminals; those committing fraud (e.g., welfare fraud) against the government; and fugitives from justice, including juvenile fugitives and those fleeing the consequences of militant revolutionary activity. It found by

> a random sampling of 500 cases in which a fugitive was being sought by the FBI ... that *in every case* the fugitive was known to have used at least one alias. In 75 of these cases, the fugi-

tives had previously been identified under five or more aliases, and in one case the subject is known to have used more than 30 different false identities.

The report detailed the adventures of a Chicago "welfare queen" who "used 250 aliases in 16 stores to steal more than $150,000 from social welfare programs. She used 331 different addresses, three Social Security numbers, and records of eight 'deceased husbands.'"

A cornerstone of social and community life, a name is offered as part of the context of trust within which further conversational, emotional, and economic exchanges acquire substance. Birth and marriage certificates place one within a web of family and geography. Thus, much as personal identity documentation typically marks a unique individual's name, address, and physical characteristics, it is also a strong contemporary measurement of kinship.

In some sense, a person's identity is the nexus of the overlapping circles of identity represented by each emblem of status or group membership. However, ID is conventionally proffered in more subtly hostile or in strange contexts as a badge of belonging to those who would question one's status and consider one an outsider by default. M. L. Shannon's *The Paper Trail: Personal and Financial Privacy in the Nineties* details how private citizens are surveilled by "them"—government agencies and profit-seeking bodies, such as marketing and insurance companies. The book conceives of personal documentation in the context of a personal liberty to determine how and to whom information about the self is conveyed. It links the creative construction of identity and its detection, both telling the reader how to "disappear," or rid oneself of an obtrusive, damning, inconvenient, or outgrown identity, and how to find others who would rather not be found.

Books on new identities such as *Scram* and *The Paper Trail* typically have a paradoxical duality. In their prefatory remarks, they conventionally offer the admonition that the techniques they teach are not to be used for illegal purposes, but rather for maintaining one's basic rights as a citizen, say, by the identity hobbyist or prankster. And then they go on to make very practical suggestions for advancing to more legally questionable applications. While initially identity books author "John Q. Newman" avers he is not providing information to those who are interested in more than ordinary "privacy," by the first chapter of his book he offers information that will help "new identity seekers" to "evade taxes, arrest, regulation and supervision" and "reap a wide spectrum of benefits and privileges that are bestowed on those people the system likes." Marvin Barnes, the author of *100 Ways to Disappear and Live Free*, was arrested in 1979 for filing forty-seven fraudulent tax returns.[8]

In *The Paper Trail*, Shannon distinguishes among three types of forged IDs, based on how they might be expected to be received by potential viewers. In the first category are documents made to resemble actual IDs. Where these IDs belong to government agents, presenting them can constitute a crime of impersonation. The second category of forged IDs presupposes an audience awed by authority (and authoritative-sounding organizations) and insensible to fine detail. An ID that was issued by the made-up "Federal Bureau of Instigation," for example, stands a chance of being passed over by an inattentive authority. An ID from the "International Bureau of Intelligence" is an example of the third type of ID, in which the name is entirely made up and designed merely to *sound* official, by the maker's calculation that carelessness on the part of the reader will allow it to be mistaken for an existing agency's identification.[9]

This third category—the invented ID—is the one most fully treated in many of the books on escaping and establishing a new identity through documentary means. These books offer information about how to provide a plausible Social Security number, one that won't automatically be recognized as concocted. Their tone makes sense of why many of the books on becoming an identity fugitive are sold side by side in the catalogs with tax evasion manuals and bomb cookbooks:

> It is against the law to make up an SSA number. Apparently this constitutes *giving false information to the government*. Of course, it's OK for the government to give false information to the people. They have been doing it since 1776. Meanwhile, as far as I have been able to determine, there is no law, federal or otherwise, against having a poor memory.[10]

During the 1970s, books such as *The Paper Trip*, as well as numerous printing presses dedicated to the production of counterfeit IDs, made the technologies of paper ID available to an ever-wider public, and deluged federal, state, and local law enforcement agencies with a new kind of work. Americans' increased mobility was making it important for merchants to be able to more accurately identify strangers in commercial transactions. Public alarm about illegal aliens was also growing. Were identity tricksters entering the country in large numbers, and then defrauding the government of social welfare dollars, using false ID to gain access to personal and confidential records? This was the context within which the United States Department of Justice began investigating the use of false identification. In response to these and other trends, in 1974, the United States Attorney General formed the Federal Advisory Committee on False Identification. In 1980, the first major federal undercover investigation of the diploma mills, Operation Dipscam, was launched.[11]

In 1985, a hearing of the United States House of Representatives showcased evidence that the use of fraudulent credentials, particularly in the health professions, was a growing and significant national problem that disproportionately impacted older members of the population, the principal users of health-care services in urban hospitals. In their attempt to determine the scope of the use of fraudulent credentials, investigators of the Select Committee on Aging made contact with all the state licensing boards and with 250 college and university registrars. They concluded, "About 500,000 Americans have secured, and many are employed on the basis of, credentials they purchased but did not earn." That figure included the astonishing number of 10,000 doctors, "or one in every 50 physicians, practicing with falsified or questionable credentials." Government agencies themselves were by no means shielded from this practice. The subcommittees found possessors of fraudulent professional credentials within the ranks of the Departments of Defense, Labor, Justice, Commerce, and State. Notably, the Army, Navy, Air Force, Treasury, Veterans Administration, and the U.S. Postal Service—typically the front line of defense against diploma mills—were not immune to these jobholders.

It didn't help that the states had anything but a uniform approach to professional licensing. As Representative Don Bonker, the chair of the Subcommittee on Housing and Consumer Interests, explicated,

All States license barbers and cosmetologists, and yet not all States license psychologists and physician assistants. Kentucky, we are informed, licenses watchmakers and auctioneers but does not require licenses for psychologists. The great State of Maine licenses tree surgeons and movie projectionists while not requiring the same of ambulance attendants or occupational therapists.[12]

States' reciprocity arrangements, whereby credentials earned in one state could routinely be accepted in another, further eased professional practice on the basis of fraudulent credentials. Without national cross-registration, a person wishing to perform a fraudulent professional identity could present fake credentials from a state known for its stiff licensing requirements and have them be recognized as more than sufficient in one that did not license at all. In addition, reciprocity arrangements allowed a professional identity to resurface in an adjoining state, should it fail in the first one.

In a market glutted with overeducated workers, scanning for possession of a graduate degree proved a handy way to manage a swelling applicant pool. As the opportunistic "Southwestern University" profitably put it,

Unless you possess a degree you like many other highly motivated and qualified individuals may never be given the opportunity to even compete for well deserved promotions, raises, and prestige that you have earned through hard work and achievement. ...

Our degree program has no fixed curriculum or set time schedule ... Degree requirements are based on a minimum requirements system considering that many mature adults have, through various achievement [sic] gained an educational EQUIVALENCY and have become fully qualified in their chosen field of interest. ...

It is possible that you may already possess all the requirements to qualify for a recognized degree award from Southwestern University. ... Much of [your] existing knowledge and valuable experience in your present position may have passed unnoticed and may be considered of little value to your present employer when evaluated separately. These existing achievements, however when evaluated and consoli-

dated into a single college transcript, can earn you your degree.[13]

The unprecedented numbers of adults pursuing higher education
in the 1970s and '80s demanded different forms of education than
did more traditional-aged college students, who may have lived on
campus, gone to school full-time, and answered to few outside responsibilities. Working adults seeking degrees needed coursework
that could be completed in the evening hours or on weekends and
that required minimal on-campus time, as well as institutions that
recognized the additional educational value of working experience.
Correspondence courses certainly promoted the kind of physical
anonymity that could pave the way for mail-order, "expedited," or
otherwise outright bought credentials. When the "Elysion College of
Liberal Arts," based in Mexico but operated from a San Francisco
post office box, printed its catalog, it made a boast that would have
attracted both these nontraditional learners and seekers of fraudulent degrees: "Studying is truly independent." (As the House of
Representatives report commented caustically, "In truth, studying is
truly nonexistent."[14])

Like the mail-order degree, the mail-order identity was a pre-domi-
nant paradigm for identity creation of the 1970s, '80s, and early '90s.
Identity-change manuals, offered through the "personal privacy"
departments of publishers and distributors such as Loompanics Unlimited of Port Townsend, Washington and Paladin Press of
Boulder, Colorado, explained how it should be done. Whether for
gain, opportunity, escape, or fun, the identity artist who wished to
invent a new self on paper followed a systematic progression by
which he would "develop" the four major pieces of identification—
the birth certificate, driver's license or state identification card, Social
Security card, and passport. Obtaining the key pieces of paper ID in
a specific order, the identity artist would use the earlier pieces to establish the identity needed to obtain those pieces with more stringent
requirements.

The birth certificate is inevitably the bedrock of a paper identity.
"The only truly unique document that a person possesses"—as name,
date, and place of birth can all be shared—the birth certificate

says, in effect, that *you* were born on a certain date, at a certain place, and of two specific individuals. This document also contains information as to your race, sex, if you were a twin, and if you have other siblings. Even identical twins' birth certificates differ because the birth record will show the birth order and the time of your arrival in the world. Both of these facts will differ slightly from your twin, even though all the other data is identical.[15]

Because of the ease in many cases of ordering a birth certificate by mail, it has been a convenient way to generate a new identity.

The Infant Identity or Infant Death Method, one of the best-known methods of the late twentieth century for birthing a new identity, involves obtaining a false identity by using the name of someone who both died in childhood and whose death records have been kept in an obscure place in a county separate from the county of birth. The United States of the 1970s and '80s was a hospitable period for the Infant Identity Method because of the unlikelihood of a person dying in the same county in which he or she was born; statewide cross-referencing of births and deaths was only attempted, and only to a limited degree, in the 1970s. One of the difficulties stemmed from the amount of information available at the time of a person's birth, as opposed to at the time of his or her death. Clerks had to err on the side of keeping an identity "alive" if they had insufficient information to confirm that the identity recorded as a birth was identical with that presumed at a death, particularly in a case where a person had died without family or friends nearby. From the perspective of the identity changer, the ideal birth certificate:

> should be of the same sex, approximate age, race, and general background as yourself. If possible, you should try to select the certificate of a child who had no brothers or sisters, or alternatively that of a first born. ... Another possibility is to use the birth record of someone born where lots of people who are from other places have babies, but have no ties or relatives in the community. (Las Vegas, Nevada would be one example.) This is because you want there to be as few people as possible around who could ever debate "you" being "you."[16]

The potential identity artist would scan local genealogical records rather than clip a higher-profile newspaper obituary. Choosing a less conspicuous identity better safeguarded against the possibility of a conflict with another identity trickster's using the same identity.

The second foundation document, after the birth certificate, is either the Social Security card or the driver's license. One school of thought recommended using the birth certificate to apply for a Social Security number and card. These ready, one could apply for a state ID card, which made getting a driver's license that much easier.[17] Alternatively, Social Security cards could be obtained as a second-order form of identification from the "breeder documents"—typically the birth certificate and driver's license.

Numerous identity-change manuals offer recommendations about numbering forged Social Security cards plausibly. However, the Social Security Administration's "Project Clean Data" hunted for numbers that had never been officially issued, as well as kept track of Social Security numbers held by people long deceased.[18]

What James B. Rule calls the "documentary interlock" among the data represented in identity documents is played out daily in almost any face-to-face encounter in which they are exchanged:

> Oh, you wish to pay by check? Let me see your driver's license; Do you have some other ID? What is your home address? What is your phone number? Oh, a credit card? What is your Social Security number? What is your mother's maiden name? Oh, I'm sorry, but we aren't set up to take cash. Don't you have a Visa? *Everyone* has a Visa. Fill out this form. That form. Don't worry, it is confidential. What were your addresses for the last five years? Oh, I'm sorry, but you left this blank. *You must fill out the entire form.*[19]

Because of documentary interlock, new identity seekers were also advised to circumnavigate government-issued identity documents when they presented proof of age in applying for a Social Security number. Baptismal certificates worked well, particularly in areas where the Catholic Church was securely entrenched. Hospital birth certificates proved handy because untraceable: originals would be destroyed within a few years. However, a cover story to explain why the baptismal certificate was all one had had better be *original,* wrote Shannon, tongue in cheek:

> One old trick is to explain that you lived in a different country for most of your life. Your parents were missionaries in South America, and you traveled with them through the Matto Grosso teaching the natives that the world is full of evil. An old trick? A *very* old trick. It's been published in practically every book on the subject of alternative ID, and the people at SSA have heard it many times before. ...
>
> There are some other possible ways to get a card, which may or may not work. One is that your parents supported you until recently, when they discovered you:
>
> Are going to join the Moonies,
>
> Are gay and coming out of the closet,
>
> Are joining the French Foreign Legion,
>
> And so they cut you off. Disinherited you ...
>
> Or perhaps you were a prisoner in a state penitentiary since you were 18. You were just released, have "paid your debt to society" and are (yet another person who is) ready to become a productive member of society. With a birth certificate ... and some "official" prison documents straight from your laser printer, it just might work.
>
> Along those lines, you might tell them that you worked for cash all your life, as you didn't believe in paying taxes. ... But, as have so many other people in this book, you have changed your ways ...[20]

The last of the four basic forms of ID is the United States passport, the only document for American citizens that serves simultaneously to establish citizenship and identity. It is a highly prized piece of identification and needs to be applied for with great care, as many safeguards are in place to prevent passports' being issued to fabricated identities. Many of the manuals advise letting a new identity "harden" for at least eighteen months before applying for a passport, especially as passport agents were trained to be suspicious of applicants presenting only recent ID.

Published in 1993, *The Paper Trail* is one of the earliest books to deal with the forging of ID in the age of desktop publishing, an era that has made the forging of everything but passports, Social Security cards, and driver's licenses far easier than ever before. It makes a crucial point about audience skill in "reading" ID: when creating one's own identity documents, one must also consider whom one aims to fool; connoisseurs should never see works they would be qualified to judge negatively; a cop, for example, should never be handed a forged driver's license.

As a vital safety strategy, identity change books further recommend separating the trail of evidence for each of the four major items of ID. The time to do this is when applying for a driver's license—preferably in a state that does not rely on the Social Security number as the driver's license ID number. And one must be economical in one's applications for IDs, obtaining only those pieces that are truly necessary: "All you really require is what suits your immediate needs, and something to fall back on." Finally, ID that is kept in a drawer stays "fresh" longer than ID that is used. The identity artist can age his fake ID by brushing the edges of the paper with lemon juice and lightly baking it. If he only needs to buy a little time, he can plausibly backdate the documents. Simple lamination adds the patina of permanence to any ID.

As a place to start, the Infant Identity Method was deemed best suited to a young person wanting to establish a new identity. Someone older, facing expectations of employment and credit records, would have to adapt the basic strategy. He might, for example, choose someone who had died at about his own age but was likely still to have records, as well as contacts who believed the person still to be alive. Such people would be able to provide letters of reference, while the identity trickster could use the new name to apply for a business license and begin to establish a history.[21]

An alternative method would be to borrow the identity of an "alter ego"—someone who is alive, lives in one's area, has the same (at least last) name, occupies a low-profile position in his work and social life, and has minimal access to computers. Such a technique can blur a trick-identity trail nicely. Art forger Elmyr de Hory's crooked brokers obtained a Canadian passport for him in the name of Joseph Boutin, an insurance clerk. Boutin was still alive but did not appear to be much of an overseas traveler. Sending for a copy of his birth certificate, de Hory's representatives had a lawyer apply for a passport, which combined Boutin's name with de Hory's photograph. The scheme depended on two factors: there being no existing public records or notices of public accomplishment on Boutin that would contradict de Hory's presentation of himself in this false identity, and there being no occasion for the real Boutin to require the identification that the fake Boutin now held. (For a time, it worked: then, a search by the Royal Canadian Mounted Police snowballed to catch the Joseph Boutin who was wanted for bigamy and the possession of stolen property. The lesson: remembering to check for a criminal record when usurping someone else's name.[22])

A variant of the alter ego method was apparently applied in the early 1980s by Paul Arthur Crafton, a "mystery professor" who borrowed others' academic credentials and taught, under multiple identities, simultaneously at George Washington University, Shippensburg State, and Millersville State College. In Crafton's Lancaster, Pennsylvania apartment, law-enforcement found documents that supported 34 identities' worth of documents, including letterheads, passports, five driver's licenses, two Social Security cards, and almost 70 credit cards registered under various names. Most perplexing to the authorities were the genuine birth certificates and academic credentials belonging to real faculty members who were living and working in Britain, Australia, and New York. In attempting to unravel the mysteries connected with Crafton's identities and activities, investigators embarked on what the Pennsylvania State Attorney General called a "plastic and paper chase," confiscating in the process a copy of a 1979 identity manual called *The New Paper Trip: For a New You Through New ID.*[23]

To complete the picture offered by a paper-house ID, one must also prop one's wallet with the supplementary ID that will support the perception that a full life has been in progress for some time.[24] Complete backstopping involves preparing documents that support full educational, work, medical, insurance, credit, and automobile histories. These can include voter registration cards, county hospital ID cards, student IDs, and telephone company calling cards, all of which can be obtained with minimal basic ID. Identity-change manuals advised having on hand "official company forms, such as a semi-annual employee evaluation, employee of the month award, and articles about 'you' cut from a company newspaper," as well as "letters of appreciation from non-profit agencies in recognition of your years of volunteer work."

ID known to be hard to get can help to lock in a new identity. For example, a cab driver's license can be a useful piece of ID to have on hand in case of being stopped for a traffic offense. Its utility hinges on police knowledge of what it typically takes to earn such a document and on the decentralization of the units that issue these licenses. Thus, the combination of the proliferation of cab driver's license styles and the common knowledge among law enforcement that the presenter would have to have been fingerprinted in order to obtain such a license, typically results in an easy release. The presentation of virtually any ID with fingerprints on it adds to the apparent veracity of the card—but for reasons of traceability, these marks should never be one's own. Almost needless to say, there are tremendous advantages to never having had one's fingerprints taken.[25]

Rather than supporting a new identity, certain forms of ID, including those issued by New York City's Forty-Second Street-style "spy shops," can brand a person as attempting to operate under a false identity. Propping can be considered criminal, "preparing false evidence." "Pocket littering" has also been associated with espionage.

Investigators and undercover agents naturally need fake IDs to substantiate the pretensions they make in their work. As far back as the eighteenth century, Vidocq used standard identity documents—birth certificate, passport, and a certificate of half-pay—in order to support the performances he planned. And during one of his escapes from prison, Vidocq considered becoming a soldier, but realized that he would need "certain papers, which I had not." In the 1950s, when Vizzini, as a Federal Bureau of Narcotics agent, decided to portray an Air Force major, he used contacts in Georgia to get a full complement of material identification, which included "a flight card, an instrument rating card, a Geneva Convention card in case I got 'shot down' over enemy territory, dog tags and an Officer's Club card. I was put on the official roster..., complete with a form for 'notification of next of kin' and got a San Francisco APO address."[26]

Much of what was written in late twentieth-century identity change manuals was certainly applicable to the work of investigators and undercover agents. At the very least, the Private Investigator & Security Catalog offered ID blanks and "easy do-it-yourself lamination" to help an investigator shore up his story that he was, for example, a press photographer, auto repossessor, security consultant, executive bodyguard, missing persons investigator, special investigator, or ironically information broker. During the 1980s and '90s, one private investigator used commercially printed business cards that effectively and variously established his identity as a "process server, insurance adjuster, insurance agent, real estate broker, fire extinguisher inspector, and delivery person."[27]

The home agencies of law-enforcement workers about to go undercover have standard means to provide them with birth certificates, Social Security cards, car registrations, and driver's licenses that reflect, support, create, and to some degree constitute their undercover identities; in the late 1970s, the Federal Law Enforcement Training Center also assured its agents that it would provide laundry markings, personal correspondence, monogrammed clothing and jewelry, and photographs and family pictures to substantiate an undercover's identity.

Undercovers who have documents for more than one trick identity are well advised to ensure they carry only one identity at a time.[28] In a training session I attended, the instructor recommended that the undercover, like an identity fugitive, prop his wallet with all the fake junk IDs that will add credibility to his trick identity: video rental cards, library cards, the phone numbers of fictive friends. He explained, "All you're doing is building your credibility, just the way an actor would dress a certain way or would carry accoutrements that would enhance whatever his image is. All it is is props. Props allow you to become who you are."

Above all, the law-enforcement identity trickster must remember to remove incriminating documents and props, including his badge, any credentials, notebooks, cards, and letters: they show off his home identity in law enforcement. Undercover officers for the Washington, D.C. Metropolitan Police had their identities protected by also having their ordinary personnel history and their badge and revolver data deleted from the central computer system, the payroll printout, and the police photo file, and placed in a safe.[29]

In cultural context, the paper method of certifying a trick identity has force in a pre-electronic culture of identity, where whatever ordinary citizens assert to be true of themselves frequently does have a document behind it. (As a lawyer once told me in the early 1980s, "Don't you know? The world is composed not of people, but of documents.")

The documents are all-important when authenticating works of art. Getting at an art work's authenticity does not lie in understanding its artistic essence in the present moment, what it seems structurally or formally to "speak," nor in how it affects particular viewers in specific contexts of viewing. Rather, this form of authentication seeks to lay bare the chain of ownership or physical possession that all but falsifies the notion that the work under discussion could be anything but an original. Clive Wainwright has written about this process, as distinct from looking at the style of the work and from performing tests on the work's materials, as a "purely scholarly" one, in which knowledge of the history of fakes is as vital as knowledge of the history of original works: one of the successful outcomes of a provenance search is to have traced a work to a time prior to one in which any fakes are known to have occurred.

A seller's presentation of documentation of an aristocratic and unimpeachable provenance—essentially, an art work's identity papers—is going to be his most authoritative effort at authentication. Mocked-up documentation from a work's prior owners can establish a trick history for the work. Elmyr de Hory's paintings

> always came with impressive documentation—certificates from the family of the painter, a record of sale at some auction house like the Parke-Bernet Galleries, and often a statement of authenticity by one of several Paris experts, formally recognized by the French government as *experts auprès du tribunal*, which meant, in effect, that their word was law.

Elmyr de Hory's success in selling works in France may be due in part to his broker Fernand Legros's assessment of the system of obtaining authenticating documentation for his paintings:

> From the very beginning, since he was in the business of selling high-priced goods, Fernand's technique relied on the concept of the expertise—a proof of one sort or another that

what he was offering for sale was the genuine article. The French government recognizes certain individuals as experts *auprès du tribunal,* which means they have the legal right, gained by years of study and superior knowledge, or their relationship to the deceased artist, to provide for a specific work a certificate of authenticity. In return for this they receive a small fee. Fernand, who appear[ed] to have been gifted with a nose for the weakness in systems as well as people, went right to the heart of this one. He simply raised the fee. He later said to a friend: "I wasn't trying to bribe anyone. I just dropped a thousand dollars on the table. If the man didn't pick it up, I dropped a second thousand dollars. I found that people preferred round numbers."

Of course, de Hory himself sometimes forged his own certificates of authenticity as well as paintings, including one that read "This painting is by me Paris 24 May 46 Picasso." David Stein typed what he thought would be believable authenticating documents for his fakes using a French typewriter, and ordered a set of rubber stamps that matched those employed in French galleries.[30]

Provenance in the art world can be said to correspond roughly to the rules of evidence in law enforcement, which ensure that officers maintain a tight documentation showing the passage of material evidence from one hand to another in order to ensure the admissibility of events in court as having authentically occurred and having been permissibly obtained. In the United States, undercover agents are typically given special training in record-keeping, particularly in how they document their drug buys. The buy report gives credence to the tale the prosecutor will want to tell about how drugs were obtained from the bad guy, and establishes that the drugs exhibited in court are identically the ones that have passed, through sanctioned custodial practices, from the hands of the undercover directly to safekeeping. Testing of the drugs, e.g., by the undercover's supervisor, as a condition of hand-to-hand exchange further underscores their identity and authenticity. In both art and law, the reports and documents of exchange point to the identity and authenticity of the original artifact, itself a trace of an artistic or criminal action or event.

Disguise Artists and Detection

Working in his pre-technologized universe of evidence, Vidocq
leaned hard on visual and vocal markers of identity. The identity virtuoso was a quick-change artist with a sweeping array of plausible
roles in his repertoire. Vidocq's techniques and bravado inspired
French and British writers of the nineteenth century and elevated
disguise artistry as a critical strategy for creating the figure of the detective.[31] In one extraordinary day, in a segment of his tale Vidocq
names "Disguises on disguises," he begins his identity subterfuge by
exiting his hideaway at suppertime in a frock and pantaloons with a
dish of mutton on his head; obtains by threat the costume of one of
his denouncers; next dons a workman's costume; and finally pur-
chases the costume of an invalid, explaining to the broker that he is
planning to act in a play. Vidocq goes to a friend's house to complete
the "metamorphose":

> In less than five minutes I was converted into the most
> maimed of invalids; my arm laid over the hollow of my
> breast, and kept close to my body by a girth and the waist-
> band of my breeches, had entirely disappeared; some ribbons
> introduced into the upper part of one of the sleeves, the end
> of which was hung to a button in front, joined a stump ad-
> mirably deceptive, and which made the disguise most
> efficient; a dye which I used to stain my hair and whiskers
> black, perfected my disguise, under which I was so sure of
> misleading the physiognomical knowledge of the observers in
> the quarter St Martin, that I ventured there that same eve-
> ning.

Vidocq's physical disguises did not stop at alterations to his costume
and his apparent physicality; part of his remarkable gift was his ability
to alter his physical structure. Having taken tobacco juice, expecting
to induce a high fever in order to get himself transferred to the
prison hospital, he next devised a scheme to be able to remain there
a while:

> At Bîcetre, I had been taught how to produce those wounds
> and sores, by means of which so many beggars excite public

pity, and get those alms which cannot be worse bestowed. Of all these expedients, I adopted that which consisted in making the head swell like a bushel; first, because the doctors would be certainly mistaken; and then because it gave no pain, and all traces of it could be removed by the day following. My head became suddenly of a prodigious size, and great was the talk thereof amongst the doctors of the establishment, who, not being as it appeared blessed with a superabundance of skill, knew not what to think of it. I believe some of them spoke of elephantiasis, or of dropsy of the brain. But, be that as it may, their brilliant consultation ended in the prescription most common in hospitals, of putting me on the most strict regimen.[32]

The culmination of an outstandingly successful 1845 London exhibition of Vidocq's disguises was a display of the unique physical capabilities of the virtuosic identity artist himself. As one viewer wrote:

The principal curiosity in the collection will be found to be M. Vidocq himself ... He is a remarkably well-built man, of extraordinary muscular power, and exceedingly active. He stands, when perfectly erect, 5 feet 10 inches in height, but by some strange process connected with his physical formation he has the faculty of contracting his height several inches, and in this diminished state to walk about, jump, etc. ... From the flexibility of his features, and his powers of varying the expression of them, he would make an excellent player in such representations as require an actor to sustain several parts.[33]

Close observation was the predominant investigative means of Vidocq's era. In the *Memoirs* he opines, "A man without memory is like a Venus without buttocks." In London, the Bow Street Runners' John Fielding was reputed to recognize 3,000 criminals simply on the basis of their vocal qualities. Vidocq would periodically go out into the prison yards during the men's exercise periods and memorize their faces. He boasted that his memory permitted him to solve mysteries others could not conquer:

> How often I struck with astonishment someone who came to
> me to report a robbery: he had scarcely mentioned two or
> three circumstances than I was already ahead of him; I either
> completed the story for him or without waiting for more de-
> tailed information I rendered this oracle: the guilty parties
> are such-and-such. [34]

One of Vidocq's contributions to the history of detection was his creation of a systematic filing system that treated the physical features, histories, and modus operandi of the criminals in his domain. With recordkeeping, the individual observations of a single detecting mind could be shared with others in the profession, thus eliminating total reliance on an individual's recognition capabilities and memory. It gave multiple detectives the ability to scan the entire collection of records each time a new criminal actor presented. It also enabled multiple perceptive faculties to contribute to this early data bank, adding perspective (as well, arguably, as an additional likelihood of error or distortion). Perhaps most importantly, it articulated a criminal's peculiar style of working, the narrative of crime that was uniquely his. Precisely because law enforcement relied so heavily on the visual (and to some degree aural) signs of identity for the early stages of recognition and criminal identification, disguise became a chief means of evading such detection.

By the early nineteenth century, the attention to disguise, on the part of both criminals and detectives, evolved into an increased attention to modus operandi, in part because of the growing importance of "style." Similar to the late twentieth-century practice of criminal profiling, the concern with modus operandi focused attention on the imprint of a recognizable criminal hand that was thought to reveal favorite ways of constructing criminal situations. [35]

In the mid-1970s at the FBI, Howard Teten began profiling criminals. His methods later featured in Jonathan Demme's 1991 film, *The Silence of the Lambs*, Teten constructed gestalts of perpetrators from the kinds of conditions that pointed to a discernible modus operandi. His criminal profiling was a last-resort method of developing suspects, and would consist of examining the photographs that represented the conditions of a crime scene in order to determine what kind of personality would both be capable of and have a motivation for carrying out the crime in a particular way. Using this method to determine what kind of car the perpetrator drove or where he would be likely to relax in public could help locate a suspect. Likening his project to market research, Teten and later criminal profilers used the method to narrow their search to types of potential perpetrators.

In making positive identification of specific perpetrators, physical identification was the dominant mode law enforcement used during the second half of the twentieth century. A suspect would be known by discrete, essentially unalterable physical markers such as fingerprints. However, unlike earlier periods in history, when physiognomic characteristics were thought to reflect a propensity for particular criminal acts, physical features were verified by techniques of physical evidence and by witness descriptions.

A typical 1991 security officers' catalog of physical identifiers for suspects permits identification by "20 commonly used points of personal physical description": race, possible national origin, and ethnic group; sexual identification; height; weight; build; head shape; face shape; complexion; hair, including color, texture, style, dressing, and hairline; facial hair; eyes, including color, special type, noticeable defects, and characteristics of eyelids; eyebrows; nose; mouth, including lip thicknesses and shape and condition of teeth; chin; ears; scars, birth marks, pockmarks, needle tracks, warts, moles, tattoos, partial paralysis or immobility, amputations, or naturally foreshortened or withered members; deformities; blood type; and medical defects.[36] Such a list provides the sense of those variables of physical identity that law enforcement might regard as salient for the purposes of identification.

The more easily an element is changed, the easier it is to detect. A criminal will choose the means of disguise that are least complex and most convenient, while law enforcement must discern which means have been selected by precisely these same criteria of simplicity and convenience and are thus likely part of a disguise. Similarly, while the criminal needs to misdirect a crime witness or victim into perceiving an easily altered feature as a dominant and permanent one, the police artist's job is to extract from that same witness or victim the defining features of the perpetrator.

Police artists are taught to attend both to gestalts and to details. Because their discovery of information is frequently indirect, mediated by the perceptions of such others as crime victims and witnesses, police artists must focus on principles that allow them to differentiate relevant from irrelevant data, gross from minor effects. Crime victims' perceptions are famously unreliable, subject to distortions in the moment of assault or threat.

When in danger, a victim undergoes drastic perceptual changes. His field of vision focuses and condenses, minimizing his peripheral abilities. Thus, a victim might "see the weapon in great detail but everything around it becomes blurred like the image in out-of-focus binoculars."[37] The fight-or-flight syndrome also makes chaos of the victim's ability to prioritize remembered elements, or to recall elements in the order in which the interviewer asks about them.

Through judicious interviewing, the experienced police artist should be able to discern which features are more and which are less subject to willful change—and are thus more or less significant as disguises. According to a 1990 manual, good police artist should attend to elements in the following order:

A. Things that cannot be changed.

B. Things that can be changed only with time, effort, or considerable expense.

C. Things that can be changed easily and cheaply.

D. Things that can be discarded altogether.[38]

In this system, race, sex, and age, as well as the shape of facial features, can be disguised only with difficulty, and are thus the most important identifiers. From an identity fugitive's point of view, this perception of inalterability means that those who are successful in disguising these elements become extremely difficult to detect.

With enough time, weight can be gained or lost, often with excellent disguise effect. And because it cannot be altered or unmasked by others, dieting is regarded by disguise experts as a superior means of changing profile and facial contours. Given the popularity of books with such provocative chapter titles as "Foreskin Restoration," one might guess that fugitives commonly turn to cosmetic surgery. However, disguise manuals aver that it is actually extremely rare that criminals attempt to make any changes through plastic surgery, generally regarding it as an impracticality. The real utility of such surgery lies not so much in calming down exceptional distinguishing features as in changing their style.

Simpler mechanical means, such as mouth and nostril inserts, dental plates, and even body padding, however, can change the appearance of a fugitive's basic equipment. Although clearly the manuals for both detection and disguise assign sharp priority to visual signs, occasional mention is made of aural methods of disguise, such as altering one's vocal resonance by stuffing cotton in the cheeks or inserting nose plugs. Altering how one hears is touted as an easy way to alter how one's voice sounds.

Most readily changed—and, importantly, reversible—are facial and head hair and clothing. Accessories such as sunglasses, hats, cigars, and strategically placed scarves have the advantage of being easily discarded and may "dazzle" the crime victim, thus distracting him or her from hardier features of the criminal's appearance. Disguise of gestalts gets right at how figures are commonly recognized; thus, a hat is an expedient disguise not only because it distracts attention from facial features but because it changes the gestalt of the face, its apparent shape and size.[39]

In a manual for would-be police artists, case studies exemplify the utility of attending to deep-lying physical features. Though she "projects, with equal ease, the image of scrubwoman, pretty secretary, gun moll, housewife, and hippie," case example Marilyn Jean Buck's face is a sea of irregularities, including exceptionally wide-set eyes, a doubly pigmented left eye, uniformly outsize or undersize glasses frames, a nose that has probably suffered a number of injuries, leaving it with nostrils of different sizes, and a face that carries weight differently on its two sides. Similarly, Chicago gang member Melvin Edward Mays's face is memorable for its irregularities, among them an unusually long distance between nose and mouth, and distinctive, ill-paired eyebrows. An examination of these two faces demonstrates that

> Once we have passed beyond the basic elements (head shape and critical distances), any human face can have an almost infinite number of variables because no face is in perfect balance. When we have identified four, five, or six of these variables, we probably have enough information so that

whatever face we encounter is not likely to match many others anywhere on Earth.[40]

The very belief in immutable physiognomic features makes it possible in some cases for some fugitives to slip between the cracks. Seemingly incontrovertible physical identifiers valuably lend the authority of objectivity to an identification process. As Erving Goffman notes,

> "Identity tags," namely officially recognized seals which bond an individual to his biography ... [constitute] the class of certificates which are designed to establish someone's claim to something through marking of some kind that is openly given the function of being unforgeable. These documents constitute a kind of open challenge.[41]

Believed in the late twentieth century to be among the most accurate of the physical methods of authenticating identity were retinal blood-vessel patterns, hand geometry, and fingerprints.

Fingerprinting, first widely used in the first decade of the twentieth century in the United States, is conventionally accepted as linking evidence and identity with a high rate of accuracy. Fingerprint matching can serve as seemingly conclusive proof of identity, providing abundant opportunities for unquestioned fraudulent presentation in physical documentation, especially by such means as building up false fingerprints with latex. Forensic dentistry has had similar force as an "absolute" identifier:

> Based on the theory that because human adults have 32 teeth, each with five anatomic surfaces, there are 160 dental surfaces that may contain identifying characteristics and which create the individuality of your dentition. In addition, facial structure, occlusion, and the shape of the teeth and jaw also identify and are difficult to disguise.[42]

Since dental records became admissible as evidence in 1975, they have been regarded as being especially useful in the identification of human remains, deceased persons, missing children, and people with amnesia.

Vidocq made putty of the so-called unalterables. Operating on a similar principle, though on a more mundane level, in the 1970s it was well known among New York criminals that the New York Police Department required officers to be at least five feet eight inches tall. Bad guys thus never expected to be "made" by shorter male officers, actually making these males excellent candidates for undercover drug buys.[43] The fingerprints of Paul Arthur Crafton, the professor with multiple active identities and university teaching positions, were worn so smooth that police had difficulty bringing them up for identification. No doubt this aided his successes in working under several identities simultaneously.[44] Widespread confidence in the solidity of biometric identification in both cases was the very thing that permitted identity play.

Increasingly, performance-based methods link an unalterable physical pattern with a unique person. Signature verifiers attempt to match the movement, pressure, speed, or sounds of the act of signing one's name. Keyboard dynamics recognition equipment measures the speed and touch of typing. Voice recognition equipment matches inflection and rhythmic patterns. The means of foiling these sophisticated identification devices have at this point yet to be treated by the "privacy" presses, though they almost certainly shall.

Through such identity markers as voice tempo and rhythm, detectors of disguises begin to look at how identity lives in time. One list of features to observe embeds behavioral markers among the other signs of identity: speech patterns, including quality, accent, defects, speed, and pitch; walk; preferred hand dominance; habits, such as gum chewing or finger drumming; nervous disorders that manifest physically; narcotics use; alcohol use; tobacco use; sexual behavior; and mental disorders.[45]

What identity artists on both sides of the law typically *do* in order to appear to be someone else can be thought of as belonging to two broad classes, simulation and dissimulation. Writing about magic technique, Dariel Fitzkee explains, "All forms of disguise are either simulation or dissimulation: Consider the distinction in the two words. Simulation is a positive act. It shows a false picture. Dissimulation is a negative act. It hides a true picture. One reveals. The other conceals. What the first reveals is false. What the second conceals is true." When one simulates, one "imitates [the object's] external identifying indications such as characteristics, marks, symbols or other signs." Conversely, dissimulation is the concealment of gestalts or details. [46]

Most forms of identity change involve varying degrees of both dissimulation and simulation, of both concealing the real and presenting the false. Vidocq certainly both added and removed telltale signs. About his experience in captivity, he noted, "Whoever passes any time at the Bagne, drags habitually and involuntarily that leg to which the fetter has been fastened." A fugitive planning an escape would need to represent, or simulate, this condition. Vidocq's addition of disqualifying signs—another type of simulation—also aided in his disguise work. He noted that with his "hat off by reason of the heat, they saw my hair curled, which could not be the case with a convict." [47]

Contemporary undercover cops dissimulate when they turn in their badges and weapons for safekeeping before going under, thus eliminating the chance of these identifying objects' revealing their professional identities and sabotaging their trick ones. Further, because "most policing depends upon the authority of a uniform," undercover work depends on discarding one. [48]

To adopt a social role of "urban camouflage," in which not-being itself draws no undue attention, one chooses roles with a low profile in the realms of authority and sexuality, roles whose low social status would make them most readily dismissible: according to a 1984 manual, these include: servants, waiters and waitresses, housewives, gas station attendants, construction workers, businessmen, students, mailmen, and UPS men. [49]

Federally protected witnesses must both simulate and dissimulate, keeping as their "overriding goal ... to pretend not to have been who in fact they were, and to pretend to be who in fact they know they are not." In their case, a complete "social death" of their previous identity is necessary for their protection. [50]

Identity manuals generally recommend to the fugitive, the less disguise, the better. The elegance of a "chameleon disguise," for example, is that "it doesn't look like a disguise. Done properly, it doesn't look like anything at all, ... [and] is suitable for quiet mingling, surreptitious scrutinizing, and any situation in which you want to be present but unnoticed." Physical alterations that can be construed as "natural," such as dyeing one's hair or changing or shaving facial hair, as well as employing costume elements that go on and off at the wearer's will, are preferable to those vulnerable to mishap (wigs being the most common—and comical—example). Thus, a beard is a natural-appearing disguise for a chin of unusual shape; similarly, an everyday strategy of variety, such as a woman's change of hairstyle, makes a good disguise for simple evasion purposes. In sum, the best disguises are "able to cover up your individual, or characteristic, features; generic and commonly available; easy to put on and take off; and easy to dispose of."[51]

To use one of these simpler disguise techniques effectively, the would-be disguise artist needs to have a fairly clear-eyed appraisal of his own physical make-up. One of the key pieces of equipment in his "pocket disguise kit," along with a rolled-up hat and a pair of sunglasses, is a mirror. Videotaping is also recommended as a means of seeing oneself in motion as others might; video is touted as "technology's gift to the disguise artist." Canny self-analysis is at least as vital: does one's given physical make-up suggest that a disguise strategy of blending in or of standing out would be the more believable?

Camouflage has been dramatized as "the disguise of not-being," and compared to something readers likely experienced at an early age:

> Think back to what you used to do in school when you didn't want the teacher to call on you. Probably, you cleared your mind of activity as much as possible, you held still and kept quiet so as not to attract attention, and you avoided looking at the teacher. Right? Now remember the *feeling* of trying not to be called on. This is basically the state of *not-being*.[52]

Every seamless roleplay, whatever its combination of simulation and dissimulation techniques, takes as its model the practices of passing, wherein members of one group (usually of low status) attempt to be known and accepted in practice as members of a higher-level status group. Goffman identified a "cycle of passing," in which the passer moves first toward expanding consciousness of his act, then toward increasing planfulness, and finally toward total pervasiveness of his passing identity in his life. This journey describes the parallel

motion of the passer's subjective sense of him or herself within a new
social role and the achieved level of external success demonstrated by
passing within that role:

> The cycle may start with unwitting passing that the passer
> never learns he is engaging in; move from there to unin-
> tended passing that the surprised passer learns about in mid-
> passage; from there to passing "for fun"; passing during non-
> routine parts of the social round, such as vacations and
> travel; passing during routine daily occasions such as at work
> or in service establishments; finally, "disappearance"—com-
> plete passing over in all areas of life, the secret being known
> only to the passer himself.[53]

Just as identity play as a whole is more prevalent in societies in
which identity is highly valued, passing is not uncommon in cultures
that oppress particular categories or classes of their citizens.[54] Typically, members of an underclass have a survival motive in becoming
expert readers of signs produced by more powerful groups. Passing
has received most attention for what it reveals about the politics of
visibility with regard to race.[55] It also concerns those who, though not
necessarily immediately visually identifiable, want to assimilate to a
dominant culture, for example, religious or sexual minorities. Ann
Morrow, a sixteenth-century British woman who, under male disguise, married three different women, exemplifies certain aspects of
this repression.[56]

Passing is the domain of much undercover work. The following
description of the United States's Office of Strategic Services spies
during World War II applies equally well to the attention for detail
that undercovers must pay, particularly when entering a culture far
different from their own:

> An agent traveling in an occupied country must wear clothes
> of the occupied country. The slightest variation will give him
> away. An American laundry and cleaning mark, for example,
> would be tantamount to a death warrant; yet those cleaning
> marks are impossible to remove. They had to be cut out and
> patched over, an improvisation which was suspicious and not
> entirely effective. Other give-aways are: the manner in which
> buttons are sewn on—The Americans do it in criss-cross,
> Europeans in parallel; the lining—European linings are full;

the adjustment buckles—in Europe they bear the mark of the country of origin; suspender buttons—no matter what European country they come from, they bear the imprint, "Elegant," "For Gentlemen," or "Mode de Paris."[57]

In addition to knowing how to reproduce the signs of the target culture, one must also know the degree of perceptual subtlety available to those in it, and gauge one's own performance contexts appropriately to those perceptual arenas. Thus, while having keen insight into one's own appearance, one must consider just how close and how expert the audience's scrutiny will be.

One undercover training system involved having trainees roleplay as members of a gay male subculture, as members of subcultures generally have readier access to crime and criminal information. The preparation for infiltrating this particular subculture was especially useful in the training of undercovers: it threw the trainee directly into the study of dress, props, and body language and their appropriate uses in the gay community, which was of necessity highly skilled in reading nonverbal cues and signals. In addition, so long as social conditions prevail that make passing advantageous, knowing how to infiltrate the community means being able to gather incriminating evidence that can be used for blackmail.

Knowing how far to go, depending upon who's watching, also applies to undercover work performed in alien contexts. Though RCMP undercover Murray Simms had done extensive identity work in Europe, he regarded himself as an unlikely candidate to portray a fashionable character, since he did not yet have the ability to read the subtle meanings of knot size and collar shape as they are affected variously by members of the fashionable class. He could, however, bring his version of those trends back to North America and be credible in the United States or Canada as a dandy.

While the deft manipulation of stereotypes is an important tool for the identity trickster in general, this is especially so for one who would pass. Players, however, had better differentiate between building disguises upon the stereotypes others hold—a superior technique once mastered—and venturing into an alien group performing one's own stereotypes of it, especially before understanding how group members perceive themselves. As one advisor roughly put it:

If you want to disguise yourself as a Dutch boy in wooden shoes, don't try it at the national tulip festival in Holland, Michigan. Don't attempt to infiltrate a Muslim meeting in blackface, or a Daughters of the American Revolution meeting in a dress cut from the American flag. Don't throw around expressions like "Hey, let's all toke down," and "This stuff is going to blow your mind," when talking with a drug pusher.[58]

In some forms of identity work, such as police decoys, the performer *wants* to distinguish himself from his social context, while playing directly into stereotype. Identity tricksters who wish to stick out should choose such highly visible states as "danger, good fortune (especially wealth and fame) and bad fortune (disease, injury, extreme poverty)." They might also elect to play out such stereotypes as "prostitutes, racial types other than one's own, hippies (outdated, but still part of many people's stereotyping system), nuns, priests, rock musicians, pregnant women, mothers, [and—notably] police officers."[59]

A juicy combination of presenting visible signs, while withholding the presence of the identifying body, is the act of staging the residue of one's presence, using costuming and propping. Infiltrating the world of a heavy-hitting Mafia man, Sal Vizzini anticipated that his undercover hotel room would be searched. He therefore carefully propped it—creating what the Soviets once called a "secret exhibition"—so that materials supporting his cover would be there to greet the breakers-in: "They found exactly what I wanted them to find—a couple of letters postmarked 'New York, N.Y.' and addressed to Pasquale Lombardi in Rome; a photograph of a big-chested girl inscribed 'To Pasquale, With Love'; and a pair of cuff links with the initial L." Arranging props to perform his identity in his absence helped Pasquale Lombardi establish that he was as he professed.[60]

Functioning as one's own costume and set designer is not always as successful as this. In 1924, David Rowland MacDonald decided he would fake his own death in order to allow his emotionally distant wife to spend a happier life without him. He propped a bundle of clothing on the bank of the Allegheny River, close to Pittsburgh, and scripted a suicide note that enumerated his failures as a businessman and a husband. After his departure his wife collected on three insurance policies, and quickly remarried, while MacDonald reincarnated himself in Pasadena as John Edgar Davis. The single identity of MacDonald and Davis came to light when, on a minor charge, the defrauder was picked up and his fingerprints taken. The bundle of clothing was part of the staged package that "dressed" his event. In the end, touched by McDonald's story of having done it all for his wife, the insurance companies did not prosecute him. A writer who wished to embark on an acting career staged a publicity stunt by which he propped his own body to suggest an entire scenario. In 1935, Caleb Milne, IV staged his own kidnapping, and was found several days after his grandfather received his ransom note asking for $50,000. (Kidnapping oneself is not itself a crime.) The 24-year-old Milne was "tied up, his eyes and mouth taped and his wrists fastened to his knees. The sleeves of his coat had been torn off, and there were needle marks in his arm." All of this corroborated his tale that he had been kidnapped, drugged, and transported to a deserted farmhouse. Notably, it was a propping—or costuming—element that brought the lively story down: "Milne said that his watch had been taken immediately after the kidnapping, but he said he knew what time it was when he reached the farmhouse by looking at his watch."[61]

During the 1980s, New York Police Department decoy officers were advised to draw freely on such costume and prop elements as "crutches, canes, wallets, handbags, wigs, dresses, hardhats, coveralls, changemakers, nurses' and other hospital uniforms, T.A. [Transit Authority] uniforms, [and] utility workers' uniforms." In the same period, undercover officers in Phoenix received along with their new assignments any extravagant clothing and hairstyle requirements they were to incorporate.[62] Despite these somewhat operatic disguise measures, the decoy is supposed to stick out by showing just how typical he is of those people who are believed to make a good mark, or potential crime victim. In designing a decoy role, law enforcement assesses how criminal perpetrators "qualify," or cast, their marks, and then take the mark role on directly. Charles Beene played right into a suspect's vision of a real mark for a mugging, and successfully dispelled his assailant's fears that he might be a police decoy. As Beene lay in a doorway in a sleeping pose, his wallet in easy reach, several bills exposed, the potential mugger read the drops of (fake) blood on

Beene's house slippers as the decisive sign of a truly injured person rather than a cop, and went for the wallet.[63]

Goffman would call the decisive drops of blood "body gloss," a "constellation of appearance-related techniques" individuals use to "make otherwise unavailable facts about [their] situation gleanable."[64] A 1980s disguise-manual author provided an outstanding example of body gloss when he recommended to those who wished to infiltrate drug gangs a special method for faking needle tracks

> by spreading a thin layer of Elmer's Glue-All or surgical adhesive in a line a half inch to an inch long following the line of a vein. The glue will cause the skin to wrinkle slightly. When it is dry, blue-gray, brown, and maroon shades of cosmetic pencil or eye makeup can be brushed on. Keep the coloring irregular and shade it into surrounding skin to achieve the effect of a deep scar. A thin coat of transparent nail polish will seal the track, making it more long lasting. Blend the edges of the polish into the surrounding skin for added realism.[65]

Though they strive for some degree of subtlety, decoy officers can also be classified according to how visible to potential criminals, versus how investigatively active, they are expected to be. A decoy proper is someone who is supposed to be highly visible, while not being expected to witness accurately the perpetrator or the details of the crime. Slightly less visible but with greater responsibilities for observing and reporting is the "backup," who, in order to provide proper testimony, must see without being seen. The back-up must "blend into all types of areas, be close to the decoy (for the decoy's safety) without being noticed, and be able to make the arrest and testify in court." Least visible and most responsible for detached surveillance is the "blend/observer," who must "get into high-crime areas without being recognized in order to on-view violent crimes, while being especially alert for armed and wanted felons." For each of these roles, the performers and those casting them must appropriately balance the cop's visibility and his or her ability to see what may become relevant material for legal testimony.[66]

The aesthetics of a particular decoy performance are certainly bound to the sensibilities of its law-enforcement culture. During the

1970s, when decoy programs inviting crime at the street level received a lot of press, an especially stagy approach was adopted. Law-enforcement officers who wished to act as decoys relied on the more spectacular of theatrical make-up techniques, including building scars, altering the shape of facial features, and constructing age make-up for cops in their twenties. Even the top guy was closely involved. At a Seattle police station,

> One corner of the commander's desk holds a makeup case containing various lengths and colors of hair for instant beards, mustaches, and sideburns, wax pencils, cement for sticking on false beards, and nose putty to create misshapen bone structure. Gauze bandages and iodine are used for obvious "injuries"; crutches convey "victim" helplessness and therefore attract street muggers.

> With the commander acting as "makeup man," the decoy squad arrives early for its 7 p.m. to 3 a.m. shift and immediately begins its transformation.[67]

The techniques could not by any stretch be thought of as naturalistic:

> The officer who is to become the next victim stands 6'2" tall, weighs 200 lbs., has blonde hair and is clean shaven.

> First, the officer's hair is quickly transformed with the application of non-toxic white liquid shoe polish ... Next, theatrical make-up is used to provide a slight beard, an abrasion on the right side of his face and the appearance of a recent injury to the officer's right hand.

Costuming added to the effect of weakened age:

> Clothing will consist of worn trousers (clean but slightly wrinkled), a sports jacket that does not match with shoulder pads removed to give a stoop shouldered impression, worn shoes with holes cut in the sides to provide relief for an apparent arthritic condition, a shapeless fedora and, as a final touch, a pair of glasses with one lens cracked.[68]

In designing the physical accoutrements of their performances, identity artists on both sides of the law build up the plausibility and the richness of how they will appear to their potential audiences. It makes sense that the surreptitious aging of identity documents, or of art works, and the planful staging of a disappearance or appearance, would occur in something of a social vacuum: such things have to be in place for the identity to have a chance to be performed at all.

In an actual audience encounter, however, things of course are considerably more complicated. So, anticipating an extended contact with an audience, the performer constructs a detailed image of how the interaction will play out that includes how the ineffable elements between performer and audience will be built up and made to suc- ceed. Most important of these is trust, which is about much more than the way in which the physical props act reciprocally with per- formed assertions and behaviors to establish an identity and context for interaction. Trust has also to do with manipulating the symbol- ism of interaction, the way in which an offer of identity is made—by extending a paper ID when it is demanded; by asserting—or defend- ing—a document's or a personal identity's authenticity; or by standing behind the assertions made in prior performances with the same audiences.

Making it possible to invite others into increasingly incriminating interactions has been the province of law-enforcers, law-breakers, art pranksters, and even of fairly serious artists. Identity is a form of cur- rency: it's only "good" if the other person agrees to accept it. In the next chapter, we look at the structural elements that make audience contact possible in perhaps the most virtuosic of complex identity work, the con game, a close relative of the undercover storefront op- eration in its extended development of relational trust.

4

THE CRAFTY EXPEDIENT:

CON SCENARIOS FOR PASSING TRICK IDENTITIES

The people who get on in this world are the people who get up and look for the circumstances they want, and if they can't find them, make them.[1]

—George Bernard Shaw, *Mrs. Warren's Profession*

It's funny, though, how these transactions [of my money art] are themselves a lot like drug deals. The same sorts of questions come up: Is it real? Is it a con? Is it good stuff? Is it worth it? Is it legal?

—J. S. G. Boggs

In fact, the picture that emerges when one studies a large number of swindling and selling techniques is of a society by and large profoundly skeptical about the possibility of love and gifts, at least from strangers.

—Arthur Allen Leff

D amn! It's happened again.
I'd just had a most agreeable Friday lunch meeting with an editor I usually find intractable, during which we exchanged thoughts about my own relationship to the deceptions I write about in this book. Anticipating a productive afternoon of reading and pa-

perwork, I settled into my favorite coffeehouse. An amiable, vaguely homeless African-American man in his middle years strode into the coffeehouse, settled into the midst of this upscale Chicago neighborhood (not mine), and staked out his territory. He hovered near me, around the living room-style arrangement of oversized armchairs and sofa, steering clear of the intent people screwing up their eyes at tiny laptop screens at the tables.

"You own the place?" he asked my grave-looking, grey-haired white neighbor, whose nose stayed buried in the *Chicago Sun-Times*. "I own a lot of places." Forbidding stop. The black man didn't push him. He spied me.

I decided not to write him off, though I had a stack of computer printouts I wanted to thrash through: there was actually something appealing about him. I made light conversation, and accepted his compliment about how polite I was: I must not be from here. (My politeness is frequently noted by people with whom I'm having a first conversation; for some reason, good friends never mention it.) "You *fine*," he told me, looking me up and down with that standard hook of the neck. I don't mind hearing that once in a while, even if it is a line. No harm: I liked pretending he means it.

When I shared my cookie with the con, I could feel the sharp disapproval coming from my neighbor. "You just inherited him," he warned. But I'd gotten the cookie for free: my friend at the counter had thought it wasn't fresh enough to sell. Seemed only right to share my good fortune.

Once I set up to work through my papers seriously, the con turned his attention to a young college student up at the counter ordering a latte. He convinced her to join him on the sofa, learned she was the daughter of missionaries (she's a goner!), and got her to pray with him. (Yes, I was eavesdropping.) Eventually, she gave him a few dollars. My steely-eyed neighbor behind the tabloid seethed lightly. I felt as though I wanted to "save" the young woman—in a more secular way than she and the con were talking about—but I also recognized this very warm interaction was actually making her day. Though this college student could probably scarcely afford to be parting with the money she gave him, she did what she probably thought her parents would have wanted her to do, and left the coffeehouse and the con's company before she had the chance to be disillusioned.

After both the con and his mark left, my disapproving neighbor behind the newspaper turned to me. Every newspaper looked small in front of this 6'6" retired police lieutenant. He knew this guy's game, and he described it to me in detail.

The Con Scenario: In Tacit Tandem

Biblical, military, and political histories offer innumerable scenarios of cons and clandestine information-gathering.[2] Non-Western history has also made much of the identity trickster. During the fourteenth century, for example, in order to gain lethal information about enemies, Japanese ninjas assumed the identities of samurai, as well as of merchants, servants, and farmers. The serpent in the Garden of Eden story has proven a popular metaphor for both undercover operators and con artists: as the first con artist, the serpent "convinced Eve and through her, Adam, that they could gain knowledge, immortality, prestige, and equality with God by eating from the fruit of the tree. The serpent knew very well that they could only lose, and that only he would make a profit."[3]

Any actor would rather play the seductive, complex serpent than one of the white-bread human innocents. Like Robertson Davies's magician character Magnus Eisengrim, who believed that illusions should be celebrated as art rather than denigrated as frauds, we might see the con artist's ability to manipulate contexts and techniques to deceive a viewer as a demonstration of his artistic virtuosity. Even though a con game's principal aim is virtually always monetary, clear artistic elements can't help but shine forth. There's the rigor of the dramatic structure; the coordination and juxtaposition of plot elements that appear spontaneous; and the orchestration of the mark's emotional responses, combined with a scenario that flexes with those responses and yet inevitably wins. According to Richard H. Blum, con games have

> a strongly theatrical quality ... The confidence men play roles for which they rehearse and make up, they hire one another to do bit parts, they set up stages for action and, when all is ready, they invite the victim not only to be an audience but to participate as an actor in the star role. The victim, in ac-

cepting the invitation, moves from the humdrum into a world of impersonation and fantasied gain. It can be amazing to see how readily ordinary folk enter these dramas, how easily the theater begins, and how practiced they are in impersonating themselves as they would be if they were what their hearts desired. One must not overlook the fact that the dramas are destructive ones in which at least one person is hurt, yet that action, too, is not foreign but familiar, and both perpetrator and victim may respond to harm with an unexpected fatalism if not grim humor, as though it were a practical joke. In one sense it is just that.[4]

Both the object of our admiration and someone we can see as being not all that unlike ourselves, the con does artfully what we all do every day, asserts Sanford Levinson:

Our ability to distinguish the con artist's false identity from the "real" one rests ironically on our knowledge of our own multiple selves. We could not recognize, accept, and even admire the illusion of the con if we did not relate the multiple identities to our sense of ourselves as both public selves ... and private selves.[5]

As similar as professional liars are to everyday ones, the one skill that distinguishes the con artist from the amateur is his fluency in the stock plots that make up his trade. The con game's fidelity to an overriding structure governs both the overall game to be played and the performative "bits" that come up. An American con artist described the con as a national currency reliant upon standard methods of improvisation:

Any two con men from anywhere in the country can work together, once they talk a little and get the lingo. The important thing is to put something together that works. There are different names for the same set-ups, and you can add or take off a little on any of them, but a good team can intermix elements easily and quickly, depending on how things are developing.[6]

Con games have proven so resilient as to permit a seemingly infinite number of variations: in the early 1980s, a Special Committee of the United States Senate recognized over 800 con schemes. The longevity of many stock schemes attests to their viability and flexibility as performance scripts. The original con game, the Pigeon Drop—still one of the Ur-con games—is believed to have originated in China, where paper currency was first printed in the fourteenth century. Many more games have survived at least several generations. The "Spanish Prisoner" was popular during the 1930s and '40s, and continues to be successful as it has migrated to the Internet; it was even the eponymous star of a 1998 movie written by David Mamet.

Performed correctly, a con game cannot fail. As I've suggested, the star of a con scenario is not so much the identity player as the play itself, refined over time to optimize results. The work of the con is to cast a mark who will play his part so as to let the scenario play to its triumphant (for the con man) conclusion. Thus, if one is familiar with the structure of the con, the moves of the con artists are predictable, staged in a standard sequence to gain an expected response from the mark.

A single mark is the con game's typical object. The game's collaborators divide up the functional roles so that the force of the social reality acts powerfully on the mark; increasing the number of people on the operative side of a con game often only enhances the believability of the presented reality. When the con game is played well, the mark has no thought but to step into a persuasive scenario, doing just what will provide the most profit to the bad guy.

A short con—usually a couple of hours in duration at most—is "fast moving, of short duration, high mobility, and a high frequency rate." By contrast, long cons can take weeks or months in the set up and up to years in the cooling down. While long cons aim at a fair portion of the mark's total assets, short cons generally go after whatever money the mark has on him.[7]

At the center of many short cons is the staging of a "good faith" gesture by the mark, a proffering of some of his own money, seemingly to demonstrate his trustworthiness with the greater sums hinted at in the fictitious scenario. Ruses vary in how they ensure that the mark does bring this money forward. In the Pigeon Drop, the mark withdraws his money and submits the bills so "the serial numbers can be recorded," thereby showing that he's prepared, for example, to pay taxes on the money received. In the Bank Examiner scheme, the mark exhibits his readiness to aid in an honorable cause, the collection of evidence against a supposedly swindling bank employee. The anxious-to-help mark goes to the bank, withdraws all his money, and turns the bills over to an out-of-sight executive who, the mark is told, is recording serial numbers but is in fact making off with the bucks. In the Latin Charity Scheme, the mark puts up money of his own against the money he has offered to distribute to prove he has his own wealth and will not steal the South American's. In the Texas Twist and the Filipino Card Cheating schemes, the mark shows his own money to prove that he is prepared to pay should he lose at cards. In the Tainted Money Scheme, a fortuneteller convinces the mark that the curse that has been on him will be removed when he brings in half of all he owns to be cleansed.

Possibly the best known of the scenarios that feature the good faith gesture are "switch schemes," a group of games that

> follow a carefully rehearsed script and are dependent on the ability of the swindler(s) to develop trust and confidence in his victim. The con man misleads the victim into believing that he is going to receive a large sum of money and persuades him to display his own money for a short period of time. The victim will eventually end up with a sealed package of some type (envelope, knotted bandana, locked bank bag, paper sack, etc.) that will contain worthless scraps of paper.[8]

In the opening sequence of the classic 1973 film *The Sting*, the character of Hooker (played by Robert Redford) trains his mark, who is carrying a bundle of money, to conceal it by stuffing it down the front of his pants. Hooker's demonstration of ideal bundle placement allows him to swap out the mark's real bundle of money for the con man's "boodle." In a variation called the Jamaican Switch, the hitman plays a superstitious Jamaican who acts afraid to place his money in the "white man's bank" or finds another way to elicit an act of trust or a demonstration of a higher rationality from a white mark. His accomplice—and usually the mark as well—reassure him with heavy withdrawals and shows of money outside the bank, which by sleight of hand are switched out from the mark and replaced with play money.

Thus, the con artist is an expert artificer of contexts, tightening every feature of the scenario around the mark's purse. Like a magician skilled in misdirection, he is

> adept at disguise and attention control. He employs physical disguise with his apparatus. He employs psychological disguise—simulation, dissimulation, maneuver, ruse, suggestion and inducement. He exercises absolute control over the attention of his spectator by forestalling it, by catching it relaxed, by dulling it, by scattering it, by diverting it, by distracting it, and by openly moving it away.[9]

In magic, "the conjurer directs your attention to what he does not do; he does not do what he pretends to do; and to what he actually does he is careful neither to appear to direct his own attention nor to arouse yours."[10] The bracketing of the scene of which the mark is a part resembles that used in stage magic, which allows the magician to start a new trick before the audience is even aware of its having begun.[11] The presentation of a "misdirection of strong compulsion"—like setting something on fire!—puts the audience's attention where the real trick is not.[12]

In maintaining the illusion that nothing significant that happens has been planned in advance, the overall style of performance is crucial: it must be "natural." Naturalness' immense utility to the magician is that it proves to be "an anesthetic to attention," a way of pushing and pulling spectators' sense of the significant. "Interpretation" is how the magician teaches his spectator what to expect by directing his construction of reality. He may employ a "ruse," a "crafty expedient" that "divert[s] attention from the magician's real purpose." In some sense, magic theorist Fitzkee admits, "all magic is a ruse." The ruse performs two critical purposes: It "makes it possible for the magician to do an unnatural thing naturally. The ruse also makes it possible for the performer to do a natural thing under a guise other than the true one." A natural performance of a *deceptive* act is one in which the performer has trained himself to think—or to appear to think—as he wishes the spectator to believe.

In con games as in magic, rehearsal for the presentation of the natural is a necessity, though an oxymoron. Regarding a money-changing trick, Fitzkee importunes the reader:

Putting the check in the envelope is done exactly as if the check were placed in an ordinary one. There is no need to do it in any other manner. The magician actually is putting it in an envelope.

The signed check is placed in the flapless envelope and the performer immediately grasps the flap of the second and pulls it away. There is no need to do it in any manner other than a natural one. The performer is actually pulling an envelope from the stack. Any false moves at this particular stage of the proceedings would only result in suspicious surveillance unnecessarily.[13]

Knowing when to clothe the most significant part of the trick in utter banality can be a key skill in pulling off a con game. The most significant plot elements in long cons are treated as accidental and innocuous. The con artist identifies the mark as well-to-do and vulnerable. He gains the mark's confidence, or "plays the con for him." Starting out quite like the undercovers in training with unsuspecting visitors to a local shopping mall, the con artist "ropes the mark," then steers him toward a meeting with the insideman, who appears as if at random.[14] The insideman "tells the tale," or demonstrates the method by which much money can be made by crooked means. The mark is allowed to "win" a substantial sum—called the "convincer"—which acts to prove to him that the means to riches actually works.[15]

The players "elevate the mark" as they raise his level of confidence and his expectations of return. The mark receives the "breakdown," a determination of how much he will need to invest. Prodigious rewards are promised for the mark's patience, industry, and foresight. The mark is then "put on the send" to fetch his money from home or the bank. When he's been "played against the big store" and "fleeced," he must then be gotten rid of, "blown off." Ideally, the con men will try to have it appear that the investment failed because of "some chance factor" completely unrelated to the players in the con.[16]

The "wire" is the archetypal long con. In *The Sting*, the mark is persuaded he can have a sure bet on a race, since results can be transmitted to him after the race has actually been run but before they are broadcast more generally. He is fleeced when he acts on a false message.

In *Swindling and Selling*, Leff distinguishes between "single O's," games that take only one con artist, and "double O's," games that require two con artists to play out their essential plots against their mark. "Psst Buddy," an attempt to sell stolen goods at a low price, uses only the mark and a single con man. The cast of a single O is filled out by passersby. As Leff explains, a single O depends heavily on the conveying of expositional material: "To make it go at all, the characters in the play have to spend most of their time, in effect, *telling* each other another genre altogether, the short story. The action, such as it is, is necessarily mostly offstage."

American culture's valuing of individualism, personal freedom, and professional specialization make certain single O schemes particularly well suited to life in America. Although "gypsy short cons" can be performed anywhere, as John McLaughlin notes, "the United States is ideally suited to the gypsy's way of life" because of its size, population, and transitory culture, in which people customarily change jobs and locations frequently. One gypsy con scheme depended for its success on a late twentieth-century phenomenon, a rising litigiousness in accident cases. Gypsy "floppers" and "divers" would stage themselves as victims of auto accidents, appearing to throw themselves in front of moving vehicles, using to their advantage witnesses' poor night vision; the power of sound effects, such as the sound of a hand slapping hard against an automobile door; and pre-existing fractures, which appeared to provide evidence of impact from the "accident."

In a gypsy short con, the cunning artists prey upon the poor perception of witnesses (and drivers) under duress, which can include imagining they have seen more than they actually have. Pretending ominous injuries, the gypsy con artist can collect a tidy settlement from the driver in lieu of going to court. In a variant of this con, the gypsy scouts out a business establishment in a potentially unsafe area, chooses a number of expensive goods, stages an "accident," and frequently is sent off with the goods as shield against a lawsuit. Such scams predict fairly that most marks will choose to spend the lesser amount of money sooner rather than the much greater amount of money they are likely to have charged against them should the case go to court.[17]

The specialization of American society—resulting in the utter incompetence of many people to look after our own possessions—also offers fertile opportunities for frauds by apparent service people. A cautionary book, *Fraud and Deceit: How to Stop Being Ripped Off*, terms this group of cons "the art of compounding your problems," as car, home, or electronic-device problems are created by the very people presenting themselves as repairers.[18] Being a reassuring presence in a fear-filled industry can make for a good scam, as happens in fraudulent cemetery lot sales and funeral arrangements.

The very existence of an undercover "industry" has produced lucrative cons that provide reassurance to bad guys. (In a well-known law-enforcement scam, a "lawyer" extends the offer of checking out a suspected narcotics officer for a high-end bad guy for a $5,000 fee. After waiting two or three weeks, he reports that he couldn't find anything on the suspected narc, recommends being quite careful, and collects his fee. (Actually, for the lifetime of the scam, the narcs benefit, since no investigation is completed on them, and the bad guy's suspicion is allayed, at least in part, by the illusive efficacy of having paid the professional fee.)

By contrast with single O plays, in double O's, with two or more con artists and a mark to work with, "the onstage action can really begin."[19] The numbering and positioning of characters is anything but accidental. The canny division of functional roles permits a naturalistic array of events and a believably timed introduction of new personages to the mark. Though the device that catches the mark may vary from one game to another, the emotional functions each of the players takes on are predictable.

In a con employing two artists and a mark, the roper keeps himself far from the character who's got access to the means of making a quick buck. After the roper establishes rapport with the mark, the two of them casually run into a "capman" (known variously in different games also as the catchman, hitman, sounder, steerer, fake, or drag), who attempts to elicit the mark's cooperation in ganging up on the roper, or "lame." Of course, the mark doesn't understand that the dynamics of the threesome are working against not the roper, but himself. A temporary exit for the roper is staged, providing the "in" for the capman to make his move on the mark. The switch ensures that an apparently secret plan can be made between the capman and the mark, while decreasing the likelihood that the mark will become suspicious, as might have occurred had all three remained together throughout. In the switch,

> the initial topic which brings the victim and the bunco artist together is adroitly abandoned and a new topic substituted. The switch serves to allay suspicion, since the new topic is presented in such a way that the con himself is not seen as having introduced it. Ideally, the switch allows the victim to sell himself rather than to detect that he is being sold.[20]

The Found Ring Scheme shows clearly the benefits of the division of functions. In this game, which typically takes place in a convenience store or gas station, the attendant receives a phone call from a frantic "customer" who has just lost a family heirloom ring while pumping gas or using the restroom. The customer assures the attendant he'll be right over, and offers a substantial reward if the attendant can find and hold the ring for him until he arrives. His accomplice—the "office"—finds the ring, but is impatient about waiting. He offers to leave the ring with the attendant if he will just give him half the reward amount—the attendant can collect the full amount when the owner arrives. Naturally, the owner never appears, and the attendant is left with a worthless ring.[21] The physical separation of the accomplices—as well as the fact that only one of them appears in person and then only briefly—helps create the perception that the scenario is unfolding naturally.[22]

In contrast with the relational backstopping that undercovers engage in to underscore their trustworthiness, partners in a con game must establish the *lack* of a prior relationship between them. Creating other kinds of distance between the accomplices allows a hospitable entry point for a mark. In some periods and climes, two apparently better-educated white people, the capman and the mark, might readily see their advantage, as well as some sort of moral justice, in ganging up together against a seemingly illiterate black man, who is actually the roper. As one con artist advised, "Work their hatred. Everybody has hates. Just find out what it is they hate and agree with them. When the heart takes over instead of the brain, then the sucker is beat."[23] Building naiveté into the roper role—having him appear to be a country bumpkin or a foreigner with unsophisticated ways, such as carrying all of his cash on his person—is often a key element in inducing the mark to feel protective or superior toward him—and, in the end, to feel that this stranger could be cheated easily and without consequence.

In addition to making it easier to work the mark, the separation of roles in con games also serves as a means of protection for the members of the con band. Members of an early twentieth-century forgery crew, for example, received well-defined cuts of the take, made possible in part by the harsh separation of their roles. The backer or capitalist "very rarely allows himself to become known to the men who 'present' the forged paper at the banks." The forger, or scratcher, maintains a separate office. The only functional role that knows all the players is the middleman or go-between, who

> receive[s] from the forger or his confidential agent the altered or forged paper. He finds the man to "present" the same, accompanies his confederates on their forgery trips throughout the country, acts as the agent of the backer in dealing out money for expenses, sees that their plan of operations is carried out, and, in fact, becomes the general manager of the band. [24]

In addition to ensuring that only one figure in the band knows all the chief other functions (protecting each against the others), in choosing the middleman the band picks someone who is "staunch" and who has at least one conviction against him, so that his testimony would have to be corroborated by at least one other person.

Games requiring three or fewer con artists are often constructed as short cons, which operate lean, using pure aesthetic economy so that "strangers are made to appear as nearly as possible *necessary* to each other, irreplaceable members of the same cast." In addition to the roper and the capman, a third figure may be introduced: "The houseman always plays the role of an unbiased spectator, one who stands to gain nothing in the swindle but nevertheless supports the capman in convincing the victim to participate in the scheme."[25] The introduction of this third player helps stack the numbers in favor of the con team, much as a second salesperson may help tip an uncertain customer shopping with a friend into buying the jeans she's parading in front of the three-way mirror.

In plotting out the course of a long con, an insideman is a tactical leader. He plays the choice contact with the mark, sizing him up so as to determine how to have the scenario proceed. He handles the blow-off, the closing stage of the scenario in which, the mark, having lost his shirt, is persuaded it is in his best interests to wave it stoutly goodbye. The insideman is also the director of the whole scenario in several important respects: he selects the game to be played out against a particular mark; determines which other roles need to be filled in order to have the game play; and establishes the setting of the game. And, just as an undercover operator may, in order to divert suspicion, stage his own arrest alongside that of the suspect, the insideman preparing for a successful blow-off may also stage his own losses in the game, sometimes gaining the mark's sympathy by appearing to have lost even more than him.

The manager, or bookmaker, finds physical and human form for the insideman's ideas. He may prop the setting for the big store, cast the other roles that are to be played, and stage manage and shepherd the concept. During the Depression, Joseph "Yellow Kid" Weil set up a big store to run in a single day in order to con a multimillionaire. Weil rented the former Merchants National Bank of Muncie (Indiana), inheriting tellers' cages and other marks of plausibility:

> Weil then secretly established his own bank. He printed deposit and withdrawal slips and put them into desk slots in the foyer. Streetcar conductors were hired as bank guards and tellers and other bank officials were culled from the ranks of some of Chicago's most notorious confidence men and women.[26]

The Sting features a casting scene in which the manager interviews the men who wish to be cast in an upcoming big con, one of whom has brought all of his own costumes, like an itinerant nineteenth-century actor. Roles for those in the con mob may have interactive possibilities with the mark or be principally decorative. Typically, the work of the manager involves having prepared believable documentation for each of the roles as well, paralleling the backstopping of the paper ID for an undercover identity. The manager *frames* the big store and creates the atmosphere of prosperity and swank recklessness which goes with dignified, large-scale gambling. ... He is responsible for all the spurious documents to be used in any kind of con game which the mob may wish to play—fake personal bonds for the con men, fake membership cards in secret or fraternal organizations, fake newspaper clippings, betting slips, stock sales and purchase orders, credit slips, ledger sheets, and numerous kinds of letterhead to be used in any sort of phony correspondence which may be necessary. ... He keeps on hand various stock letters, copies of which can be "received" by the con man and shown to the mark when necessary. And, most important of all, he has official custody of the *B.R.* or *boodle.*[27]

Once he gets the con rolling, the roper makes a proposition that will bring the mark to the big store. He "convinces the victim or mark that the insideman is a true genius or man with special power or information that makes the deal a sure thing."[28] Consistent with the separation of roles, the roper rarely appears to have much to do with the activities at the big house.

Frank Abagnale combined elements of the long con—the elaborate work with identity documents, costumes, and supporting players—and the short con, working without accomplices. However, after a long period of cashing bad checks as a lone Pan Am pilot, the con artist found himself wishing both for more consistent companionship and for the additional air of plausibility that traveling with others could afford him:

An aircrew—and I thought of an aircrew only in terms of stewardesses—would lend concrete validity to my role of airline pilot. I had learned that a solitary pilot was always subject to scrutiny. Conversely, a pilot trailing a squad of lovely stewardesses would almost certainly be above suspicion. If I had a beautiful bevy of flight attendants with me in my travels, I could scatter my valueless checks like confetti and they'd be accepted like rice at a wedding, I thought. Not that I was having any trouble passing them at present, but I was passing them one at a time. With a crew behind me, I could cash the sham checks in multiple numbers.[29]

To set up his plot, Abagnale presented himself to the University of Arizona as a Pan Am pilot recruiting female students for a glamorous public relations mission. The young women would be placed on salary and chaperoned on an all-expenses-paid jaunt to Europe, where they would be photographed for glossy airline brochures. If selected to become actual flight attendants after this "pre-training period," they would receive support for their final year of college. From the thirty young women he interviewed, he selected eight who seemed to him most likely to succeed in the roles he had invented—and the least likely to ask questions.

Abagnale gave his new employees the strictest instructions. They were to wear their uniforms or civilian clothes as he determined, but always to identify themselves as flight attendants. If they ran across real flight attendants, they were to say they were on a special public relations tour with the New York office, not real attendants too, and to limit any questions. They would be paid biweekly and were to allow him to cash their checks for them rather than send them back to the United States to be deposited. (They could send any money they wanted home by purchasing a separate money order.) Abagnale made sure to hire photographers in each of the cities to maintain the premise of the trip, and regularly cashed the young women's "paychecks," bluffed-up expense checks, and his own counterfeit cashier's checks.[30]

This inventive form of summer stock netted Abagnale about $300,000. When he returned the young women to the University of Arizona, he "cooled out his marks," making sure any suspicions they might have, upon leaving his company, would be allayed. This crucial closing element of con games ensures that the mark will not, as E. H. Sutherland puts it, "go to the police or make a fuss in other ways." Goffman has noted that one means of achieving this is to provide "instruction in the philosophy of taking a loss."[31] Thus, at the end of Abagnale's summer with the co-eds, he insisted they keep the uniforms, check stubs, and identification cards, in case Pan Am should decide to hire them upon graduation. (He assured the young women it wouldn't happen *until* graduation.) The con master's deft manipulation of his unwitting accomplices is undoubtedly virtuosic, his story giving us a simple portrait of the process of propping a con game with supporting characters to make it believable.

A storefront operation designed and acted by undercovers takes on many of the illusionary and role parceling techniques characteristic of the long con: it is decoy work at the scenario level. On the criminal side, these schemes take place in "big stores"—in betting houses, poolrooms, stockbrokers' offices—or, in the games of the more distant past, telegraph offices. Using many of the same techniques as the big store, the storefront operation makes victims of crooks, in venues as varied as auto repair businesses, head shops, gold and silver exchanges, or liquor stores. Used to capture a wide variety of criminal behavior, including white-collar crimes, murder, arson, drug dealing, and vice, storefront operations may be run from a network of telephones, a van, or a literal storefront. They may function fully as businesses, or just appear to do so, again by using documents, sets, props, and supporting players. An Albuquerque-based group of detectives once maintained a print shop as a storefront façade:

> We went to great lengths to create the illusion that the shop was a functioning business. ... When the storefront was open ..., the printing equipment was churning out the product. Paper was streaming off the press—of course, nothing was being printed and the same paper was used over and over. We donned our work aprons and always had ink on our hands. Bundles of printing packages, as if sent out to clients, were strategically placed ... When appropriate and properly timed, ... customers (other undercover investigators) would enter the business and place or pick up an order. If legitimate customers did enter the storefront, they were simply told we could not handle any more business and they were directed to a competitor. When targets entered the storefront, they were truly under the impression that this was a functioning business.[32]

Some storefront operations start out as a generic business and then tailor the business's products and services to what its customers seem to demand. A clientèle can be generated through face-to-face contacts, both cold and through informants, as well as through Internet marketing. Undercovers can prospect by anticipating industries or products that might appeal to national or international markets. One undercover predicted well the success of a coffee and tea warehousing operation aimed at both Asian and South American markets.

Royal Canadian Mounted Police undercovers Chris Mathers and Murray Simms developed elaborate, multilevel storefront operations that ran as active businesses, attracted crooks, and furnished themselves with real business skills they might choose to employ upon retiring from law enforcement. As they prepared to run a financial services corporation, Simms read books such as *The Ten-Day MBA*. The corporation had the full customary founding documents. A law-firm partner was able to provide plausible deniability. A paper trail established a history of profit.

As Mathers, Simms, and their staff progressed in their work with the storefront, they found that money laundering services—frequently hinted at under the aegis of "currency exchange"—provided a pathway to other clandestine financial activities. Over a four-year period, the storefront had moved into second, third, and fourth-generation, apparently separate, businesses, each set up for as long as it could retain the integrity of its identity without discovery by the bad guys. While Simms handled the warehousing operation, Mathers ran the financial side. They designed their cover stories so they could make customer referrals to each other, as Simms explained to me: "We had a long history together, we had an interest in each other's companies; therefore, we could vouch for each other." Their staff, which consisted of between two and five people, had some more confusing roles to play: at various points, they would be staffing both sides of the operation, as well as operations that were different generations down from the start-up business.

Whether staged by law enforcers or law breakers, the con game cannot be presented as a purely altruistic gambit, but only as one that provides both parties with enhanced opportunities: "Anyone shaping a deal must write a script which persuasively sets up a situation in which both parties gain but neither's gain is at the other's expense." The con artist must not appear to be acting against his apparent self-interest, as the "most fundamental principle of selling credibility" is "thou shalt not appear to be making a gift."[33]

The collusion entered into by con artist and mark thus represents a system in which the advantage to be had is taken from those outside the system:

It is a perfectly rational and widely recognized model of general economic organization which identifies the source of "our" boodle as "them." If we together can form a team that outperforms, outdeals, outthinks, or even outsteals outsiders, they can be exploited by us, very much more successfully than either of us alone could exploit them, and usually much more profitably than we could exploit each other. We "need each other" still, but this time the source of our symbiotic gain is not the "thin air" of comparative advantage but the more down-to-earth "their stuff." ... The ur-plot for substantially all selling scripts, crooked and otherwise, is this attempt to dramatize the creation and operation of a "firm" in which the buyer/mark has a useful, and preferably necessary, role to play in the plunder of someone else.[34]

The mark's complicity is scripted into the con structure, as in Abagnale's stewardesses' agreeing to his cashing their paychecks. At the turn of the twentieth century, medical quack Albert Abrams sold fraudulent electronic diagnosis and treatment machines to customers who were warned never to break the seals on the boxes or to "try to operate them with a 'skeptic' in the room, since the treatment would then prove useless."[35] This tactic quite effectively isolates the mark, as it aligns all his social interests with those who appear to believe in the power of the machines. The structure of the Pyramid Scheme likewise makes it "in the victim's best interest to become a promoter and transfer his loss to another," thus making the original perpetrators very difficult to prosecute.[36] In the Found Ring Scheme discussed earlier, the gas station or service station attendant, having handed over money directly from the cash drawer to the con accomplice who "found" the ring, when the time comes to face his boss has to align himself with the con artist and to lie—believably—that the money he paid for the ring was stolen, or probably lose his job.[37]

The con game stages a form of audience participation whose arguably cruelest feature is that the mark doesn't know he's watching a performance designed to put him through the most practical kind of catharsis. After all, con games are, according to one pithy definition, "carefully rehearsed plays in which every member of the cast except the mark knows his part perfectly"; they are literally incriminating.[38] Moreover, the mark's participation is framed on multiple levels not as the opportunity either to engage or to refrain, but merely to select from among the available ways of participating: First of these levels for the mark's participation "is the constraint to play. Once in, he cannot decide to disdain the play or postpone it; his doing nothing itself becomes, in effect, a choice and a course of action." Second, the number of choices is limited. Third, a choice becomes a commitment to a specific course of action. And fourth, "a tight connection exists between the game and the payoff."[39] The final tip-off is the illusion often purveyed of the victim's being in charge. In con games, as well as in undercovers' building of cases against suspects, the mark or criminal target is subtly steered to feel he is "leading" much of the conversation. In ensuring a steady progression from one step to another, holding the mark's trust is crucial:

> The important thing is never to let the mark catch you lying. That means that everything not only has to ring true but that everything you tell him comes true during the play, everything but the big thing, the delivery. That's the way you build his confidence, you get him to trust you, since what you say turns out that way.[40]

All games convey the notion of unavoidably limited business partners and create the mark as someone specially necessary to the proposed activity, which Leff calls the nexus of monopoly and monopsony. The game "Psst Buddy," in which supposedly high-value stolen merchandise is offered furtively for a low price, works because the con artist conveys to the mark the notion that he needs him, that because he cannot openly offer his stolen wares for sale, he depends on those to whom he does reveal his product.[41]

Perhaps the deepest level on which the mark's role is laid out for him is the means by which he is exited from the stage, in general before the play is entirely over, before all the players break frame. Certainly one of the more colorful methods of blow-offs uses a "cackle bladder":

> In a raid or faked attack on one con man by another, a blank is fired. One of the con men has a bladder, or balloon, filled with chicken blood or some reasonable facsimile inside his mouth. He falls, acting as if he had been shot, and allows the

blood to trickle from his mouth. Afraid of implication in a murder, the mark flees the scene.[42]

Less threatening closures to cons, as we have seen, involve simply cooling out the mark. Either way, the ultimate job of the mark is to disappear, a role he typically performs quite willingly.

Many theatrical performers—stand-up comics, dramatic artists, members of improvisational comedy troupes, and, of course, magicians—recognize that performances with audience participation usually carefully choreograph the possibilities available to the audience-member-as-performer. Just as the "pick a card, any card" ploy allows the magician to subtly foist a pre-selected card toward the "participant," performers who bring audience members up on stage, ostensibly to participate, know they know the stage terrain better than do the audience members and so will be safe in expecting to guide audience members to appropriate parts of the stage. They also control the microphones, so have a good deal of power over extraneous verbal expressions. Audience participation thus might be more accurately termed audience inclusion in a performance script for which audience members misguidedly believe they are co-authors.

The con artist guides his audience to feel that it is acting and believing of its own free will. When the mark is permitted to find the con artist's wallet for him but will accept no reward, the con has the opportunity to return the favor by placing a bet for the mark, invoking the principle of not incurring any cost for himself but potentially yielding up good for both; the mark has also to accede to this offer in deference to a code of graciousness. Such an appeal to the mark's higher instincts effectively provides the all-too-seductive illusion of freedom. Some people are suckers for that.

Qualifying the Mark

The term "mark"—as it refers to the victim of a confidence scheme—derives from the circus con practice of literally marking those who had either already been taken or demonstrated the signs that they could be. On adults deemed ripe for carnival swindles, the placement of the chalk mark indicated where its bearer carried his money. In a nineteenth-century carnival and circus scam for selling more balloons,

> The operators ... hired assistants to blow tacks at balloons after purchase to create an instant demand from howling children for replacement of their busted balloons. In some cases, frustrated parents were forced to make a third purchase.

> As some parents grew irate if more than one balloon popped, astute operators developed the custom of consoling a child by patting him on the back while filling the reorder. The operator's hand would be covered with chalk so that some would remain on the child's back. This mark informed the balloon busters that the child's balloon had been popped enough.[43]

The exercise in roping mall shoppers and trying to get personal information from them, as described in Chapter 2, is similar to the process of qualifying marks. In our class exercise in a real-life environment, student narcs did not waste their time with people they'd sized up as "no" people, and went right for those whom they could fairly assume to be "yes" or "maybe" people.[44] Similarly, selecting marks for his *Candid Camera* and *Candid Microphone* programs, Allen Funt generally found men more amenable to his outrageous scenarios than women. Funt hypothesized this may have been because women knew the most bizarre interaction would never come to blows: "a woman, not having to face this eventuality, is more likely to react" and to give him a hard time, often to humorous effect. Had his objective been to get away quickly rather than to engage in a witty conflict, Funt might have preferred male marks. When, however, Funt played the role of expert, women proved as passive as the men, a finding no doubt tied to larger cultural themes of the 1950s, juxtaposing male experts with the female consumers of their advice.

Street muggers spend a good deal of effort determining who would allow them to seize money and property and escape without getting caught or identified or losing a physical fight. Street criminals look for

> the lone people, those who take the shortcut through the al-
> ley or park and are out of sight of the general public, or those
> who seem to be careless about the way they carry their purses,
> wallets, or other property. In addition, crooks are looking for
> someone who is weaker than themselves.

> Based on these criteria, then, the potential victim might be
> elderly or very young, injured, small in stature, retarded, in-
> toxicated, or giving off any of a variety of signals that he is
> not paying attention to his surroundings.

The appearance of carelessness can be the sign that attracts the bad
guys, as

> Street crimes are generally committed impulsively, and the
> victims are chosen at random, except that the more defense-
> less a person appears to be, the more likely he or she is to be
> victimized. In the same way, carelessness, which the criminal
> often sees as "a mistake made in his favor," increases the
> odds that an individual will become a victim.[45]

Writers on cons estimate it typically takes five minutes to qualify a
mark for a short con, several hours for middle cons. When qualifying
marks for long cons, the con artist must ascertain that the candidate
is open to new people and "ready ... to accept the conditions of the
investment opportunity, namely to enter into a conspiracy with another person, to agree to secrecy, and to be willing to live with [the]
confusion" inherent in a long con.

In the 1960s and early '70s, particular types of marks were regarded as highly preferable:

> older men or senior citizens, well-dressed men who were
> drinking or are drunk, soldiers on travel orders and those re-
> turning from overseas, travelling salesmen or convention-
> goers, travelling pro-athletes, Chinese, lower-class young men,
> Negroes, business and professional men, middle-aged men,
> lonely women and members of religious orders.[46]

One con player told the police the categories into which she men-
tally placed marks. In addition to the lonely, there were also the
"greedy and larcenious" [sic], the "honest," and the "gambler type."

The "religious type" believes his coming together with the con artist is "most definitely God's work." The "prior victim" is a key category: "You find out how they were beat the first time and play them an entirely different way. You can sometimes get them on a religious tip as God is sending back to them what was taken the first time."[47]

As we have seen, isolating the mark is relational as well as physical. Con artists look for those whom they can isolate from a reality-providing frame of reference, such as caring friends or family members. Wealthier marks are less likely to arouse the suspicion of their close associates when they become involved in unusual new financial activities than are victims of more modest means.[48] Blum's interviews revealed the method for the selection of marks was apparently

> to exclude those who were protected by the presence of possibly critical or protective others, to exclude those whose ongoing activities would rule out a casual intruder and conversely, to seek isolates, aimless groups open to distraction, those open or receptive to intrusion and those pairs where one would be vulnerable to show off to the other.[49]

Goffman has written that two marks are harder to work than one.[50] Similarly, Funt found that people would be much more willing to go along with his outlandish *Candid Camera* schemes when he effectively isolated and cornered them:

> Bring in a third person, and the whole equation is changed. I met a man who wouldn't say "boo" when I borrowed a cigarette from him, used his lighted cigarette to get a light for mine, and then threw his away. But if the same thing had happened in front of that man's wife, a friend, or even a stranger, he would have said plenty. For in the presence of a third person the whole outside world makes itself felt. This man can no longer allow himself to seem like a coward. He thinks of what other people expect him to do more than what his private feelings dictate. Suddenly he begins to pour out righteous indignation. He's a little more vain and pugnacious. He's a little more like the people in movies and plays.[51]

David Maurer talks about a con artist's "grift sense," the "undefinable ability to sense the readiness of some people for certain con games and their probable responses to each part of the conning process."[52] Vidocq gave the name *drogueurs de la haute* to those who worked hard-luck stories on the sympathies of the rich.[53] Some con games are specifically aimed at occupational types who act out predictable patterns. A scam aimed at realtors preys on this profession's willingness to woo high-profile customers. The con artist blows into town, and lets his plans to buy high-ticket property be known. Allowing the realtor to show him several appropriate properties and to buy him expensive meals, the con lets it drop that he owns several racehorses and knows about a "sure thing" in a race the following day. He invites the realtor to join him in a bet. The realtor—not wishing to offend his customer and lose a potential commission—is willing to risk part of his expected commission on the race.[54]

One author remarks the many schemes that found success among devout Mormons:

> Ironically, the very qualities that distinguish the Latter-Day Saints as fine, upstanding citizens proved to be their financial downfall at the hands of con artists. Because they were religious, law-abiding, and community- and church-oriented, they tended to be sheltered and trusting. They took the word of those they looked up to in the community hierarchy—law preachers, bank officers, and well-heeled businessmen—rather than researching the facts for themselves. Officials of the Church of Jesus Christ of Latter-Day Saints have issued warnings to church members, but Utah remains a prime hunting ground for many a bunco artist.
>
> Says Frederick A. Moreton, a vice-president of Kidder, Peabody & Co. in Salt Lake City: "If it works in California or Colorado, it's bound to work in Utah."[55]

Some schemes prey on the mark's sense of himself as an altruist or a good sport.[56] In their book on gaining information from others under false pretenses, E. Roy Slade and James R. Gutzs highlight the value of preying on the altruistic impulse. Their hard-to-resist blood-bank telephone ploy offers a flattering good-citizen role to the person on the other end of the line:

> "Hello, this is Walter Jackson with Medical Alert. We're trying to reach Mr. Steve Jones who is registered with us as a blood donor for emergency purposes. Yes, Mr. Jones is or has

A- blood, a rare type that is now needed because of an accident involving this blood type. Mr. Jones last donated blood
approximately one year ago and we're now trying to locate
him again as he is one of the few donors we have in this area.
If he is no longer living or working there, would you please
give me any information you have that will help us find his
current employment or new address?" [57]

The mark is highly motivated to cooperate with the caller; after all,
the man is seeking information in order to save a life!

Cons have a telling name for marks who engage in a scam repeat-
edly—addicts. One con man, a veteran of the marriage bunco, found
that he succeeded by finding "women who've been lied to. I like
those who've been lied to and wronged many times. They don't believe the truth anymore. So if you lie they believe you."[58] Thus, like
con artists themselves, marks may "specialize."

Like the undercover role that serves as a receptacle for the target's
fantasies, a con game that meets a deep-seated need of the mark
makes other types of deceptions possible, including spiritual and
healing hoaxes. Franz Mesmer, for example, helped his female clients, whom he had diagnosed as hysterics, into a hypnotic state by
having them sit around a vat, where they touched each other as apparently stunning young men stimulated them manually to further
the "magnetism" along.[59]

The fortuneteller is perhaps the clearest, most distilled example of
how the con artist embodies the mark's hopes and fears. The successful fortuneteller "provide[s] the customer with the information that
he or she wants." Embarking on a long con, the fortuneteller typically combines the making of sufficiently vague statements and
characterizations as could be applicable to anyone while fishing for
additional information about her mark's station in life and concerns.
By the careful combination of these two techniques, over time the
fortuneteller can gauge some of the customer's important issues: as
the fortuneteller "provides a series of [general] statements, [she]
watches the customer's reactions to each. It is assumed that the customer will most actively respond to those statements that deal with
his or her real concerns."[60] Con artists generally follow this method
of recalibrating their scripts based on their careful, ongoing observation of their marks.

Like the storefront operation, undercover decoy work bears an important resemblance to con games, particularly in its selection of unwitting co-actors. An undercover decoy places himself in a role in which a potential criminal might qualify *him* as a good mark. Role-plays described in 1992 by San Francisco Police Department decoy officers included:

> a female officer walking near a hospital with her arm in a fake cast, a senior citizen with a leg brace leaving his apartment for his daily grocery shopping, a female stranded with the hood up on her car near a high school where purse snatches were increasing, and a disoriented person trying to catch a bus in a high-crime area.[61]

In some ways conceived more as objects than as agents, the decoys are sometimes referred to as "bait," like the senior citizen decoy in the street mugging scenario: "First, there is the bait. It's Grandpop with painted-on wrinkles, hobbling across the street, always in sight of his back-up team. He acts and looks like an easy mark and his vulnerability seems to cry out."[62] Detective Mary Glatzle, nicknamed "Muggable Mary," is pictured in an issue of the *FBI Law Enforcement Bulletin* appearing evidently careless of her personal effects. She rides a bicycle with a double-strapped handbag dangling off her right shoulder. A cigarette is poised in her right hand as she steers. A windbreaker half pours out of a broken-down basket hung over the front handlebars. Her wide bell bottoms could get caught in the machinery below at any point, distracting her from approaching muggers.[63]

The Street Crime Unit of the New York Police Department, whose techniques received a lot of attention during the 1970s, placed "blending and decoying" officers in locales where they would be expected to have a better-than-average chance of attracting perpetrators. Without weapons, the decoys had their back-up teams carefully placed so as to be available to read prearranged hand signals while staying out of the bad guy's suspicion range.[64]

From the criminal's perspective, the excitement of seizing an "easy mark"—as the decoy appears to be—can be a huge motivator in street crime, perhaps more central than the amount of money likely to be gained. Muggers report feeling seduced by their object: "That wallet was like hot apple pie on a window sill" and "If I passed up an easy mark, I couldn't live with myself."[65]

The reversal of agent and object may in fact be the hallmark of the con game, where the mark becomes con artist as well, believing he's the one duping the con. Darwin Ortiz differentiates between a normal instance of cheating, in which a person believes he has a good chance of winning against a hustler, and a con game, in which the mark thinks he's actually cheating the hustler: only the second is a true con game, as the mark must try to outsmart or cheat the con. The game of Three-Card Monte constitutes a con because of the bent corner of one card:

> When the sucker sees the bend in the corner of the winning card and assumes the broad tosser doesn't know it's there, he is willing to make a bet he might not otherwise have made. He is no longer gambling, he is plotting to cheat the monte operator and, in the process, is setting himself up for the con.[66]

As Joseph "Yellow Kid" Weil is reputed to have said, all his victims "wanted something for nothing." Instead, and more profitably, he "gave them nothing for something."

Certainly, greed, mixed with laziness, are key motivators in street cons such as the Pigeon Drop, mail swindles such as the Spanish Prisoner, and fraudulent job offers such as work-at-home and pyramid schemes, as well as in animal breeding plans and the diploma mills described in Chapter 3. The greed of the so-called victims of con games is evident in the scheme enacted in the 1940s by con man Jake Max Landau, who sold "secret" insurance policies to relatives of the deceased.[67] Customers' greed also enabled Elmyr de Hory to sell his art fakes at prices that would have been ludicrously low for an original work; buyers were trying to outsmart the dealer.[68]

Emphasizing the active complicity of the mark in the con game, Katz argues that

> We need to change our view of the prankster's "victims." When someone is involved in the fabulations of a prankster, the supposed "victim" is actually a partner in a potentially exotic adventure. It is my view that the good initiator of a prank should not ask his partner to do anything he would

not do himself. ... Therapists currently stress the importance
of role-playing and gamesmanship in lovemaking. To manipulate another, you must also manipulate yourself, especially
psychologically.[69]

That fraction of con victims who do report to the police often "re-
grettably distort the elements of the crime in order to appear totally
blameless for their involvement or because they hope to gain restitu-
tion for their losses. Unfortunately, by lying, they make the crime
more difficult to solve."[70] Notably, to erase their own complicity in
the event, many victims appear to withdraw from their roles as actors
in the drama, repositioning and recasting themselves as witnesses or
passive victims.

One con artist characterized the mark as "just another con man
too—and it's your money he wants. What you're doing is jacking each
other up and the first guy to get the other's wallet is the winner."[71]
The switch scheme from *The Sting* mentioned earlier in this chapter
preys on the mark's sudden inkling that he has a chance to con the
con men. In this switch scheme, the cons bait the mark about why
they should trust him with their money. The mark bites and, in so
doing, loses his ability to distinguish between the moment when he
thinks he is being handed real cash and that moment when he loses
his own (real) cash. The mark's complicity in his own victimization
may be constituted by his dogged persistence in unrealistic perceptions about his relationship with the con artists.[72]

Funt's *Candid Microphone* fans would frequently send in suggestions for scenarios to revenge-victimize people with whom they had
some history: "School children asked us to trap their teachers in un-
dignified or compromising situations; ordinary citizens want us to
catch policemen and other authority figures unawares; little businessmen plead with us to capture the off-the-record attitudes of their
larger competitors."[73] Funt invited *Candid Camera* viewers to write
him at NBC with suggestions of people upon whom they would like
to see hoaxes played. In these kinds of situations, Funt became the
instrument through which others qualified marks and even helped
design their own hoax scenarios.

After being conned, marks may be more than willing to participate in deceiving others. P. T. Barnum billed an empty freight car as

"The Great Unknown." After people paid to view its nonexistent contents, they typically complied with Barnum's "fervent printed request not to reveal this marvelous secret to later customers!" Through their compliance, victims may have "achieved a certain absolution, graduating from the ranks of the hoaxed to that of the hoaxers."[74]

The infamous Pyramid Scheme is actually designed not around sales per se, but referrals. Thus, the final, and ultimately most useful, role for the mark is to keep the game going, often by turning, in collusion with those who have victimized them, to enlist others. A frequently asked questions sheet, probably intended for those beginning to doubt, explains the advantages of staying in an envelope-stuffing scam:

> I didn't know that I had to spend more money to put these plans to work?
>
> There's an old saying "it takes money to make money" ... To get into ... mail order it takes less money than any other business that we know of and the chances of succeeding are far greater; if you know how to go about it. ...
>
> Unfortunately, a lot of people who order our programs will lay them aside and never put them into action. ... Smart people, like yourself, will put our programs to work per our instructions and make money.

The language of opportunity—that is, to take advantage of those not yet in the in-group—can form another pitch:

> It may seem strange to buy a program and then start out by selling it to other people. You might think that everyone would soon have one. This is *not* true! Many people who buy this program won't ever follow through—when they realize that work is involved and someone is not going to simply hand them a thousand dollars, they lose interest and go back to watching television and feeling sorry for themselves. Those who do follow through, however, will have the last laugh because it is they who will succeed.[75]

Built well into the Pyramid Scheme, and a form of mark-proofing, is marks' structural unlikeliness to complain early in their involvement;

they "can recoup only by shifting the loss to others."[76] Someone who's bought a diploma from a diploma mill in order to advance materially loses much if he rats on those who provided him with the bogus certificate.

Con artists of all kinds depend on the relational discomforts marks will experience if they pull back from the world of the scam. A dealer who tries to pass a fake along to a new buyer or who avoids telling a collector he's purchased a fake colludes with the faker. Art dealer Fred Schoneman is said to have admitted:

> It's an ugly thing when you have to tell a client he's bought a fake. Of all the things in this business—it's a kid-glove business—the thing I dislike the most is being called in to tell if a painting is right or wrong. I'll do it only for clients who are very close friends. You have to do it gently. If you say "fake" you insult a man's intelligence, you wound his vanity, and you probably lose him as a customer."[77]

That so few of those who bought fake paintings by Elmyr de Hory came forward to prosecute may be a sign that these collectors were prone to a similar vanity: "The buyers themselves can scarcely be expected to come flying forth from anonymity and say 'I'm the idiot who ...' and 'Yes, I took a tax writeoff back in '63 on. ...'"[78]

Yet something "more than embarrassment" seems to be involved in marks' failure to report on their predators, "for in some cases, even after the ball is over, the victim may admire and even protect the man who has cheated him."[79] The confidence game is the mark's placing of trust outside himself, in the con artist. Sometimes the con's ability to inspire confidence even outlives his own unmasking. Nowhere is "confidence" better exemplified than in the quack doctor whose patients remain loyal to him even once he has been exposed, as Gale Miller notes:

> The quack manages a superb bedside manner. Since he can't really provide a cure if major disease is present, he vends promises, sympathy, consideration, compassion. The patient responds to this attention. This helps explain one of the odd paradoxes relating to quackery, that failure seldom diminishes patient loyalty. When regulatory agencies seek to prose-

cute quacks, the agencies have a difficult time getting hapless users to testify in court.[80]

When a con artist adopts a victim role, the mark is even more likely to identify with him. Like a magician, the con artist models the emotional reactions the audience must have. He makes believe along with his marks that he is in terrible straits, and appears to be just as surprised as they are when things turn out badly. The medical quack, for example, typically stages his practice so as to lead "the patient to assume that he is being treated by a knowledgeable and competent person who is being unfairly attacked by other physicians and by the state."[81] The setting and the physician-performer's manner lend legitimacy to the performance. The ailing and desperate or frustrated patient readily identifies with the misunderstood and suffering but compassionate doctor. The con artist's adoption of a victim stance inhibits any further tendency on the part of mark to attack.

Britain's "master hoaxer" of the early twentieth century, Horace de Vere Cole, was said to have hoaxed "compulsively," and, "like all who have that calling his main fear was not that he would be found out but that he himself might become the butt of a hoax."[82] A career deceiver's basic gullibility may help him recognize (other) good marks; in some sense, this essential vulnerability of the con artist underscores the flexibility of positions within the criminal con game, the fluidity with which roles may be assigned and taken on.

Many con artists consider themselves not only expert marksmen, but also easy marks. It may be, as Blum proposes, that "certain people are more at home than others with deception—in giving and receiving lies, in responding to pretense and impersonation and in sharing unrealistic aggrandizing fantasies." Carl Sifakis maintains that many hoaxsters get their start, in fact, by being hoaxed by others. Indeed, one con man assumed that those who con can also be conned, as he affirmed the importance of casting a mark by knowing well one's own persona: "The best qualifier is for the con man to be as near like his victim as possible. The same dress, the same speech, the same class—and the more alike in interests, the quicker the rapport. The qualifying comes naturally because the con man knows his victim already."[83]

The predictable "turning" of the mark from victim to co-perpetrator finds its parallels in the "muddied identities" of both the enforcers and the perpetrators of crimes. In the former case, an undercover operator may slip into identifying more with his target than with his law-enforcement role and purpose; in the latter, an informant, once caught, may be strong-armed into serving the other side's purposes.

In the next chapter we examine the blurring of these bad-guy: good-guy boundaries, focusing on the roles of the cop gone bad and the criminal informant turned over to the police side. It is here, in the blending of identity work and the playing of the scenario and context for what they're worth, that undercover work is most like con game.

5

MUDDIED IDENTITIES

The number one rule I've always had as an undercover operator, and I always tried to give this to the young kids, and this rule is what I use to evaluate people in my mind's eye is, when you do this work—when you become a con artist, or an actor, or deceiver or manipulator, whatever—all the techniques that you're taught, or that you develop yourself (and some of them are quite effective)—you know on Star Trek, when they're not allowed to go down on the planet and mess with those people down there, they've got to let them do their own things? The same thing applies to this: The prime directive has to be, never use the techniques that you've learned and developed on the people that you care about, or the people that you work with or work for. Those techniques are for the crooks. Lie, cheat, manipulate: do whatever you have to do, but don't turn around and use them on the people you love or love you.

—Chris Mathers

According to Bill Taylor, the greatest thrill for an undercover operator is when there's a close match between him and his target. He told me, undercover work "is the last frontier for a police officer; it's you conning the con man. ... You've literally penetrated their whole world, and been able to convince them that you're somebody that you're not. It's kind of like walking out there in the street in the old days of Texas, and it's you and him." Acting out this kind of match is not unlike a romantic seduction—The undercover finds, once he has "literally wooed, conned someone out of their life," that his work "*is* a seduction; you are literally seducing them out of their livelihood."

Admiration for one's opponent—the sense that the two of you are well matched because you're both the best at what you do—increases the emotional and technical stakes of the game. The FBI's Howard Teten displayed the kind of respect for the elusive criminal characteristic of a master gamesman. In our conversation, he mused, "The truly skilled [criminals] we've never met. ... You never know they were there."

The matching of wits and abilities on either side of the law invokes a nearly chivalric code of conduct similar to that of eighteenth century dueling matches, hunting competitions, or games of chess. In the virtuosic chess games popular in eighteenth-century Paris, elaborate means of "giving odds" signaled the amount of respect fairly due one's opponent. The eighteenth-century chess world was governed by an

> unwritten "code of condescension" ... Only having to accept odds of 1½ points from an opponent entitled a player to the opponent's respect. Only having to accept odds of 3 points, usually in the form of a knight, entitled a player to what might be termed "consideration." Having to accept odds of 5 points, usually in the form of a rook, entitled a player to nothing but disdain.[1]

Vidocq's late eighteenth-century crime connoisseurship elevated the audacity of identity performances to the level of art. He held in high esteem the "craftsmanship" of Fossard, the thief of the Medal Gallery at the Bibliothèque Nationale, who made a perfectly circular cut in a wooden panel with a gimlet to gain entrance, as well as intricate schemes involving the substitution of false valuables for authentic. Vidocq also exhibited a nostalgia (combined with shameless self-congratulation) for the great period of roguery that had already passed by the time of his writing: "A new generation has sprung up, but they can never equal in dexterity Bombance, Marquis, Boucault, Compère, Bouthey, Pranger, Dorlé, La Rose, Gavard, Martin, and other first-rate rogues whom I reduced to a state of inaction."[2]

Without sufficient challenge, identity play is hardly worth the effort. De Hory found motivation not only in the money available to him from faking the work of famous painters, but in the challenge of taking on the more obscure ones: "Utrillo and Corot had been copied so much I never even bothered. I never did Miró either—it seemed to me so terribly easy that I never did dare to try it. Even the real Mirós look like fakes." De Hory pursued the art dealer Paul Rosenberg in 1951 to have him authenticate his fakes:

> I had to know: am I as good as they are or not? Can I do it as well as they can do it? I knew of course that Picasso had invented something new, and I was merely following in his footsteps—but if Rosenberg, who was the greatest recognized expert in America on Picasso, who was Picasso's dealer, who for the last forty years was handling Picasso exclusively—if my drawings were good enough for such a man, then it meant that in their quality they were certainly as valuable as Picasso's. It's a sort of recognition by the highest authority.[3]

The copying of Picasso is an act dwarfed by the hoodwinking of a worthy living opponent, Picasso's dealer. This suggests that the highest distinction for the identity performer motivated by scaling is being able to dupe a member of the innermost circle. Only sometimes, he fools himself as well.

Rotting Cops

> *There are cures only to be effected by the aid of poison, and perhaps the leprosy of society can only be extirpated by similar means, but in this case the poisonous dose administered was too powerful, and the proof is, that nearly all the secret agents at this period were caught in the very act of committing crime, and many of them are still at the Bagnes.*
>
> —Eugène-François Vidocq

> *[The criminal world] is a world of corruption, debauchery, and downright evil. Right and wrong are reversed. The honest, hardwork-*

ing individual is considered to be a fool, and the best liars, thieves, and killers are respected.

—Jerry VanCook

By the mid-1980s, undercover operators and their supervisors had unearthed the work's procedural and ethical complexities. Its personal costs had also become more evident. The popular *Miami Vices* depicted such complexities dramatically. How does an undercover balance his desire for intimacy with his responsibility to accomplish his mission, a duty that hinges on his ability to deceive and to carry secrets? Can a cop recognize any codes of right and wrong outside of established law? Why is it that many bad guys don't *seem* so bad? Who's really the boss when it's the guys on the street getting things done? How do conflicting loyalties play themselves out in the criminal world, as against the world of law enforcement? (And, do these worlds really differ?)

Cops vary in their reporting of the prevalence of undercovers' "crossing over to the other side" and losing their primary identification with law enforcement. One undercover instructor insists that "dirty cops" were already so before they became cops. Another attributes "going bad" to individual cops' modus operandi: undercovers who get into danger "start cutting corners the way the bad guy would." Chris Mathers minimizes the frequency of cops who have difficulty making transitions back to their regular identities, and likens the process, for himself, of adopting a fictive identity to something as black or white as turning on a switch: thus, the process of reverting to a home identity should simply be the flicking back of that same switch. He maintains it is more the excitement the notion of cops's going bad carries with it from novels and film, with their own narrative and characterological conventions, than actual practice, that makes such muddied identities a source of such intense interest. However, when it does happen, it is no less dramatic than in media treatments.

It is in the nature of undercover work that "particularly in small- to medium-sized cities ... the police and the bad guys are on a first-name basis. They know each other well, and each team knows how the other plays the game."[4] Fred Buckminster, longtime accomplice of the legendary Chicago con artist Joseph "Yellow Kid" Weil, was a well-known cop gone bad. Reportedly, Buckminster crossed over through a simple but sizeable show of money:

> The meeting of these men was classic. At the turn of the century, Buckminster was a member of the Chicago Police Department, a detective working in the bunco squad. He trailed Weil about for a few days and saw him work some short cons. He arrested Weil on State Street, telling him he was going to run him in for practicing confidence games. The two men strolled toward a precinct station. At the corner, Weil reached into his pocket and pulled out a wad of money, all in large bills. Without a word he placed the money into Buckminster's hand.
>
> "What's this?" Buckminster asked, staring incredulously at about $8,000.
>
> "That?" asked Weil. "That's just walkabout money. I made that in two hours this morning."
>
> "In two hours?"
>
> "Yes, and so can you. I can use a guy like you, one who knows the ropes. Put that in your pocket." Weil stood staring straight ahead as he talked to Buckminster. "Go ahead, it's chicken feed to me. You can see that kind of dough every day if you throw in with me."
>
> Buckminster clutched the money, then took his badge from his vest and looked at both the money and the badge [as the story goes]. He pocketed both and shook Weil's hand. He quit the police force then and there and joined Weil.[5]

Undercover FBI agent Patrick Livingston's personal difficulties from playing his trick identity undermined his investigative successes in exposing a pornography ring operated by organized crime between 1977 and 1980. Though his investigations resulted in a slew of indictments and several convictions, he continued to establish bank accounts and to introduce himself under his working name, Pat Salamone. Even during the operation, Livingston recognized he was having difficulty distinguishing his trick identity from his home identity, and sought out the help of a psychiatrist. He was arrested for shoplifting from a Louisville department store in 1982, and had two other unspecified "brushes with the law." Because of his identity problems, 14 of the indictments resulting from his undercover investigations were dismissed without prejudice.[6]

VanCook provides an image of undercover cops as "Explorers" whose inherent personality characteristics predispose them (like Vidocq and Abagnale) to engage in their own illegal activities early in life. For VanCook, law-enforcing and law-breaking personalities are one and the same:

> Most often the young Explorer grows out of them as he matures and finds other avenues to explore. Those who do not and continue to break more serious laws after reaching adulthood are called criminals. But some adult Explorers redirect their adventure drive into more socially acceptable channels, and these people are called cops. Often, they are the best cops around.[7]

Others argue that the undercover's shift to the bad guy's worldview may come as less of a playing out of an inherent emotional tendency than as an occupationally necessary cognitive stance. In undertaking this process, the undercover not only thinks *like* the bad guy, but—because they are co-performing, co-present and co-active in time—thinks *with* him.[8]

Whether or not many undercovers self-select to be readily comfortable performing on either side of the law, the qualities that support them in the work also may hinder their moving smoothly out of it, as psychologist Michel Girodo cautions:

> Some [agencies] look for outgoing, highly extroverted, and risk taking officers not knowing they are at the same time tapping a personality factor associated with poor impulse control or a personality more likely to subsequently manifest a conduct disorder. Others look for good acting ability, this time attracting those who also load more highly on neuroticism and hysterical features of personality. Indeed, in many respects the extreme qualities thought to underlie some of the talents required for operational effectiveness are the very ones which are more likely to be associated with emotional distress, personality disturbances, and difficult readjustment.[9]

NYPD Detective Dave Huang was a young Chinese man who had lived in the United States since the age of six. Although he did not ultimately cross over, he was powerfully affected by his induction into a secret Taiwanese gang. As Korean-American Detective Robert Chung, a member of his team, described the ritual:

> They did it in English on my behalf. But there was this elaborate ritual with candles, a bowl of rice and incense, a portrait of Guan Di, which is, ironically, the historical person of loyalty. Yellow Bird pricked our fingers and we put some blood in the glass of wine and we all shared it. Dave's name was White Dragon and mine was Black Dragon.
>
> It's foolish, but to a young teen who's probably very alienated in this country and feels totally out of place—*boom*, he's part of this historical thing that goes back thousands of years—the secret brotherhood, all these rituals.[10]

An us-them mentality associates one set of techniques with the in-group, another with those outside:

> We deal with people who operate in a world of cheating, fraud and con games. In order to collect the information we need on them, we have to play their game. ... You can not check out the sly scums of the earth that pry [sic] on innocent people by being a goodie two-shoes. You have to think like them, sound like them and smell like them. You have to out smart their lies, con games and cheating. You have to get and stay one step ahead of them.[11]

As a factor contributing to a possible crossover, roleplaying is undeniably persuasive in and of itself. One undercover preferred the expensive cigars, another the fine hotel rooms his undercover role demanded, and both continued to indulge in these pleasures even when off-duty: their masks left residues. Roleplaying is not a superficial or a technically "clean" act, even when it involves a more-or-less wholesale replacement of the personality with the role, as in much stage acting. How much more danger of role contagion is likely in the case of the undercover whose trick role has much to do with his home identity.

The greatest danger of going bad comes when a fictive identity has become adaptive, serving purposes closely identified with the performer's own, separate from his work function. Goffman observes, "When an individual acquires a new and stigmatized self late in life, the uneasiness he feels about new associates may slowly give way to uneasiness felt concerning old ones."[12] Thus, it may come to pass that the new peer group of dealers may be more reinforcing than the old group of uniformed cops.

Mathers played a role that to all accounts would have been hard to relinquish, that of a rich mobster who got to spend money freely, smoke choice cigars, and enjoy a certain flamboyance. He credits his clarity while in role to family members and friends who let him know if he showed any signs "of being a dick." (And for most of his own undercover jobs, he went home to his own life and identity each night.) Girodo notes, when the undercover agent's "social reality" swings between bad and good guys, the compatibility between an agent and his cover men may also support an officer's staying on the side of good.[13] However, when an undercover's trick role is designed to be in perfect complementarity with the bad guy, provides a variety of symbiotic rewards, and requires staving off contact with any of his home-identity associates, anything less than reciprocal strengths and complementary personalities on the undercover's "home team" can make it more satisfying to be a bad guy than a good.

Cops working in an underworld setting report their sense of who the "Other" is shifts along with them. As Goffman painstakingly points out,

> Stigma involves not so much a set of concrete individuals who can be separated into two piles, the stigmatized and the normal, as a pervasive two-role social process in which every individual participates in both roles, at least in some connections and in some phases of life. The normal and the stigmatized are not persons but rather perspectives.[14]

Cops who spend a good deal of time acting from within the criminal element may carry their sense of center and a need to stigmatize others along with them. From a vantage point within criminal culture, of course, the uniformed cop is the Other. In Abagnale's internal mental drama, the cops became the bad guys. Relatively late in his impostorship career, the con artist describes having lost "sound judgment" about the purpose and efficacy of his acts. He was, he remembers, "driven by compulsions over which I had no control. I was now living by rationalizations: I was the hunted, the police were the hunters, ergo, the police were the bad guys. I had to steal to survive, to finance my continual flight from the bad guys, consequently I was justified in my illegal means of support." An undercover associating with or portraying such a personality might well make a similar identification.[15]

When a cop's customary loyalty hierarchy starts to erode, he is in danger of going bad. Two training academy instructors defined for us a standard judgment by a police officer about whom to protect as radiating out first from the self, the one whose safety and well-being must be preserved at all costs; then to one's partner; then out to other cops. Citizens come just afterward, and the "scumbags" are only to be protected after all others' needs have been dealt with. When the positions in a cop's sense of this hierarchy start to turn inside out, and the bad guys are the first to be protected, it's a sure sign of an operator misidentifying.[16]

Police officer James J. Ness and his wife worked undercover narcotics together in the late 1970s and did experience some confusion of allegiances, which they were eventually able to resolve:

> At times we wondered who we really were and what we were doing. When befriending people we could possibly arrest someday, we began to wonder were they really that bad. They also had families, dreams and needs, but sometimes they crossed over the line between right and wrong and then we arrested them. In general they were ordinary people trying to stay alive by doing things they knew best, just like we were doing."[17]

Uniformed cops commonly regard undercovers with suspicion, and may treat their undercover comrades more like the criminals they both fight than as colleagues. The tension between uniformed police officers and undercovers is summed up in Vidocq's telling line: "Joining chorus with the thieves and malefactors, all the agents who were not successful as police-officers, assailed me with the utmost virulence."[18] Thus, an undercover who keeps a trick identity afloat long enough to make his case may come back to his home identity with a sizable hurdle remaining—that of protecting his psyche against the rejection of his comrades.

One can, of course, become lost in role with varying degrees of severity. What Girodo calls the "Medalist Syndrome" is typically experienced by a younger agent who has experienced some success in deep cover. Having gathered critical evidence against major figures, he may develop "an inflated ego, an exaggerated sense of importance, and an idyllic but spurious sense of entitlement which is communicated through deportment." He may lose all interest in the more mundane aspects of uniform policing. In the graver "Primate Syndrome," the agent fails to restrain impulses and may present behavior or discipline problems.[19]

Agents may also exhibit a high degree of paranoia or post-traumatic stress reactions. While a very tiny proportion of agents may actually suffer from a true split personality, many more may "carry out the role of having a split personality." Typically, these are the performers

> who fail to obtain recognition for their efforts and who are assigned to mundane tasks ... in their home departments, [and] persist in their undercover role as a way of drawing attention to themselves when the strokes are insufficient. Or they perform some impulsive anti-social act, or speak with the same accent, or use the same vocabulary, not out of a schizophrenic break but rather as a way of making a statement.[20]

That undercovers are psychologically able both to perform in intimate roles with those whose worlds they infiltrate and to pull away when time comes for an arrest is remarkable. Indeed, many of the television and film portrayals of the undercover role touch on the trope of the undercover whose loyalty is divided. Yet those who appear to have no trouble separating themselves emotionally from their target may still, from the outside, have questionably tangled up their lives with his. In the 1950s and '60s, Vizzini exhibited little concern about the dangers for himself of losing the ability to distinguish between his own side and the other. He boasted, "You forget about the badge and the flag. You think like a criminal, you act like a criminal, and you catch a criminal." Yet Vizzini appears to have been constitutionally unlikely to allow mixed feelings about a target to interfere with his ability to remain loyal to overall government objectives. His target

> Charlie Lucky Luciano was a murderer, drug dealer, at one time even a stool pigeon. I'd have shot him without a moment's hesitation if I'd had to, especially if he ever pulled that Beretta on me. He was also a cool, in-charge guy. He had a sense of humor, except about himself and the rotten deals he felt he'd been given. He'd "buried 100 guys" and waxed sentimental over a picture of his lost love and her surviving dog. He was a simple man and I think a complex one at the same time. I'm not going to lose any sleep over him, but I'm also not going to forget him. ... I know I won't forget the thump I felt seeing his death notice in the Miami *Herald* over my morning coffee. I was wearing his gold cuff links at the time.[21]

The image of Vizzini wearing his target's gold cufflinks while reading his obituary undercover economically encapsulates the image of the friend-cum-predator. Vidocq himself was profoundly aware of the predatory aspects of his new official role, and waxed on his guilt at using his knowledge of the criminal underworld, before he dwindled into rationalizations:

> The share of self-satisfaction produced by the feeling of having been instrumental in rescuing a fellow-creature from destruction, was but a slight compensation for the misery I experienced at being in a manner compelled by the stern duties of the post I filled, either to send a fresh succession of victims to ascend the scaffold, or to mount it myself. The quality of "secret agent" preserved, it is true, my liberty, and shielded me from the dangers to which, as a fugitive galley-slave, I was formerly exposed. ... I therefore strove to reconcile myself to [my condition] by arguments such as these:— Was I not daily occupied in endeavouring to promote the welfare of society? Was I not espousing the part of the good and upright against the bad and vicious? ... My reason became convinced; and my mind, satisfied of the upright

motives which guided me, regained its calmness and self-
command.

Romantic relationships quickly put the undercover in a double
bind, as when a female informant becomes interested in the male
undercover for whom she is working. Practically speaking, he can
neither ethically respond to her attentions nor brush her off. The
conflict between duty and desire is frequently played out in dramatized scenarios about undercover life, as in a 1985 ABC *After School
Special* entitled "High School Narc," whose central conflict takes
place within Andrew, a youthful undercover who first infiltrates a
high school to investigate its drug-dealing scene and then falls for an
appealing young woman who happens to be one of the dealers.

Sexual relations with the other side are a predictable way, both in
actual undercover work and in Hollywood scripts, to compromise
allegiances. Gary T. Marx draws attention to the distinctive similarities between sex and undercover work as a whole: both are bound up
with impression-making; are private; and involve secrecy, temptation,
and intense bonding. Sex may also invoke roleplaying or pretending;
undercover work generally has a voyeuristic component; and the excitement of undercover work is often described as a sexual thrill.
Indeed, in some undercover infiltrations, especially during the 1960s,
one major strategy to disrupt the unity of groups under federal investigation was to insert undercovers into customary loyalties between
established sexual partners. Infiltrating the Ku Klux Klan, government undercovers were specifically instructed to tell members that
their spouses were cheating on them, as well as to encourage informants to further such infidelities.[22]

Goffman gives much attention to the work of double agents, who
may turn from working for their country of origin to helping the
country they have infiltrated, while appearing still to be loyal to their
home countries. An agent known to have turned can remain useful
to his home country, as he can be used to feed false information un-
knowingly to the other side, making "the most valuable spy to the
target country [the] one under their control, who feeds false information to his handlers." In fact, "an agent will have to go through many
turnings before his value is entirely used up." The figure of the double agent concretizes the oscillation between the appearance of being

one of us while actually (perhaps) being one of them, that characterizes not only the supposed good guys—the cops—but also the most
devious of the supposed bad guys—the informants.[23]

For both Vidocq and Abagnale in their lives as criminals, it was
advantageous to "turn over," to reduce their sentences by helping law
enforcement. After spending four years in an American prison, and
then being paroled to menial labor, Abagnale was offered a reduction
in sentence if he would agree to use his knowledge in the service of
banks and law enforcement, the con artist chose to become a white-
collar crime specialist, lecturing and consulting widely to financial
institutions and law-enforcement agencies on fraud prevention, and
preventing businesses from being further duped by check forgers like
him. (The CEO Club described him as "the con-man voted best talk
in CEO history.") He liked this new profession as much as the old, in
part because it satisfied his ego needs:

> If I did not do what I do today—if I had stayed a pizza cook, a
> grocery executive or a movie projectionist—I might very well
> be back in prison today ... Why? Because there's no glamour,
> no excitement, no adventure and nothing to fulfill my ego in
> those vocations.
>
> What I do today, on the other hand, fulfills all my needs. I
> get up in front of thousands of people, and I know they're
> listening to what I say. That's an ego trip. I appear on dozens
> of television programs annually. To me, that's a glamorous
> life. It's an adventuresome life, because I'm constantly being
> challenged by white collar criminals who come up with new
> gimmicks to defraud clients—and I know they're out to put
> me down as much as they are to make a bundle.
>
> Actually, I haven't changed. All the needs that made me a cri-
> minal are still there. I have simply found a legal and socially
> acceptable way to fulfill those needs. I'm still a con artist. I'm
> just putting down a positive con these days, as opposed to the
> negative con I used in the past. I have simply redirected the
> talents I've always possessed.[24]

Similarly, art forger David Stein emerged from prison ready to apply
his first-hand expertise for the benefit of the New York Police Department as it established its first art forgery division; he lectured

widely on the techniques of forgers. These exceptionally visible and sought-after informants, however, are the exception to the rule: most informants find it necessary to lie low, lest they not serve long.

Going Good: Informants

How pitiable is the condition of a fugitive galley-slave, who, if he would not be denounced or implicated in some evil deed, must be himself the denouncer.

—Eugène-François Vidocq

Betrayal is the name of the game. A traitor betrays his country. The spy takes advantage of contacts he makes within the target country, and betrays friendships. The spymaster may betray one or more of his agents, including an entire network, to serve what he considers a higher purpose.

—Tony Lesce

The world's biggest gossips are school teachers, cops, and criminals.

—Jerry VanCook

Undercover work is an expensive means of investigation, chosen only when the investigator has to infiltrate the target group if he's going to gain information. Going one step better is using someone who actually *is* an insider, a member of the criminal coterie who is personally motivated to aid or even guide the investigation process.

During the 1970s and '80s, the FBI used as an informant an accused murderer, Michael Raymond, to such a degree they dubbed him a "cooperation expert." It was precisely because of Raymond's immersion in criminal activity that he was deemed so vitally necessary to the investigation. As his lawyer put it, "To get the goods on corrupt politicians, you need people who are wallowing in corruption, and one of those people was Mike. He's a mercenary, he's never made any bones about it."[25]

The figure of the criminal who's crossed to the side of good, yet can still appear to travel with the bad guys, was a trendy nineteenth-century literary theme. Vidocq was the inspiration for the central characters of many nineteenth-century novels, including Honoré de Balzac's Vautrin in *Père Goriot*, Edgar Allan Poe's character Auguste Dupin, and Victor Hugo's Javert in *Les Misérables*, who at the very least closely link the criminal and the tireless detective identities.[26]

Whereas the undercover operator is an outsider who pretends an insider status, conventionally the informant is a recent insider who must not give out that he has moved to an outsider's function and formed a "coalition" with his own former enemy.[27] The active informant leads what Goffman would call a "simple double life": he lives in two worlds, only one of which is aware of the existence of the other. The double status of informants as the lowest class of citizens who can be functionally identified with the law-enforcement side—coupled with their extensive experience in the status plays that come with street buys—makes them, in many undercover operatives' estimation, the wiliest and most clever roleplayers. They are arguably more skillful even than the most experienced law-enforcement officers, particularly so because the agencies provide these identity workers with no material documentation such as the driver's licenses they routinely create for cops working undercover.

Following his own turning from convict to law enforcer, Vidocq successfully hired ex-convicts as prison spies for the French Criminal Investigation. (When they had collected sufficient information, he would arrange for them to "escape" or would have them fake their own deaths.)[28] Whereas in Vidocq's time, an informant was essentially a spy, a twentieth-century undercover like Levine would say he used an informant chiefly to "get me in" in his undercover role so he could gather his own evidence:

> If you use him for anything else, for surveillance or to make a buy or to sit in on some deal, then he'll probably have to testify to it later on, and that can cause problems. Like, he won't do it. And even if he's willing, he's probably got a worse record than your average war criminal, and defense attorneys like that. Gives 'em something to work with. Besides,

if you make him testify, he's gonna get burned as an informer and maybe get himself killed. So either way, he's not
gonna be much use to anybody after that. You gotta do it
yourself. Whenever you can. That's the golden rule.[29]

VanCook states the case for informants boldly, calling them "the key
to successful undercover operations" because of their ability to make
introductions and social inroads with the bad guy on law enforcement's behalf. In Vizzini's bids to infiltrate the Mafia, he recognized,
"Everything ... would start—or end—with the introduction. The guy
that vouches for you is what counts, especially with a Sicilian. ... The
go-between does it. He dukes you, builds you up, he brags on you.
Hell, you can't very well do it yourself."[30]

The undercover prepped informant Sam Cook to play his role
ably in the seemingly chance introduction to Lucky :

> The script was fairly simple. Cook would be in the San Fran-
> cisco Bar and Grill in Naples, owned by Luciano, talking to
> Luciano when I happened to drop in. He would recognize
> me as a pilot he'd known when he was a cook back at an air
> base in Kentucky (which he was). I was a guy who shot crap
> with enlisted men on pay day—or anybody else who had
> money to lose—and wasn't too fussy altogether about rules
> and regulations. A swinger.

> It would be a brief but obvious reunion. He would call me
> Mike and maybe remember I'd once swiped a bottle of Chi-
> anti from the Officer's Club for him. All this would be for
> the benefit of Lucky and whoever happened to be with him.
> One of his lines would be: "Hey, Major, you've come up in
> the world." Then he'd turn to Luciano and say something
> like, "He was a lousy lieutenant but a helluva guy when I
> knew him in the States ... meet my friend, Major Mike
> Cerra."

This simple script, like the development of the Cerra identity in the
first place, was clearly keyed to answer to the prime areas of suspicion
Vizzini anticipated from his target: Where did this guy come from?
Which side was he on? It established the principal characterological
features that would be necessary to have Luciano regard Vizzini with
friendly eyes: Cerra was none too particular about principles, he was

ambitious and motivated by profit, and he went way back with some-one Luciano knew well.

When it came time to perform this scenario and Vizzini walked, as planned, into the San Francisco Bar and Grill, he was surprised that Cook appeared not to recognize him, only later realizing that the performance only made sense with its appropriate audience, and Luciano was away at the moment. It took another take to bring about the introduction.[31] Completing the venture was Vizzini's perform-ance of not knowing that this man was *the* Lucky of international crime fame, asking others, after Luciano had left the scene, what his last name was.

In addition to introducing him to the bad guys, the informant provides coaching to the undercover that would be unavailable from any other (comparatively safe) source. One informant offered valu-able advice to a NYPD officer, who remembered with gratitude the informant's telling him: "'That gun you're carrying is too big.' Next time he came, he actually bought a pistol for me, a Colt .380. At the time, I was carrying a Beretta. In that world, that is probably about as righteous a thing as a man can do for another man."[32]

Law enforcement gains its informants by the "flip and roll," a pro-cedure by which lower-level players are caught in a criminal act, arrested, and given their options, the most palatable of which is to aid the investigation. Michael Levine was particularly skilled in flip-ping informants. His attitude only helped him:

> Lady, I have your life in my hands, his attitude said. I'm
> gonna fuck it up completely, and doing it won't mean a thing
> to me because you interrupted my lunch. So right after I
> make sure your life is in ruins, I'm gonna go out, get some-
> thing to eat, come back and do this again to somebody else.
> And it still won't mean a thing because I got more important
> things to do. Like getting a shoeshine.

With a Colombian woman who had been caught transporting two kilos of cocaine, Levine performed his routine in "bored, impatient, flawless" Spanish:

> Lady, come in here and sit down ... I know they told you
> we'll only throw you out of the country, but that's not so.
> You've broken the laws of the United States, and for that

you'll be tried and punished. So don't give me any shit. If
you want to talk, talk. If you don't want to talk, don't talk.
But let me tell you this. If you *don't* talk, you are going to jail.
You're going to do seven or eight years of very hard time. ...

All right. I'm not going to say another word. You've got one
chance to help yourself, and that's by giving up everybody
you know. I'm going to walk out of here now, and it's up to
you to stop me. Because if you let me go through that door,
you will never see Colombia again.[33]

Almost invariably, Levine's hard-line technique worked. An informant who can be effectively blackmailed with his own collusion in
law-enforcement activities—most blatantly, by publication to the underworld that he has turned over—is less likely to divulge
compromising information to a target.

The most structured program for the cultivation and protection of
informants is the United States Marshals Office's Federal Witness
Protection Program. Formally instituted in the early 1970s, by 1991
the Federal Witness Protection Program had assigned fresh identities
to approximately 13,000 of the most entangled criminal informants
willing to testify against their more seriously involved associates.
Some critics considered the Marshals Office's apparent collusion
with these lesser criminals reprehensible:

In a sense, the government ... decided to capitalize on errors
that criminals make—their failures, squabbles, and divisions.
Criminals who are rejected or double-crossed by their colleagues, who are apprehended by the authorities, or who just
"want out" constitute 95 percent of the program enroll-
ment.[34]

Banking on the assumption that on the street, loyalties shift—even as
they introduce training and supervision procedures to reduce the
likelihood of their own employees' loyalties' changing—law enforcement agencies build some of their more difficult cases, for example,
against organized crime.

The cop-informant relationship has been aptly characterized as
that between a parent (who can provide money, food, and immu-
nity/forgiveness) and a manipulative child (who should be expected

to push for as much as he can get). An informant who truly fears for his safety will act when threatened, and "the officer should never hesitate to exploit this imbalance in the power relationship. Giving the informer the impression that the officer will cut him loose by withdrawing protection if he doesn't provide total cooperation can often stimulate effort."[35] As the cop maintains the power balance in his favor—essentially, by ensuring that the informant always has more at stake than he does—he knows he's made the informant as reliable as possible. A trainer presented the informant as just a tool to be used, always in the most expeditious way possible: "You can lie to the C.I [confidential informant]. You can tell him anything he wants to hear, as long as you don't promise him anything."[36] Echoed a student: "You have to be a politician." "Exactly."

Befitting his taxonomic impulse, Vidocq grouped informants according to how useful they made themselves to investigations. Some were

> only paid according to the captures they made. There were also thieves who constantly followed their profession, and whose presence was tolerated on condition of their giving up to justice the malefactors they might by chance fall in with; sometimes it happened that for lack of other objects, they would denounce their own comrades. After these tolerated thieves, came, in the third or fourth gradation, that swarm of abandoned profligates who lived with girls of infamous character. This ignoble caste occasionally supplied important directions for the taking of pickpockets and swindlers; generally, they came forward and offered the most useful information when they were anxious to procure the release of their mistresses who chanced to fall under the surveillance of the police. The women who lived with well-known and incorrigible offenders were useful auxiliaries, constantly furnishing accounts which enabled the police to send off from time to time numbers of these lost creatures upon their travels to Bicêtre.[37]

Experienced undercovers emphasize the importance of sizing up an informant's motivation in order to use him or her most skillfully. The "rollover" wants to help the police in order to work down the charges against him. Alternatively, the "businessman type" will seek to turn in his competitors as a means of increasing his own share of the market, while keeping a close eye on the identities and practices of agents with whom he works.[38] "Good citizens" have seen the error of their ways, and are eager to stop other wrongdoers. (This sounds suspicious because it is: the good citizen motivation in many cases may be a cover for some other motivation.) Revengers "believe that if they can 'do' (set up) their victim and chalk up a few brownie points with the cops at the same time, they've killed two birds with one stone." The "mercenary" bags guys for the money. A mercenary "will call any law enforcement agency and ask them how much he could make by doing a case. He will continue calling agencies until he gets the highest bidder."[39]

Payment to informants takes into account the level of risk, how involved the informant was in the case, how much evidence was collected on the basis of the information he provided, the significance of the target, and whether the informant will testify.[40] Law-enforcement agencies often forbid discussion with informants of specific dollar amounts as a means of preventing them from shopping around. Indeed, the session on paying informants was one of the few lectures at the undercover training academy from which I was barred. Nevertheless, Vizzini offers one early benchmark: in the early 1960s the United States would pay up to $20,000 for information leading to the location of the plates used to make counterfeit bills, more if the information allowed investigators to seize the plates. Informants could bargain their rates up if they had information that would lead to a seizure of the manufacturing plates.[41]

Each type of informant motivation implies an ideal method of handling him. The revenge-motivated informant, for example, may need to be worked quickly: "Just remember to squeeze him up front if he's got a grudge, because you never know when he's gonna get back together with whoever it is he's informing against." In the event he and the target make up, this informant may not only dry up as a source but also actively seek to obstruct or sabotage the investigation.[42]

Another set of distinctions characterizes informants by their position within the criminal hierarchy on which they inform. For law enforcement, this distinction is one of the determining factors for whether an informant's identity can be protected should the case go to trial. The informant who provides information from the position of witness or victim is to be differentiated from the one who is "a co-conspirator or criminal associate who provides information for money or to secure another advantage." Unlike a witness's identity, an involved party's identity cannot be guaranteed protection.

A tipster informant "merely points the finger of suspicion at one who violates the law but neither witnesses nor participates in the crime"; it is in these cases virtually certain that "his identity is not material to the defense and disclosure will not be required." Police will be able to build evidence and establish guilt independently. However, a defecting informant moves away from the site of criminal activity, and generally "burns his bridges behind him." He is a "go-between" whose identity must often be disclosed. An undercover operator can also have an "agent in place, or snitch, who informs secretly"—and dangerously, because he is close at hand—while never "relinquish[ing] his status in the criminal hierarchy." Most damningly, the "agent provocateur" helps to build evidence by engaging in crimes with the target, an activity forbidden to police officers. These sorts of informants can rarely be protected, as their testimony may be required to ensure a fair trial.[43]

Useful to cops only until their loyalties—that is, their functional identities—are burned, confidential informants become defined in the terms of their ability to cloak their own motivations and to present believable pretexts. Here, the ideal informant—full of the dirt and ready to spill it—is someone who has been "in" but now prefers "out"—say, an ex-spouse, lover, business partner, or client.[44]

Some agencies have assigned the most dangerous missions to informants, making them a kind of despised extension of the undercover's own body and powers. Because J. Edgar Hoover was afraid that close associations with the underworld would prove or even appear corrupting to undercovers, he used informants all the way through FBI deals, as he saw their characters as already being contaminated. One serious problem with this method was that the FBI could never be sure of the informant's loyalties: would he in the end serve the ends of law enforcement, his own needs to maintain ties to the bad guy, or a personal profit motive?[45]

Even as he painstakingly guarded the lives of his colleagues, Levine would willingly risk those of informants. He would have the informant wear a wire in high-risk situations in which he would never place an undercover, because the informant was "expendable." Levine told his students, "A good professional narc is like a good professional hunter, and the stool is his bird dog. You train him, work the shit out of him, and when he's all used up, you trot him back to the fucking kennel." Levine admonishes undercovers to keep an eye out for the informant who's a "law-enforcement buff":

> You're the coach, and he's desperate to get on the team. Loves the work. Loves to hang out with the guys. Makes him feel good. Helps him live with his own nasty, backbiting, larcenous nature if he can tell himself he's doing it for *us.* Makes him feel like James Bond. A guy like that can be worth his weight in arrest warrants if you keep him on the leash. If you don't, sooner or later you'll find he's using you, using his connection with the Man to protect himself as a trafficker. If he gets caught he'll either say you knew about it or you let him do it.[46]

Essential to maintaining informants' understanding that they are inferior characters, despite their (currently) being on the good guys' side, is keeping up with the power rituals of working together. Informants are searched for drugs and weapons each time they meet with a law-enforcement officer, and may be spoken to in terms that reinforce an inferior status.[47] One undercover told me, although informants are key tools to the work, trusting them is inevitably charged with risk: they "can make you or break you."

One experienced undercover recalled using a pair of female informants who had begun working for the police for sport and ended up staying for ten years, jokingly christening themselves "Housewives With a Hobby." Although the informants made traditional gestures of collegiality and friendship to their police contact, e.g., presenting homemade gifts when his daughter was born, he maintained his distance in order to reinforce their subordinate position. Conscious of how he acted toward them, he tried to convey the message, "Well, yeah, I appreciate you two, you've been around a long time, you've made me a star, you've done a lot of good cases—*but* we still must maintain that professional relationship." He explained, "I've never given an informant my phone number; they don't know where I live.

You see them in the mall when you're with a family member, you avoid them like the plague. You don't introduce them to family members, because they are the criminal element." He insisted on the necessity of this distance, despite there being no criminal or drug history for these "housewives who party hard," simply because of their serving in the informant role.

Maintaining the requisite distance doesn't always feel natural. Levine cautions, "A lot of these worms can be likable. After all, they gotta have something going for 'em or they'd never get *close* enough to anyone to do 'em. But it cuts both ways, and that's what you've got to watch out for."[48] An undercover can never become comfortable enough around them that he lets his guard down and reveals something they could use to exploit him; he must assume that they will always be looking for a crack in the veneer. If he does regard them as somehow subhuman—or, in Levine's case, subterranean—he must also be on the lookout for a natural tendency to say things in front of them as if they wouldn't fully understand, all too often a fatal mistake.[49]

As in undercover work, the secrecy surrounding the use of informants can lead to corruption. Informants' identities are generally protected from the targets against whom they are helping build a case; however, this very protection may lead them to provide false information for revenge or other purposes. Law enforcement may also bend the secrecy associated with using informants to ill purpose. A cop may cultivate an informant as his sole property and prevent his being accessible to the police force as a whole, or he may use the excuse of protecting his informant to cut corners as he builds his case. Nevertheless, some argue that the secrecy surrounding the cop-informant relationship leads to a freer flow of information, since the informant has better assurance of who has personal information about him and thus can be more secure about his safety.[50]

When starting out with a particular cop, an informant undergoes a testing process much like the one bad guys put undercovers through. Whereas undercovers have to show support for the truth of the identity and motivations they have presented, informants have to demonstrate that they actually have, and will continue to provide, actionable information. Informants are to be regarded as "untested" until they have proven that they reliably provide information that can lead to investigative action.[51]

The general word to the undercover about working with confidential informants seems to be to proceed gradually, never assuming that he and his informant are on the same side:

> Recruiting informants is a fairly universal procedure. You dangle the carrot and eventually the conversation gets around to cash. Nobody works on promises, and you don't want to play Santa Claus either. So you compromise. If the prospect seems to check out, you front him $500 and say, "O.K., let's see what you can do." If he doesn't check out so good, you lay some money on him but take his watch or his car keys as collateral. You play it close, hope for the best.[52]

At the moment when the undercover tries to flip him, the informant may try to negotiate, not as a businessman, but as a guy with a trail of incriminating evidence behind him. Like many other informants, David Kwastel tried to bargain with Levine. "Well, if I *did* go for this," he offered cautiously, "Will you do me a favor?" Levine's response was unwavering—he knew both how much power he had and what could happen if he surrendered any of it:

> No favors. No ifs, buts or maybes. The deal is, either work for me, and I'll see the judge gets to take that into consideration when you come up for sentencing. Or *don't* work for me, and I'll see you pull the maximum on fourteen or fifteen counts of possession and conspiracy. So suit yourself. Either you do exactly what I tell you—and do it the best you know how—or you're *gone.* Understand?

The undercover stands on firmest ground if he can rope an informant into an investigation without his knowledge of the double role he is playing. (In such a case, the unwitting informant is essentially in the same position as the mark of a con game, employed in a strategic scenario separate from, and counter to, the game he believes himself to be playing.) Levine told his students:

> That's the best kind of informant to have—a guy with a lot of knowledge and friends in the druggie world who really believes in you, in your role as a bad guy. If you manipulate

him right and, most important, make him like you and trust you as a person, you can milk the sucker dry of every last drop of information he's got without him ever knowing it.[53]

The undercover operator is not always the only one with power in the relationship. Informants can be even more dangerous to an undercover operator than the bigger criminals, as their various motives for pretending loyalty may inspire an unwary cop to essentially serve as a "counter-informant," a virtual pipeline of information to the underworld about police practices and procedures, thus potentially jeopardizing not just himself but also the safety of future operators.[54]

As a means of attracting potential informants to him in a new locale, Vizzini freewheeled his way around Europe and into information by visibly throwing money around and getting a reputation as a free spender. He also had experience with specific occupational categories of locals who were both likely to have information useful to him and to be interested in finding extra easy money: "Hustlers, cabbies, bell boys, newspapermen and cops, in that order, usually know their way around most towns."

Vizzini was struck by one of the more sophisticated networked counterintelligence systems he had seen when he tried to develop a relationship with a hustler who could provide information—and apparently already had plenty on him. "Susu" already knew that the local Marseilles police were following Vizzini, in his undercover role as Joseph Vento, and that he was keeping a gun in his hotel room. To "Vento's" expression of surprise at the wealth of her information, Susu merely replied, "Everybody in Marseilles is my cousin." Just as undercover cops recognize that even when they succeed at an operation they probably diminish the likelihood of success of future operations using the same, already exposed techniques, they are well aware that criminals, who have good reason to guard the publicity of their activities, maintain fully adequate means of gathering counter-information on those who display an interest in them.[55]

Susu "seemed to have all the qualities you look for in a good informant: knowledge, a desire to get even and a need for money. With a female, it also helps if they like you." Authors on covert intelligence work tend to regard women as uniquely agile in getting information. Advice in *The Pretext Book* reads, "Females have a way of getting things that males can not. When you need to, use a Dickless Tracy."[56] Alvarez recalled one of the best informants with whom he had ever worked:

> As it is with most women, this informant would hear things that no one else knew. She was able to tell me when, where and how much dope or money would be at a particular location. All I had to do was go and see the criminal activity take place. Informants like her can make law enforcement personnel look like outstanding investigators.[57]

In order to appeal to potential female informants, Vidocq consciously adopted strategic disguises:

> As I had generally found that, in all my undertakings, it was principally from females that I gleaned my information, whether women or girls, I soon determined on the disguise which was best adapted for my purpose. It was apparent that I must assume the guise of a very respectable gentleman, and, consequently, by means of some false wrinkles, a pig-tail, snowy white ruffles, a large gold-headed cane, a three-cornered hat, buckles, breeches and coat to match,—I was metamorphosed into one of those good sexagenarian citizens, whom all old ladies admire.[58]

Due to the transgressor status of informants generally, their use is ethically fraught and highly controversial. Using informants—like the practice of plea-bargaining—links law enforcement in the public mind with, rather than against, criminals; it also dilutes the relationship between crime and just punishment. As Brown observes,

> The American criminal-justice system is rooted in the concepts of accountability and punishment; that is, persons are to receive their just deserts for violating the law. The "buy-bust"-flip procedure by which informants are developed reduces the certainty of being held accountable for violating the law.

Even informants who are to plead guilty may have their sentencing left open, so that "his sentence will depend on what he does."[59]

Like undercover work, the use of informants also raises serious ethical issues about the right to privacy. A system of prison "snitches" in a Texas prison was used by staff to gather clandestine information in return for enhanced privileges until the practice was outlawed as unconstitutional in 1980. By contrast with the generally low status of informants, these snitches held high status in their immediate culture. The system was strongly hierarchical. "Building tenders," "runners/strikers," and "turnkeys" rose up as they proved themselves not only useful but trustworthy. Underlings in the hierarchy formed a curiously loyal attachment with those who were in a position to inform on them, much as Vidocq felt himself the recipient of a peculiar sort of fondness coming from those he had turned in.

Formalized as élite prison snitches, building tenders extended the reach of the prison guards in prison surveillance. Because they knew most of the ways that contraband could be hidden, they assisted prison guards in cell searches. One of the big dangers of the snitch system was that boredom and desire for revenge motivated inmates to create fictional scenarios for the guards, a ready audience. More gravely, they also were the cause of much prison violence.[60]

In cooperating, collaborating, or even double-dealing with law enforcement, the informant plays his dual role in front of both the most astute and dangerous audience for deceptive roleplay and the sharpest assessors of criminal intelligence possible. The thrill of "doing" both sides is probably untoppable. Because the big game is already up, the informant is free to pursue the smaller game of the identity play with whatever ingenuity he can. Much of what undercovers know about performance, they know from these betwixt-and-between—and crafty—bad guys.

The informant position shows us the infinite flux between being the one who's "doing" the other guy to being the one who's being "done"; the bad guy-informant-cop chain continually cycles the informant figure through shifting (apparent) allegiances. Even though he does the work of the good guys, the bad-guy informant retains his bad guy identity. By contrast, the undercover who goes bad finds the company of the bad guys more reinforcing and crosses over in his subjective experience of his own identity.

It is the tightrope walk between art and crime, between middle-of-the-road and outlaw cultures, and between apparent and hidden selves, that makes liminal figures such as the informant and the undercover cop—especially one "gone bad"—so compelling. Likely, it isn't going to be the most ethical among us who survive in their role long enough to win out—but the most virtuosic. One of the chief things that trick identities do is break down; the skillful identity artist controls how.

6

IDENTITY BREAKDOWN

We're mans [sic] of a thousand faces, but we tell you zero. ... You're talking to a man who has withstood the finest interrogation techniques—electrical, mechanical, psychological, philosophical, European, domestic, commercial—which is why there's no need for us to prove our valor by refusing to talk to you now!

—Izzy Moreno, informant character on

Miami Vice: Made For Each Other

Deception is actually magic in reverse. What the spectators see is magic—presuming that the performer's efforts have been successful. The identical performance, from the magician's view-point, is deception.

—Dariel Fitzkee

An undercover operator prepares and lives out a highly volatile triple secret: what his true identity is, that an investigation is going on, and that he is a part of it.[1] Unfortunately, since the bad guys track undercover identity techniques at least as watchfully as do law enforcement officers, such secrets—and possibly their performers—can have limited life expectancies. As one trainer told me, "As we got more lackadaisical, the bad guy got more sophisticated in being able to detect a narc." To be really rigorous as he prepares a role, therefore, an undercover has to anticipate that, despite his most painstaking groundwork, the bad guy will pose him unanticipated tests of identity, and he will need to save his life by improvising. In the face-to-face performance of a fraudulent identity opposite a gunman, one must do the seemingly impossible—create and enact not just identities, but also identity techniques, a leap ahead of what the bad guy can destroy.

Descriptions of undercover techniques record both what has and what hasn't survived past performances. The cautions so prevalent in the undercover manuals and training, as well as in informal transmission of techniques, respond to and attempt to transcend previous identity failures. Indeed, a principal reason those who train undercover operators are so concerned to ensure there are no outsiders in their classrooms is the techniques themselves can be narced by a single leak. Thus, to stay ahead of the changing game, the undercover operator has to develop a kind of historical consciousness. It is only as he familiarizes himself with the identity conventions and stereotypes of his own period and culture that he can manipulate them in performance with the greatest canniness possible. Nineteenth-century British con artist Alice Grey's success as a "missionary," pitting anti-Protestant and anti-Catholic factions against each other, was founded on her knowledge of the charged cultural images each side held of the other.[2]

The triumphant undercover knows and reflects back both the criminal and the larger social culture's values and behaviors. He must be consummately self-aware, able to identify and isolate the personal qualities he brings into his performance, and to know where these qualities fit within his historical period's conventions of detection. Erving Goffman observes, a social performer who is aware of his own shortcomings in performance can backstop technically as well as for his content. He "can come to strategic terms with his own weaknesses and even exploit them to improve his game. ... Here the subject splits himself in two, as it were, with one of his selves taking action relative to the proclivities of the other."

Dispensing advice as applicable to the undercover artist as to the magician, Dariel Fitzkee urges the performer to become aware of the subtle personal mannerisms by which he unconsciously draws attention to the moments of true significance in the trick. These are what con artists refer to as "tells," and include vocal habits, as when magicians "cough or grunt, exhale or inhale, clear their throats or make other audible noises at a critical moment," or when marks telegraph their next move before they take it.[3] In some sense, all of a person's characteristic behaviors—including such basic dimensions as his verbal, vocal, and tonal patterns when telling the truth and when lying—are "tells." As a framework for analyzing others' deceptive behavior, Neuro-Linguistic Programming was as available to the bad guys as it was to the FBI.

Just as a fugitive can be caught because he seeks harbor with an old lover, a narc working deep cover makes himself vulnerable when he keeps company with known associates or maintains his subscriptions to hobby magazines that are associated with law-enforcement interests. Thus, beyond mastering the ordinary disguise techniques of recognizing and then changing one's appearance, demeanor, and style of movement, one ideally also becomes aware of those lifestyle habits that may become ready tracking devices for an identity hunter.[4]

In criminal intelligence-gathering, an undercover simultaneously tries to hold on to his own secrets and to unmask his opponent's. And, while the bad guy performs his tests of the undercover's identity, he also keeps his own hand concealed (even though he may systematically stage, for others' benefit, well-placed performances of secretive behaviors). The simultaneous observation and concealment both undercover operator and target perform blur any possible distinction between identity observer and performer. As Goffman puts it, "Each seeker is therefore doubly a concealer, and each concealer is doubly a seeker."[5] The first stages of identity breakdown are inevitable, but—with skill—reversible.

Damage Control

Vidocq attributed identity breakdowns to the unnecessary sharing of information: "I have long since learnt that there is no secret well kept but that which we tell to nobody; and sad experience more and more convinced me of the necessity of acting alone in all my operations, when I could do so."[6] Likewise, Frank Abagnale credited his long evasion of detection to his never having elicited the help of knowing accomplices: "My total autonomy was the biggest factor in my success. The usual criminal sources of information for the police were useless to them in their search for me. The underworld grapevine simply had no intelligence on me." Abagnale could change course at will without leaving a trail of crumbs behind him: "While my true identity was established midway in my course, the leads garnered by police were all after-the-fact leads. I was always several days gone by the time my misdeeds were exposed as such, and officers were never able to pick up my trail until I struck again, usually in some far-off city."[7] Abagnale's techniques were still good a generation later, when identity-change manuals advise that readiness to go it alone is prerequisite to any major identity shift. James S. Martin admonishes:

> A genuine commitment to a new identity is a *private* decision about a radical change of life. If you need support from your best pal, Billy Joe, or if you are mooning over leaving your girlfriend and need to let her down easy, you haven't got what it takes to start over with a new life.[8]

The isolationism implicit in protecting an undercover identity also demands keeping it as far away from other law enforcers as possible, for their protection as well as for one's own. The fewer people—including government people—who know about the cover, the better. Vizzini recounts a rare fortunate incident in which he and a Secret Service Man from Miami encountered each other unexpectedly in San Juan. Fortunately, both had a stake in withholding any signs of recognition: "He had his job, I had mine." But that was a lucky break.

Keeping even the federal marshals out of the loop, Vizzini was taken, under the cover of "Swift Tony" Tivoli, a convicted armed robber, on a plane from New York to Atlanta, to be placed in the Atlanta Federal Penitentiary on an intelligence-gathering mission. Vizzini spent the night, just as would a real convicted felon, in a New York prison before the marshals picked him up. Once he arrived in Atlanta, the warden was the only person to have any awareness of his true identity, yet even he was "too far away to help if something [went] wrong."[9]

The "wise" are especially well placed to blow a cover or to blackmail. In Vidocq's Paris, loiterers would hang around street gambling cons and collect a share of the take for not informing to the police.[10] Those closest to you are also ideally placed to compromise a fictitious identity unwittingly.[11] Because family members can make recognitions that can prove fatal, an operator working deep cover is usually quarantined from family members and friends. Federally protected witnesses typically are also relocated: in a new place, a trick identity can be free of a well-meaning but all-too-knowledgeable backstage. Thus, the willingness to be a loner can be an essential protective element in safeguarding an identity; in undercover work, paranoia can be adaptive.

Identity presenters need to be on guard against emotional and relational set-ups. Vidocq's memoirs show repeated examples of his having trained himself to defer spontaneous emotional expression, even in the seemingly instinctual instant: "One evening as I was passing along the Rue Dauphine, to get to the Barrière Enfer, some one tapped me on the shoulder. My first thought was to run for it, without turning round, being aware that, whoever stops you, relies on your looking back to seize you."[12] In the course of one of Vidocq's many captures as a career fugitive, the officials called his mother in, assuming that the long-separated mother and son could not hold themselves back from a highly emotional recognition scene. Fortunately for Vidocq, cold-blooded practicality ran in the family. Vidocq, quickly perceived that he had walked into a trap and signaled his mother, who miraculously took his meaning. At first

> The poor woman hastened to embrace me, but I saw through the snare, and putting her from me quietly, I said to the magistrate who was present, that it was an unmanly thing to give the unfortunate woman any hopes of seeing her son, when they were, at least, uncertain of their ability to produce him. My mother, who was put on her guard by a signal which I managed to communicate to her, pretending to examine me attentively, at length declared that a wonderful likeness had deceived her, and then retired, uttering many bitter reproaches against those who had taken her from home only to afford her but a fallacious joy.[13]

Ironically, the connection between mother and son—expected by the capturing officials to be the very thing that would permit the penetration of Vidocq's pretended identity—allowed the critical physical shorthand between these long-separated family members.

Like Vidocq, Vizzini found it invaluable to be able to stifle sudden emotional reactions to surprises. While working undercover on the prominent Mafia figure Lucky Luciano, Vizzini started inwardly when he heard from his target's lips that the head of the Mafia was a man with his own surname, but was able to suppress any visible sign of his "uneasy feeling."[14]

Even in the absence of a relational stimulus, unconscious mistakes offer the highest level of threat. This can happen. When Abagnale absentmindedly wrote his real name and his father's address in New York on the back of one of his forged checks, and then accidentally pocketed and later cashed it, that could easily have been the end of his illegal adventures. (However, catching this mistake, he thought to impersonate an FBI agent in order to recapture the original incriminating check.)

Particular dangers are associated with playing young, as in undercover infiltrations of high schools in order to do anticipatory drug targeting. Sociologist Bruce A. Jacobs isolated specific behavioral displays that undercovers had to make for a high school anticipatory drug investigation in order to gain acceptance.[15] Because they gathered intelligence on drug use and drug dealing in a relatively diffuse way, by becoming accepted members of a self-contained community, operators would play their role for a significant length of time before attempting any drug buys. In a semester-long infiltration of a high school, for example, five weeks were characteristically devoted to character-establishing roleplays before any attempts to buy drugs.

In Jacobs' study, agents used three principal character-establishing techniques to build rapport with the drug-dealing population. First among these was class clowning, which "involved either rude or intellectually ignorant behavior for comic effect." Thus construed, class clowning was a means of offsetting suspicion about academic experience level. Consciously staged scenes of acting out probably also kept officers alert to the dangers of responding too skillfully to demands on their academic performance—particularly difficult since the officers were presumably encountering the material for the second time.

"Retreatism," the second of Jacobs' character-development strategies, included such behaviors as appearing to sleep during class, not paying attention to homework expectations, openly cheating, and behaving as if under the influence of drugs. Third, "troublemaking" helped to establish the deviant persona that would later be believable for a high-level drug buyer or dealer. Undercovers would ditch classes or smoke cigarettes with others. Among these techniques, "only troublemaking had a *direct* link to later tactics specifically involving solicitation of drugs. The other two merely laid the reputational base on which interactions with dealers later could proceed credibly."[16]

It is characteristically easier to infiltrate a high school drug scene if one is able to start, with the rest of a new class and a number of other "kids" who also arrive on the scene, more legitimately, during the summer. For work mid-year in the high schools, the cover story has to make sense of how and why the new kid has come to be at this high school, particularly if he has appeared at an unusual time of year. The cover story also has to address the other factors that make the new narc appear strange in high school students' eyes, such as rarely being available for after-school activities (because they're busy after school writing police reports or meeting with their undercover supervisor!); having parents who can't be introduced and a home to which other students are never invited; being remote from romantic attachments (because of institutional or personal standards about misleading innocent parties, or in fidelity to a life partner); and, as always with undercover narcotics agents, refusing drug use (simulating only as a last-ditch measure).

In addition to these behavioral displays the high school undercover must stage, Jacobs identified displays the undercover operator must *not* make if he wants to be accepted.[17] A "trend discontinuity" reflects some anomaly in the set-up of the scenario, a behavior out of step with practices of the underground marketplace. Because there is an established progression of events leading up to a buy, inexperienced narcs, who are inevitably overeager, may trip themselves up by trying to rush a timeline the bad guys own more tightly than they do.[18] They may, for example, try to buy too great a quantity or too high a category of drugs without sufficient introductions having been made or an appropriate relationship with the dealer having been established. Such "transactional overaggressiveness" may also be signaled when an undercover seems peculiarly disinterested in bargaining prices down to be in line with his budget or with current market values, when he buys from too many people, or when he attempts to buy more drugs than his apparent investment in the deal would warrant.[19] In the film *Rush,* the character of Jimmy arouses suspicion since "he turns up in October, doesn't work, buys more drugs than anyone can use and nobody buys from him." Because higher-level dealers are cautious about maintaining their businesses, they typically only sell to buyers with whom they've established a basic level of trust, which may come from doing business with them over an extended period of time, seeing them use drugs (which it is assumed that narcs cannot or will not do), or having friends in common.

The undercover must be careful about the company he appears to keep—what Goffman calls the "with relationship"— as one is naturally "contaminated" by association with suspicious others, such as the police. Of course, the "with" relationship extends to those whose reputations can enhance one's own. "Building up [my] credentials" is how Joe Pistone referred to the long work of being seen hanging out with the "right" people, the ones who would be able to help him get hooked up with the Mafia.[20]

To forestall any perception of a trend discontinuity, Pistone made sure to develop his public appearances gradually. For this undercover, "getting established is a subtle business, a matter of small impressions, little tests, quiet understandings":

> We had a list of places where wiseguy-type fences were known to hang out. ... I would cruise these places, mostly in midtown or lower Manhattan, have a drink or dinner, not talking much or making any moves, just showing my face so people would get used to seeing me. ... I didn't try to introduce myself to anybody or get into any conversations for a while. Mob guys or fences I recognized were mixed in with ordinary customers, what wiseguys call "citizens," people not connected with the mob. After I had been to a place a few times, I might say hello to the bartender if he had begun to recognize me. The important thing was just to be seen and not to push anything; just get noticed ...

Patience stood Pistone in good stead:

> You push a little here and there, but very gently. Brief introductions, short conversations, appearances one place and

another, hints about what you're up to, casual mannerisms, demeanor, and lingo that show you know your way around—all these become a trail of credibility you leave behind you. Above all, you cannot hurry. You cannot seem eager to meet certain people, make certain contacts, learn about certain scores. The quickest way to get tagged as a cop is to move too fast. You have to show that you have the time to play it by the rules of the street, and that includes letting people check you out and come to you. ... Nobody tells you if you're safe. You have to sense it. Badguys on the street are sensing you.[21]

Vizzini played his own game wisely when, in a case with a dealer of counterfeit currency, he appeared as cautious as the dealer was. Knowing when he was being offered a bum deal with the fake bills no doubt helped establish Vizzini's credibility as a real customer. So did his paranoiac parity with his target: "I complimented him, saying that by being cautious he was protecting me as well as himself, and that I wouldn't do business with anybody who trusted me. I told him that I would be interested in seeing more of his hundreds, but if they were as bad as these to forget it."[22] The power Vizzini established by being willing to walk away from a deal affirmed his proffered identity.

Physical and verbal cues of what Jacobs calls "interpersonal illegitimacy" quickly herald a law-enforcement identity to a bad guy. In various criminal and law-enforcement cultures, these can include wearing clothes that fit too well, being too well-kempt, driving cars that are too clean—even showing off particular patterns of muscularity or body mass. And, of course, undercover narcs must conceal all signs of their professional training. Officers must not, for example, "stand like cops"—weight evenly divided between feet that are spread more than hips' width apart—or use cop jargon in their undercover roles. One of Jacobs' subjects, a youthful undercover narc penetrating a high school drug scene by posing as a high school student, recalled an instance in which she exhibited her police training all too clearly:

Three of us were playing around in class one day, and the one guy goes to the other, "She's a cop and you're busted." I played along [because I didn't know if he was serious] and told the guy, "All right, put your hands behind your back,

stand up against the wall, and open your legs!" He did everything except open his legs apart, so I kicked them really hard
from the inside, like they taught us in the academy. He almost fell over! He didn't say anything right then, but later on
[after he was arrested] he told me that from that point on he
knew I was a cop.[23]

A cop must guard against using the word "weapon" instead of "gun,"
"vehicle" for "car," or "tag" for "license plate" in an undercover situation. During one of our field exercises, an undercover trainee referred to the passing by of a sheriff's car with pretended alarm, and
called it by an acronym unlikely to be used by anyone outside law
enforcement. (Fortunately, this novice actor was able to think on his
feet: when the bad guy, played by one of the instructors, challenged
him on how he had known that acronym, the student improvised
nimbly, replying that, bushed the previous night, he had stayed in at
the hotel and heard it used on the local television news.)

Support surveillance team members must also comport themselves, both on and off duty, in a way that does not mark them as
police and compromise the undercover's performance and safety.
Behaviors such as backing into parking spaces (in order to get a better view of the target), parking alone in the open, parking two cars
side by side, speaking into a raised radio microphone, talking animat-
edly to one's passenger, or driving in a flashy way can mark both surveillance personnel and the undercover.

Undercovers must be careful about their characters' vehicles. They
can draw from the police warehouse of seized vehicles, but it is safer
if they trade them with other police locales. A car identified as belonging to a cop is the most dangerous of all, so "naturally, if you
have any reason at all to suspect that your vehicle has been burned,
don't drive it. Driving a car that doesn't fit your character is far better
than driving one that may get shot at as you cruise down the street."[24]

Interpersonal illegitimacy may be perceptible by much more complex behaviors, such as acting on criminal information that may have
been passed to the undercover simply to test his identity. Paradoxically, one's very accrual of experience in role can spell danger,
making it not just the active roleplaying the undercover does that can
capsize a working identity, but also any complacency while in role:

Once the undercover agents believe they have been accepted by the violator, there is a tendency to relax, to not read the suspect's body language for trouble signals, or merely to ignore the signals. ... [Besides,] streetwise, cagey violators do not tip their hands when they become suspicious of undercover officers. Therefore, the slightest change in the suspect's behavior should put undercover officers on guard.[25]

Miami Vice portrays more or less faithfully undercovers' tendency to become careless in reading targets. As characters Sonny and Rico become more experienced at their work, they also become more jaded. Muses Sonny, "Ain't that the trap, Rico? The better you get at this job, the more dangerous it becomes. Lose your head, and you're a dead cop."[26]

Undercovers in Groups

Having a team go undercover makes certain forms of impression management easier; however, a team play also feeds the creative urges of the players, who have someone else in the know with whom to improvise. Jerry VanCook's two-man scene exemplifies a team's temptation to see how far it can push an in-joke at the bad guys' expense:

Bear in mind that I am a little under 6 feet tall, was doing a lot of power-lifting during my undercover days, weighed about 250 pounds, and have a face that I'm pretty sure my mother loved anyway. Mark, on the other hand, was about 5 feet 6 inches tall and would have been hard pressed to tip the scales at 160 pounds. When we felt a situation warranted it, I'd begin a gradual escalation of surliness that would climax with the appearance that I was about to really crack and turn the place into firewood. Then, Mark would walk over to me, reach up, and slap me across the face.

"I've had all the crap out of you I'm gonna put up with tonight," he'd say, at which point I'd begin apologizing profusely.

> No one ever said anything when we did this number, but you could see what they were thinking written across their faces: "If the big guy is afraid of the little guy ... God help us ... what does the little guy do when he's mad?"[27]

Just as Goffman detailed the differences between team performances and individual presentations of self, undercover work plays by slightly altered principles when two or more players, for example, an undercover and an informant, need to coordinate.[28] No longer can each roleplayer design his plan in isolation, thinking only, for example, of what he knows or what he can use to establish rapport with the bad guy. Rather, the most important part of each player's cover story becomes how he knows the other. The relational story—how did we meet? what made us connect?—is the spine of the preparation. A hermetic interpersonal narrative helps make the undercover narc, as the new guy on the street corner, as seemingly familiar as the longtime drug buyer (perhaps now acting as informant). Chief features of the relational story's attributes are consistency and depth. In developing an appropriate level of depth, the kind of self-insight that makes for an astute solo roleplayer also comes to the fore for a group identity play. One needs to be aware of the qualities that come across in one's own presentation of self and to collectively create narrative conditions under which those qualities can flourish and appear to emerge naturally.

In one of the simulation exercises at an undercover training academy, I listened as two "baby narcs" hashed out the features of their joint undercover identity narrative. How had they met? What had drawn them together? What had motivated each one to be interested in doing business with the other and with this particular bad guy? What was each character's drug history? Why was one in sudden need of money, spurring him on to participate in drug dealing?[29]

As they strove for both consistency and depth in their relational story, the two trainees determined they had met at a convention of fraternity brothers from different colleges across the country, held at Disney World. Since then, they had taken holidays together with their wives and children in adjacent cottages at the beach once or twice a year. And as one player's marriage began to falter—nicely providing the pretext for the sudden need for money—the two friends called each other more frequently. The students' conversation—focusing as it did on the who's, under-what-circumstances, and then-what's—was reminiscent of the building of a police report. A key element in the credibility of the story was that the momentum of the relationship did not appear to overwhelm either individual's motivation for getting involved in the drug deal.

For this exercise, the players decided it was more important to use names that they could remember easily, without having to stall, than to protect loved ones from being tailed. One selected as his last name his own wife's maiden name; both decided to use their actual wives' first names as part of their cover story, and to make it part of their package that, although friends for many years, neither could remember the names of the other's children. This enabled the players to "use" the reality that neither expected to be able to remember made-up names for the fictitious children they had elaborately concocted. The "absentminded" ploy could only be carried so far, however: Basic physical details could not simply appear to be forgotten. The two players had to have the same story at least on how *many* children the other fellow had, as well as what each of the wives looked like. The wife of a longtime friend could not be *both* 4'10½" and 5'7".

The collective tailoring of a group narrative serves a number of functions. It rehearses all members of a group undercover operation so that all respond fluidly and naturally to questions designed to test the authenticity of their presented identities. Perhaps more importantly, it gives them a common base of answers so that if individual members should be questioned separately, their story will still hold up. After the evening's simulation exercise was over, one student reported his moment of highest anxiety was while he was in the restroom, leaving his partner alone at the restaurant dinner table with the group of four bad guys. Would they question his partner to probe any inconsistencies in the joint cover story, then mess with *him*, if his partner should get up to use the restroom? Separation and interrogation should be expected by cops working undercover: it's what *they* do, whether when working with informants whose trustworthiness they can never take for granted, or when working a "reverse" sting in which they take on roles as bad guys.[30]

Sometimes the relational story can be quite disjointed, just so long as the need for one is dealt with. A pair of undercover students was able to avoid having to develop a long joint history by determining their having been thrown together, with little knowledge of the other, as a purposeful feature of their cover. The people they work for, the story was to go, "don't like an organization to get too deep, and they don't like one end getting tangled up with another, so they sent you down from Maryland, and they sent me up from Miami, because there were some problems before."

This undercover exercise extended into a second night, during which two new players took over the contact roles. Although this would rarely be done in a real operation, the exercise provided the opportunity to show how an existing story places constraints on what can be created, relevant to the real-life exigency of bringing in additional players, such as confidential informants who have been flipped. For those joining onto an operation, or hinging upon a previously established character, pre-established histories and narratives must take precedence over new coinages. One of the trainers gave the what-not-to-do example of a new undercover student who, when asked how he knew the other fellow—actually, a more experienced undercover—explained they had met while both were working on a farm. The bad guy was familiar enough with his original contact's own cover story to know he had never worked on a farm.

For the second night of the field exercise, the new players were briefed by their predecessors. As one veteran undercover put it, "Y'all got to find y'all's common things, that y'all can hit on." Early in their brainstorming session a young white female undercover listed for her partner and the support team the subjects she could speak authoritatively about: Catholic school, her two cats, sports, big-screen TV, what it was like to be raised in a town long associated with the Ku Klux Klan. Her African-American male partner for the exercise quipped, "So I wouldn't be there!" The pair therefore had to abandon its original cover story, which was that he came periodically to her town in the course of playing college basketball, and started dating her college roommate.

During its training course, the PLE Group regularly checks participants IDs. Even after hiring its undercover operators, the company conducts random drug tests and it polygraphs operators after each operation. These practices not only thwart undercovers' going bad, they model the power dynamic of being narced at any time—the reality on the undercover's ground.

Recognition Scenes: Attempted Homicide

A recognition scene, in which one person seems to reveal himself wholly to another and in return to be seen fully—is an encounter of perhaps the deepest kind. In a theatre audience, seeing disguised lovers reveal themselves to each other, or separated family members restored to each other's arms, can be deeply satisfying.[31] A wave of shock or pleasure courses over the audience when a drag performer removes his wig at the curtain call, or when puppeteers step out from behind their performing apparatus.

By contrast, while a recognition scene in undercover work may be thrilling and suspenseful to watch in a film or television show, it does not produce delight in real life for its players. In the face-to-face, high-stakes world of undercover performance, recognition scenes go beyond the dramatic to take on a primal dimension. "Getting narced" takes on additional power because of the inverse relationship between the amount of information the bad guy has about the undercover and the amount of acting the undercover is going to have to do to make the bad guy think he possesses even more. As Goffman notes,

> The more information the audience [here, the bad guy] has about the performer, the less likely it is that anything they learn during the interaction will radically influence them. On the other hand, where no prior information is possessed, it may be expected that the information gleaned during the interaction will be relatively crucial.[32]

In the literature on identity breakdown, the scene in which a pretender is unmasked can be either humiliating or exhilarating. Shoplifters interviewed for *Seductions of Crime* related their experience of getting caught as an "act of degradation." By contrast, art forger Han van Meegeren was so proud to be convicted that he insisted on having a chance to paint art forgeries for members of the court that had tried him. As the forger was unmasked, his gifts as a performer were crowned. Van Meegeren's story reveals the faker's possible drive toward personal recognition of the essence of the self. Audiences for the freaks and frauds that showman P. T. Barnum displayed remained fascinated even after the bubble of identity had been popped:

> Barnum's audiences found the encounter with potential frauds exciting. It was a form of intellectual exercise, enjoyable even after the hoax had been penetrated, or at least during the period of doubt and suspicion. Barnum understood that the opportunity to debate the issue of falsity, to discover how deception had been practiced, was even more exciting than the discovery of fraud itself.[33]

Unmasking may provide the germ of the next stage in an identity performer's career. British art forger Tom Keating gained a real following for his work once he was recognized (though not tried) as a master forger. A prolific faker of the work of Stuart Palmer, Keating presented a series of televised demonstrations of the techniques of the great painters. After his death in 1984, his work auctioned for seven times the expected price. Keating's story is not uncommon: the works of celebrated fakers may become more valuable after the faker has been exposed, his very skill having become marketable. The early nineteenth-century impostor Mary Baker, better known as "Princess Caraboo," made herself out as an exotic princess of the Far East who had been kidnapped by pirates and shipwrecked on the English coast. Even after exposure as the runaway daughter of a cobbler, Baker was able to draw crowds and to retain many expensive gifts that had been thrust upon her by merchants in the hopes that she would set fashion trends; in fact, the public clamor for the "barely literate girl [who] had been able to fool for more than a year not only the cream of society but also men of learning" was sufficiently encouraging for her, on her return to England, to perform publicly as "the former Caraboo."[34]

Whether in television, film, literature, or descriptions by working undercover operators, narcing scenes have a number of repeating features. Conventionally, the scene begins with a threatening situation, which may either build up gradually as the bad guy maintains an ongoing (and probably healthy) degree of suspicion about this new kid on the block who seems most particularly to want to buy from him, or else it may be expressed as a sudden eruption of suspicious energy. Usually, the reader's or spectator's attention is drawn to the intense emotional contortions in the undercover agent struggling to restore face when, as Bill Taylor explains, he experiences the "pucker factor," as the "anal orifice puckers a little bit!"

Once an undercover character has successfully thwarted a danger, both he and the media audience may experience a letdown. He may wonder whether the roleplay was worth the risk, and whether the role should be abandoned despite its having passed (this time). He may even engage with larger questions about the meaning of identity plays. Many of these features just represent the undercover content overlaid on standardized dramatic devices: mounting conflict as it impacts on a sympathetic character; high-stakes crisis; the expansion of the meaningfulness of specific conflicts in terms of the grander themes of the play. However, because of the inherently dramatic dimensions of discovery and recognition, and the reality that a narcing scene can mean life or death, undercover work and the spinning out of its stories seem particularly to lend themselves to these dramatic treatments.

In many dramatizations of undercover scenarios in novels, films, and radio and television programs, as well as in brag accounts by former undercover agents, the identity trickster and his unveiler are in virtually interchangeable positions, in part because the pursuer is frequently one who at another point in his detection career was himself in some form of identity flight.[35] In the TV program *The Fugitive*, the character of Lieutenant Philip Gerard is pictured as being as tormented in the pursuit as his prey is in flight; he makes a spectacle of himself by being more interested in pursuing Dr. Richard Kimble than in working on any of his other cases. Hunter and hunted are each other's best reflection, outcasts from a society whose pace has little to do with the self-fueling frenzy of the chase. In an episode from the late 1960s satirical espionage television show, *Get Smart*, central character Max meets up in camouflage with a representative of his arch enemy counterespionage organization, "KAOS." Max is dressed as an old man, Siegfried as an old woman: the little dance they do together as a natural consummation of their disguise work underscores their complementarity. Principally, however, it reinforces their recognition of their essential alikeness and unity. Likewise, in Hugo's *Les Misérables*, detective Javert is constructed as the doppelgänger of hero Jean Valjean, whom he pursues for the theft of a single loaf of bread.

Juxtaposed with the mirroring of each other by bad guy and good in these scenes is a prominent sexual metaphor in law-enforcement culture. A "penetration" assignment "is one that requires extensive planning and preparation as it involves the use of an undercover agent over a period of several months to any extended length of time. This type of assignment is geared to the eventual penetration of the higher echelon criminal element."[36] Both the narcing scene and the narrative of legal detection are about the process of discovery. In the how-to books on detection, this discovery process is marked as the shift from exterior presentation to interiority, a shift associated with touching some form of truth. The oft-referenced law-enforcement metaphor of penetration represents the admission of the identity trickster into a target culture, his gathering of incriminating information while there, and the establishment of a suspected crime perpetrator's actual identity and of the truth of his tale. A 1978 brief on undercover operations from the Federal Law Enforcement Training Center distinguished penetration assignments, which were the most involved and of longest duration, from impromptu, one-time, and "extended" assignments—the latter of which involved the maintenance of a fictitious identity for only a couple of months at most.[37]

But—not to carry the penetration image any further than it actually goes in the literature on and of law enforcement, the act can be—mirroringly—mutual. Goffman illustrates amusingly the "famous recursive problem":

> Harry must come to terms with the fact that the assessment he is trying to penetrate, namely, the one that the other is likely to make, will contain as one of its features the fact that Harry will try to penetrate it. Thus, the opponent that Harry must try to dope out is another that is known to himself and to Harry as someone trying to dope out Harry and someone whom Harry is trying to dope out.[38]

Ideally, perhaps, the undercover achieves a rapport in which the bad guy believes he's the penetrator. Vizzini describes such an interaction while investigating a target, "Big Al" Cicceroni. Big Al "wanted to know everything about me, and I made him work for what he got. I was using the old ploy of pumping him by letting him pump me."[39] Just as it is often advantageous to work on an informant who doesn't know he is one, the undercover operator cunningly stages his level of willingness to disclose information about his trick identity, while carefully staging "secret" behaviors the bad guy would interpret as authentic.

Identity games and transformations breathe fire into the drama of detection; it's as they brush with and survive danger that they become dramatically viable. And nowadays, a performer only survives if his identity does. The rise of crack-cocaine in the 1980s brought with it unpredictable behavior on the part of users and a high addiction rate, which produced a tremendous rise not only in property crimes, but also in violent crime; crack-cocaine lessens respect for human life. Officers facing a heavy-duty dealer who has become "hinky" realistically confront the most irreversible demotion of all if they misjudge how to handle a situation with an unpredictable, irascible, and violent opponent.

In undercover acting—and in contemporary training of these identity players—each choice is thus made with a judgment about how well it will preserve the life of the performer. In his biography of Michael Levine, Goddard emphasized the contrast between the risks Levine would calculatedly take in his own roleplays and the more conservative techniques he taught novice undercovers in the classroom: "When he taught undercover, he was really teaching survival."[40]

Discovery may be a danger in any identity performance, whether of an undercover agent, a fugitive from the law, or a federally protected witness; however, it has special poignancy for the career undercover operator. An identity breakdown may reduce the likelihood of future undercover assignments, an outcome most operators would regard as a demotion and a humiliation. Officers working undercover who demonstrate that their roleplaying skills, their judgment, or their ability to think on their feet is not up to the demands of the job are likely (if they survive) to be transferred back to more traditional police work, where they will have to abide by a more overtly hierarchical chain of authority, to dress and groom themselves in keeping with vastly more conservative police standards, and to give up the glamour associated with furtive, high-stakes work. As we have seen, they may also be ridiculed by cops either unimpressed or threatened by their undercover experience.

No matter how successful an undercover operation, it leaves a trace of techniques that have been exposed to varying degrees and may therefore be less likely to pass muster in future. The under-cover's paradoxical task is to learn from the mistakes of more experienced operators, adapt them to fit his own personality and what he thinks he can get away with, and then be willing to retire his own bag of tricks before it is retired for him. Because getting narced may bring to a quick close the life of a particular identity technique, one very useful debriefing strategy taught at one undercover academy was, at the close of an operation deemed successful, to ask oneself three questions:

1. What went right during the operation?

2. What can we improve in the next operation?

3. What did we teach the bad guy?

Outside forces such as the media may also press for a dramatically satisfying closure of cases, and only particular kinds of outcomes fit the model. Media typically find the heroism and ingenuity of individual police officers newsworthy, and thus pressure state and local law enforcement officers to make a news story, as well as a case.

Undercover training can emphasize how suddenly a threatening scene can arise and how quickly an operator can lose control of it. During one weeklong class, anytime one of the instructors gleefully called out, "Showtime!" and took on the role of the bad guy, his student-guinea pig would then have to step into the role of the undercover agent whose identity was being challenged. The hard lesson of one of these scenarios was to "put up or shut up." The instructor went over to one of the two women in the class of twenty-two and spoke to her as if she were a prostitute. The student accepted the role. He threw a wad of bills across the desk at her as payment for a sexual act he demanded of her. She backed down. And he won the roleplay exercise. One must only make claims that one is willing to play all the way.

The undercover's creation of a character that is responsive to the perceived needs of an investigative situation shows a sophistication in scripting, so that roles are interdependent in a system constructed not so much on plot as on final outcome. Here, too, the building of a business-dealing rapport makes any subsequent individuation of an undercover from the bad guy a threat to the investigation and to the undercover performer's life. While playwritten roles frequently allow characters' needs to come into conflict in order to produce plot, the undercover's role is based on the fact that the bad guys don't know there is a conflict in purposes.

A narcing scene changes the bad guy's frame on the activity, from one in which the two players are co-actors without outside audience, into one in which the bad guy recognizes that he may have been party to two performances, neither of whose terms he has openly known and accepted. In one of these unwitting performances, he is the unsuspecting audience for an ingenious role performed by the undercover. In the other, he is an actor slyly placed into incriminating positions that will stage him in criminal behavior for audio and video recording and ultimately presentation in court. Any notion he may hold of co-acting or co-creating the scene is disrupted by his containment by the undercover, as either isolated performer or as hoodwinked audience—much like the mark of a con game.

The sudden individuation associated with a scene of identity degradation uproots the merging of identities between the undercover and the bad guy upon which the very role development and rapport-building strategies of the undercover have progressed. In the aftermath of a narcing scene, the initial process of building rapport can then be seen retrospectively, as one in which the bad guy's performance *for* the undercover is bought with his belief that he is acting *with* him.

The members of one's own unit may be the first, either through teasing or through a set-up, to question a proffered trick identity. Partly to frighten the new undercover into the dangers of the role, though certainly as well to subject him to an initiation ritual, experienced members of an undercover unit may test him by setting up a fake drug deal; before they'll trust him, team members may make a green identity worker prove he can back them up and protect their safety. The undercover may be on provisional status until he's survived his first operation. As Girodo notes, "'Undercover operator' is an *achieved* position. Hence, regardless of the quality or duration of training, the status passage is never fully accomplished until after the trainee's first successful operation as a undercover agent."[41]

In the film *Rush*, jaded (but still handsome) undercover agent Jimmy purposely chooses an inexperienced partner from the academy. As he observes her during her training, Kristen has excellent stamina, great pluck, and appears too innocent to be a narc. As Jimmy readies Kristen to be his partner—which of course means her stepping into an undercover role as his girlfriend (and simultaneously into a real romantic alliance with him, since this is a Hollywood film, after all)—he subjects her to graduated tests of trustworthiness—what Goffman would call "vital tests"—much as if he were one of the bad guys and she the narc who had to pass muster with him. As he puts it, "One of us is fucked, the other is fucked."

Restoring Questioned Identities

In the field, undercover agents restore identities that have been questioned using a wide variety of means. A major factor in the choice is the seriousness of the accusation; this determines how much weight will need to be thrown behind a response. The inexperienced undercover operator may react aggressively at first, not always the best strategy—unless one is prepared to back up assertions. One of Lucky Luciano's bodyguards, Momo, brought his distrust of Vizzini's role to a head when he tripped the undercover in a bar. In an instant, Vizzini determined he would let the fight happen. He dropped a drink in Momo's lap, then applied his martial arts training when Momo responded by drawing his gun. Lucky could have ruled either way, especially since the gun only appeared late in the game, but he ended up by expressing his admiration for "Major Michael Cerra's" martial arts skills.

In another challenging situation, this time in Thailand, Vizzini's preparedness to suffer physically may have been what kept him alive. His readiness to withstand violence made him out to be "better than" a cop. When his captors accused him, "You work for the police," steered him toward a hotel room closet, and tried to break his hand in the door, he kept his cool, enough to say (or to imagine later that he'd said), "I will tell you anything you want to hear, whether it's the truth or not. But if you keep this up, you might as well kill me." Vizzini's cool kept him alive. When he awoke, his interrogator explained, "You must understand why we had to do this. A police agent would have cracked and revealed himself. Now we know we can trust you." Notably, Vizzini held fast to his cover as he explained to the emergency-room doctor who found that he had three broken bones in his hand and a fractured knuckle that he'd had an accident working on his Air Force plane.

Vizzini's quick movement to the offensive worked well under a variety of circumstances. He made a quick and clever decision when his veracity was challenged in a gun deal. Flanked by accomplices, his primary target said, "My primitive friend does not think you really have any gold. Ahmed says he can tell because inside you are nervous and jumpy. He still thinks we should bury you in the sand up to your neck and let him work on your eyeballs with the heated point of a knife." Vizzini made an immediate gesture that served two purposes, distracting the immediate threat and suggesting that the accusation was false. In a virtuosic act of misdirection, he grabbed one of the guns that were to be part of the deal and took a successful long-distance shot at a bottle balanced on a cross-beam fifty feet away and "the Professor's mind turned in another direction."[42]

From his interviews with undercovers who had penetrated high schools Jacobs found three major groupings of neutralization, or identity recovery, techniques: "sarcastic admission," "evidential refutation," and "belligerent denial/threatening retort." Undercovers judged instantaneously which technique would be most effective. In a split second, they would weigh the seriousness of the accusation and assess the group dynamics, including how many accusers were involved, how many neutral observers were available to be swayed, how quickly the other side was getting its information out, and the order in which each side was presenting its perspective.

Sarcastic admission of being a cop was often the smartest strategy to oppose an accusation that was only "half-meant"; a heavier-duty response would only unnecessarily escalate the situation. When performing a sarcastic admission, one of Jacobs' subjects emphasizes the value of the undercover's remaining nonchalant:

> Me and these kids ditched [class], and we were all in my car when one goes, "Is this a police car?" I just kind of looked at him, not knowing if he was joking or serious, but I just made a joke out of it. "Yeah, man," I said, "I'm a cop! My gun's in the glove box and I got the lights on top of the car. I'm John-ny Depp [actor who portrayed a fictional high school under-cover agent in the TV series 21 Jump Street], and I'm gonna arrest you!" They all just played along with it because I treated it like a joke and didn't say anything more about me being police.[43]

In choosing a sarcastic admission—on the assumption that the bad guy wouldn't believe that a sane cop would choose to make a poten-tially fatal admission of identity—the undercover can only hope that he thus zeroes out the game. At the opposite end of the spectrum are essentially passive techniques. A certain number of undercover agents survive potential identity discreditations by simply deflecting or ignoring any challenges of their identity as narcotics officers. Changing the subject can temporarily distract the bad guy from the hot issue. At best, however, changing the subject is a delaying tech-nique, allowing the undercover a short respite to consider which of the other techniques might best be applied.

A universally powerful technique of non-resistance is to play back to the bad guy *ad nauseum* a "broken record" of the suspicions he puts out, for example, by parroting back lines such as "I *am* a cop" until the bad guy tires out. It's possible to just keep agreeing with one's accuser, on the assumption that one can deflect a fight by fail-ing to engage. Playing right into the opponent's worst fears is a useful adjunct technique here.[44] One instructor advises, if the undercover finds himself in a situation in which the bad guy accuses him of be-ing a narc, he should "go [all the way] with" whatever he proposes, capitalize on his (probable) homophobia, and start to undress, invit-ing him to inspect his body for surveillance wires.

An undercover trainer conveys to our class, going with the flow can frequently be a good strategy. Like ourselves, he reminds them, bad guys make jokes, they blunder verbally, they do silly things. Remembering other ways of responding to an accusation besides the most instinctive aggressive one can resonate with some of those other qualities in one's accuser. When taken off guard, it is best to keep answering in line with the presentations already made: "As long as you base your answer on information you've already given, you're fine. But you have to keep track of what they know and what they don't know. ... Keep the story the same; don't change it." Embellishing, a temptation to any deceiver who can see he's beginning to succeed, can be the fatal blunder to the undercover, who should "Keep It Simple, Stupid" (K.I.S.S.). The triumphant undercover operator must remember the precise details not only of the behaviors he has seen (along with the times, locations, and others present) but especially of all those he has presented.

As long as one can make it all seem natural, going along with whatever the bad guy proposes need not present any danger. This strategy is not unlike the magic technique in which attention can be cast away from a potentially incriminating sign by first directing attention openly and fully toward it:

> If the magician desires to take attention away from some-
> thing, he looks at it. He puts the object down. Then he
> moves his eyes, hands, arms, body—even his remarks, and of
> course his interest—away from it. If the object is in his hand,
> he starts a line of attention to his face. Then he carries the
> attention away further with his eyes.

In the magic techniques concerned with directing attention, it is absolutely critical that the performer model "personally participat[ing] in the trick in the same way that he desires the spectator to react."[45]

To be used only in special cases is the empathic technique of mirroring the bad guy's sentiments back to him, with such dialogue as "You feel worried because we're about to do a big deal and you think I'm going to do you. I understand that." Like agreeing, mirroring is a strategy of non-resistance; however, it probably can prevail only in cases in which a baseline degree of camaraderie has been reached to permit such brotherly dialogue.

In the second technique Jacobs identified, evidential refutation, one may bring up past behaviors or assertions as support for the fictive identity. Some undercovers have bought group membership by participating in a limited (and pre-approved) fashion in non-drug-oriented criminal activities; mere participation can stanch suspicion, or support a criminal identity if the operator is being narced. In an infiltration of a private workplace, an undercover operator may decide to participate strategically in limited or token criminal behaviors when invited. If, for example, he is investigating internal thievery in a workplace, "if and when [he] participates in the internal theft operations in order to obtain evidence against the thieves, he keeps a record of all items stolen, and after the investigation is over, returns them to the company or pays for them." In general, an operator "should be allowed to participate in the talking stage [of criminal activities] only. A contingency plan must be developed to extract him from the situation before it becomes a criminal act."[46]

Though frequently discouraged in contemporary undercover practice, simulation of drug use once provided apparent behavior to which the undercover could point to demonstrate he was of the culture rather than an interloper. However, "simulation is the trickiest of ways undercover officers keep their behavior sufficiently distant from criminality so as to avoid jeopardizing investigations, yet sufficiently close to it in order to project convincingly corrupt images to those targeted."[47]

Because accepting an invitation to use drugs is a way of demonstrating that the undercover is who he says he is and not a cop, techniques for believably avoiding drug use over time are a core aspect of identity defense. To avoid having to simulate, Levine memorized and repeated many times the routine performed by one of the dealers he once targeted. When asked if he ever tried the drugs he sold, the dealer responded

> "*Me?*" Berdin looked at him in unfeigned astonishment, more than slightly offended. "I *sell* ze stuff," he said.

> Levine would use Berdin's manner, and that response in particular, at least a hundred times after that, when passing himself off undercover as a trafficker. It became his standard counter to any invitation to try the dope he was there to buy or sell, collect or deliver, when an outright refusal might have risked his cover.

When a slightly heavier-weight acting job was demanded, Levine would stave off invitations with the line, ""I'm flyin' already, okay? I'll save it for later."[48] Of course, he had to be able to "fly" believably.

Good judgment tells the undercover when to draw attention to his refusal to use drugs. As Donnie Brasco, Pistone strategized he might prevent future, more damaging scenes by making a big one early on:

> This one guy comes out of the john and comes over to me holding this little open vial. He holds it out to me and says, "Here, Don, have a snort."

> I smack his arm, sending the bottle flying and the cocaine spraying all over the place. I grab him by the lapels and hoist him. "I don't do that stuff," I say, "and you had no business offering it to me. Don't *ever* offer it to me again. I make money off it, but I don't use it. I keep my head clear at all times."[49]

The third of Jacobs' techniques, "belligerent denial/threatening retort, is best used in situations judged most likely to dissipate through escalation. Performing indignation at the very notion of being thought a liar is particularly interesting, because the technique deftly shifts the ground of conflict from the cop's identity to his character, a much less threatening region. One simple way to do this, Mathers recommends, and especially useful for a newbie, is to throw the accusation of being a cop back onto the bad guy, and see how *he* responds, making note of those techniques that seem more effective than others.

Mathers also advocates turning bad guys' own greed against them in a form of monetary aikido. He has found it effective, when accused of being a cop, just to show the bad guys the buy money. Often their greed overpowers their suspicion. Larry Wansley found that playing to the corrupt town sheriff's greed was the only way to save his life when he was "taken for a little walk" in the small town in which he had been opening investigations. With a gun cocked to the back of his head, Wansley considered the available options:

> As I stood looking down into the hastily dug grave, my mind raced. I needed a strong line of bullshit in the worst way and was having difficulty deciding what tack to take. If I told him

my mob bosses would take offense at his killing one of their own and would come looking for him to square things, it would likely appeal to his already exaggerated love of bravado. He might pull the trigger just to prove to me and everyone else that he could not be intimidated by outsiders.

And if I admitted that I was an FBI agent, he would just be more careful to hide the body where no one would ever find it.

Wansley betted everything—successfully—on the sheriff's greed:

"You dumb motherfucker," I shouted, "you're about to give yourself the biggest fucking you've ever had. I don't know where you're getting your information, but it's bullshit. Pure fucking bullshit. I've been shooting straight with you since the minute I got to this asshole town. I can make you a lot of money—a hell of a lot of money—and you're ready to just toss that away on some half-baked rumor you've heard. Goddammit, man, you're going to let the sweetest fucking deal you ever had go right out the window ...

"There's potential here you haven't even thought about," I said. "My people know ways of making money that you won't have dreams about in the next hundred years. And they know they need you to make their plans work. Fuck, it was me who told them that. Now you're standing here wanting to blow my head off. You stupid motherfucker."[50]

Wansley's technique combines Mathers' method of invoking the bad guy's greed with the Jacobs' belligerent denial/threatening retort .

When the bad guy demands the undercover's wallet, Taylor suggests challenging back, "Why? So you can write me a ticket?" The technique is similar to the typical "badass" posture described by Jack Katz in *Seductions of Crime:* When a badass attempts to "mind fuck" his victim, he in turn adopts the victim posture, thrusting his subjugated opponent into a position of guilty compliance.[51] One notes as well strong parallels with the con game, in the deeper victimization to which the con artist pretends that functions to maintain the mark's loyalty.

Although Abagnale's unmasking ultimately resulted in his leaving his role altogether, it also demonstrated what a skillful identity player he had been all along when, in Jacobs' terms, he shifted the ground of conflict from his identity to his character by nonverbal behavior alone. Abagnale's characterization and performance choices, sometimes adopted automatically, threw his identity assailants into just the position in which he would need them. In one situation, he had just used his pilot's ID to board a complimentary flight that he was going to deadhead from New Orleans to Miami, when the real pilot received a call from the ground, and asked to see his Pan Am identification card and his FAA license. It was the first time a pilot had scrutinized his painstakingly prepared professional documentation.

When the plane landed, Abagnale was greeted by two sheriffs who escorted him back to their offices. He quickly decided that irritation was going to be his best theme for the scene. Asked once again for his identification, "I slapped the phony documents down on the desk, acting as if I'd been accused of selling nuclear secrets to the Russians." The officers examined them sheepishly and then "handed them back with a nervous smile. They both gave the impression they'd just arrested the President for jaywalking." The faker remained on the offensive, which allowed him to assume the power of his captors: "I acted miffed and they acted like I should have been acting—like they wanted to be somewhere else. Oddly enough, I grew relaxed and confident as time passed, dropped my pose of righteous indignation and tried to ease their obvious discomfiture."[52]

Whatever neutralization strategy he chooses, the undercover must keep his wits about him to respond in a way that is consistent with the culture. When Pistone's Mafia targets demanded he yield up the name of a contact in Miami, the undercover felt he had to play by the culture's rules, which meant to resist strongly the desire to provide the specifics of the reference:

> I knew all along, from the time he pushed it to the gun, that I would give him a name. Because once he went that far in front of everybody, he wouldn't back off. But even among fellow crooks you don't ever give up a source or contact easily. You have to show them that you're a stand-up guy, that you're careful and tough in protecting people you've done jobs with. So I was making it difficult for them. I acted as if I were really torn, mulling it over.

Seemingly reluctantly handing them the name of an informant he had worked with months before—and hoping, a bit feverishly, that the informant would remember to respond as instructed—Pistone knew the game wouldn't be over, even if a clean report came back. To end it, he would have to shift into the dominant position:

> You can't go through all that and then just say, "I'm glad you found out I'm okay, and thank you very much." The language of the street is strength; that's all they understand. I had been called. I had to save some face, show everybody they couldn't mess with me. I had to clear the air. I had to smack somebody.[53]

Working the bad guy's knowledge and experience is what the skillful undercover does, no matter what his neutralization strategy. One undercover operator from our training group found that, by playing directly into a dealer's expectations and off of his own prior history with him, he was able to conjure up enough reversals to make a bad-cop cover story work for him. He short-circuited any accusation of being cop by admitting to being one straight out:

> I talked one guy into selling me dope telling him I was a cop. That was one of my greatest accomplishments. Well, he knew I was a cop, because he was an informant that went bad. Then I convinced him that I was a bad cop, and afterwards I'd go up and talk to him in my undercover car. I told him I was having money problems, and I was selling the product on the side. I'd find people, I'd shake them down, I'd take their dope, and I'd arrest them. I convinced him of that to the point where he started selling me dope knowing that I was a cop; he thought I was a dirty cop. And then when we ended up arresting him, he turned me in to Internal Affairs. He said I was a dirty cop; I told them that was my cover.

This player's experience demonstrates how an undercover's knowledge of the scene structure in which an undercover operative gets narced allows the roleplayer to manipulate the elements for his own success and survival.

Whatever the technique, the point of neutralizing an attack is to permit the roleplay to continue. Thus, the act of restoring a questioned identity is tantamount to clearing the channel for performance, doing the interpersonal business that keeps a scene in motion. Whether the occasion calls for more or less direct modes of allaying suspicions matters less than that it inevitably requires a split-second choice about what the most effective technique is likely to be. That fluency in decision-making is the crucial element in the performance knowledge of the undercover, calling on everything he knows about the bad guy—and himself.

Assisted Suicide

In both literature and life, some undercover identity workers seem deliberately to dance near the flame, going most deeply and most fantastically into a roleplay at the moment it threatens to go up in smoke. Some agents have experienced their identities' passing muster and surviving under life-threatening conditions. They prove they can make cases and perform their roles and their jobs in support of their national or local rules of evidence. They drop role when necessary, testifying believably in court (another roleplaying virtuosity). They earn the admiration of their colleagues as others recount their heroic and virtuosic deeds. Yet they have not yet done with their roles. These are players for whom the ego and the play challenges of their undercover role remain real temptations.

Mathers confessed that, in his undercover work, "I've said things that I shouldn't have said, because I was trying to be a smart ass. I've done things that I shouldn't have done, that, in retrospect, were dangerous and maybe not necessary." The reinforcement one gets from one's most obvious, immediate audience—the bad guy—can goad one to higher performance challenges, as in the cop who excitedly reported that he pushed the envelope in a roleplay because "they liked me, they *really* liked me."[54]

Undercovers have enjoyed testing how far they can push the bad guy's credulity and good will. One used the "obvious" name "Nick DeNarco"; he was so proud of this coinage that he kept pushing it toward the bad guy, never with any apparent recognition. In another situation, an undercover for the Royal Canadian Mounted Police signed his actual commissioner's name to a credit card receipt for a deal, again without notice from the bad guys and to the acclamation of his team members. Potentially riskiest was the sting in which the cops presented a receiving company name to which the bad guys should send their contraband liquor; any bad guy who knew his Sicilian Mafia terminology would know "Zbirri Liquors" means "Cop Liquors." All of these plays with names were ways of showing off.

Cops working undercover often play for a secondary audience as well, their back-up team and colleagues. They may devise opportunities to increase their status with their co-workers by trying to slip an in-joke past the bad guys. "What we're trying to do," Mathers explains, "is to screw each other up in a friendly way." While appearing to continue business with the bad guy, he once referred obliquely and as an in-joke to his support team to a television program aired the previous night.

The surveillance team may also test the undercover's ability to hold his own. On one occasion that Mathers was working undercover, his surveillance team called him back into the hotel room where he was about to do a deal. When he picked up the phone, they quipped, "Do you think you could put some powder or something on that bald spot on the top of your head? It's giving off an awful glare. We're getting the sun from the window in the camera." Mathers speaks with both affection and respect for his partners: "They would never do anything to jeopardize either the investigation or your safety, but they know how far to go" in their gaming. Forcing that split between the apparent and the actual audience for one's performance is one feature of a testing performance.

To dance too close to the flame may well mark the end of a role-play. However, planning rather than hubris may end a role, whether it has been played for a particular bad guy and the present scene or been played out over the long haul. Some roles, like cases, necessarily "have a self-destruct/disclosure quality with a necessary progression to discovery." The nesting of one cover story within another permits the "reveal" of a second-level cover as the outermost cover story is blown. New York Police Department Detective Sam Skeete, who was a black Latino, planned ahead for the undercover scenarios that enabled him to do cocaine deals in a bar. His partner, Alicia Parker, who was black and occasionally played the role of his girlfriend, would publicly turn on him during the take-down, or arrest, in essence blowing her cover as a means of protecting his. When the cops rushed in on the prearranged signal, Skeete would "revert" to Spanish, protest "No hablo Ingles," and hiss to the Colombian drug dealer in Spanish "*No:* Don't talk, you don't have to tell the cops anything." In a moment, Alicia would take out her badge, "and it's supposed to be, like, she betrayed me." Because the undercover was aligned on the short end of the scenario with the bad guy, he was far less likely to be suspected. Skeete would pepper the soup by threatening Alicia in English, "*You're dead.*"[55]

Informant identities can be protected by similar methods. Framing someone else in a group as an informer helps divert suspicion:

> The technique involves pulling someone in for interrogation or arresting him on a real charge or pretext. The officer then drives the person back to his usual haunt after a couple of hours. While dropping him off, the officer acts very friendly and shortly afterward he and other officers arrest or interrogate someone else in the group. This will generate suspicion against the person who was first picked up, helping to protect the actual informer.[56]

False identities and biographies may conceivably be classified as to whether discovery is inherent in them, as in many types of con games, or may be infinitely concealed. In some forms of identity performance, for example, the moment of identity disclosure is built into both role and scenario design. In Philadelphia in the late 1970s, in a confrontation with a mugger, the "'Grandpop' [decoy] suddenly straightens up, pulls a gun and announces he's a policeman."[57]

The technique of staged arrest was discovered early on. Having arranged to have himself arrested in advance of a major take-down, Vidocq came face to face in jail with a group of his former comrades:

> When I ... join[ed] the other prisoners, I pretended much surprise at finding all the party here; none appeared to have the least idea of the part which I had played. Neveu alone regarded me with distrust; and on my demanding the cause, he said, that by the way in which they had been pursued and interrogated, he could not help suspecting that I was the denouncer. I feigned much indignation, and fearing that this opinion might be disseminated, I assembled the prisoners,

and informing them of Neveu's suspicions, I demanded if they thought me capable of selling my comrades? and on their answering in the negative, Neveu was compelled to apologise to me. It was important to me that these suspicions should thus be destroyed; for I knew that certain death would be my doom if they had been confirmed.[58]

Vidocq artfully used belligerent denial and his deep understanding of group dynamics to sway audience sentiment to his side in an identity-testing situation.

In staging contemporary operations, the undercover and the back-up team often arrange to have the undercover agent arrested along with the bad guys so as to preserve, rather than burn, his cover.[59] He may be interrogated by the "outside" investigator along with the bad guys. When it comes time for him finally to leave the operation, it is ideal if he can leave in such a way that he can return if the investigation needs to be resumed, using a pretext such as the illness of a beloved but distant relative.[60] Later and inconspicuously, the under-cover agent is released from "custody" and returned to duty—with any luck, in another location. A narc arrested under this strategy must create a story about his "bust" that concurs with the timeline that the bad guy perceives as appropriate for a bad guy who got caught. He must also wait an amount of time that will seem believable in the drug culture he is infiltrating before appearing and attempting to buy again.[61]

Early in his Turkish investigations, Vizzini faced an opportunity to stage an arrest of the number-one drug smuggler in the country but needed, in this high-profile case, to preserve his cover. He therefore arranged to give commands to the arresting officers by radio from a helicopter. In another case, he arranged to have his exuberant greeting of the drug trafficker serve as the take-down signal for his armed allies to move in. Here, the drama of recognition moves to its height, as the scene of betrayal comes face to face with that of justice.

Sometimes it's all too clear when a role has reached the end of its natural life and must be retired, even if less spectacularly than in a take-down. One undercover officer had drawn on his experience as a bodybuilder to construct an undercover identity that incorporated this avocation. Throughout the time he played this trick identity, he had to continue to work out and to shave his body hair. He had to be prepared to demonstrate through the most basic outward signs that he was who he professed to be, should a bad guy insist he roll up his pant leg to show off his smooth, muscled skin. As the undercover both aged and grew tired of body shaving, he ran into more frequent challenges of his profession of identity, and it seemed wise to retire it and to develop another.

Bumping up against unintended consequences of maintaining a trick identity may also set into motion a player's relinquishing of his role. While posing as a pediatrician, Abagnale received notice on the ward of a "blue baby." Not understanding the jargon, the impostor quipped about where the green babies might be found. (Fortunately, the staff under Abagnale's supervision knew full well what the term meant, and the baby survived.) He wrote: "The incident shook me. I realized I was playing a role that had reached its limits. I'd been lucky so far, but I suddenly knew some child could die as a result of my impersonation." He voluntarily ceased playing doctors.

One has to give credit to an iconic roleplayer who recognizes when he can't keep it up. To impersonate a Harvard-trained lawyer, Abagnale had actually passed the state bar exam on his third try, and had also passed muster in fulfilling his work responsibilities. However, in choosing this high-profile professional identity, Abagnale opened himself up to the forcible camaraderie of a member of the Ivy Brotherhood:

> He was delighted to meet me. He was practically delirious with joy. I have since learned something about Harvard men. They're like badgers. They like to stick together in their own barrows. A lone badger is going to find another badger. A Harvard man in a strange area is going to find another Harvard man. And they're going to talk about Harvard.
>
> This one pounced on me immediately, with all the enthusiasm of Stanley encountering Livingstone in darkest Africa. When had I graduated? Who had my instructors been? Who were the girls I knew? To what clubs had I belonged? What pubs had I frequented? Who had my friends been?

Fending the Harvard man off for a time, Abagnale eventually realized that he didn't have enough personal knowledge to substantiate his own claim and "like the proverbial Arab, I folded my tent and silently stole away."[62]

Ego Death

Narcing scenes provide insight into the complex relations between actor and character, actor and audience, and character and audience. A weird collusion between two competing practices produces the positive constructions of the undercover role, the effacement of certain aspects of the self (such as one's police training and knowledge of the jargon), and the elevation of such others as one's real work and avocational experiences. This means that a working social identity has a singularly strong, conscious, and *performed* relation to a stylized profile of the self, and that the processes both of establishing a fictive character and of responding to an accusation by denying its fictiveness are about tantalizingly partial presentations and withdrawals that tease out our notions about the real and the whole, in body and in character. The undercover trick identity highlights the relationship between the singular bodies we inhabit and the fragments of multiple selves from which we all cobble together a working identity.

The transition issues associated with undercover work also carry implications about adaptation and adjustment in identity generally. The experience of an identity worker for whom entering a role and then exiting it are highly functional points up the ways in which identities are learned, developed, related to each other, and discarded, even for those who never consider themselves to be roleplaying in the first place. That identities may die, while players carry on, suggests that players' roles evolve, borrowing from past roles, anticipating future encounters, and blending the positions of audience and performer. The development in time of an undercover trick identity, in concert with the needs and projections of specific bad guys—or of a con artist developing his needy mark—accentuates the scenic, relational underpinnings of identity for all of us, not only for those virtuosic identity artists found plying their trades, on both sides of the law, in tacit tandem.

Appendix:

Scenario and Scenarist as Virtuosi: The "Art-Cons" of Allen Funt and James P. Coyle & Mal Sharpe

I n some sense, the con is always played for the wit of it, for the lark of creating a convincing reality and having one's opponent drink it down. The wide literature on revenge scenarios, pranks, and practical jokes—not to mention verbal jokes—attests to the beauty of a masterful blueprint for deceptions in which any material gain is negligible or beside the point. Hoaxes that provide no material benefit to their practitioners at once display the outrageousness embedded in many of these risky ploys, involve careful judgments about how "much" performance is right to accomplish the deed, and rely on precise timing between performers, as well as between performers and mark. The similarities between purely artistic hoaxes and both undercover performances and con games highlight the artistic judgments that practitioners on both sides of the law make at every moment in their personal and scenic deceptions, though their ultimate end remain in focus.

Practitioners of artistic cons are linked with popular entertainment as well as with performance art. Their methods are investigatory, exploitative, and virtuosic, their extremity and wit showcasing the qualities associated with exemplary identity and scenario work on both sides of the law.

For a couple of feral years in the early 1960s, James P. Coyle and Mal Sharpe staged what they called "taped terrorizations" with unwitting suspects on the streets of San Francisco. Coyle, a self-described con man who claimed to have talked his way into 160 jobs before he turned 24, was the ideal counterpart to the slower, hovering, deep-socketed Mal Sharpe.[1] Carrying hidden recording equipment, the pair identified marks and approached and engaged them in elaborate and often outrageous scenarios that tested the limits of credibility, rationality, trust, and morality. Coyle's function as the fast-talking, absolutely straight fellow was typically to open the conversation with their mark, while Sharpe filled in aspects of the scenario, finishing Coyle's sentences and suggestions in ways that inevitably sharpened the danger of the two's being found out, much like an experienced con team playing an inside joke possibly too far.

A scene they call "Druggist" implicates a local professional in a dodgy conversation when the two pay a call to inquire about buying a solution with which to sterilize some surgical equipment: Having read a few medical books that morning, as he says, Coyle expresses his wish to perform heart surgery on his indigent friend, Sharpe, in the back of his station wagon, which he has parked behind the shop:

> COYLE: Let me just say first of all, I'm not a doctor. I'm go-ing to perform an operation—what you'd call an operation—on this man. I think I've read enough about the thing that I can do it.
>
> SHARPE: I've agreed, I've agreed.[2]

Naturally, the pharmacist is alarmed by this proposal, and ardently tries to dissuade the pair from their plan, which, as the scene goes on, only embroils him further in the plot: If he has a moral conflict over *their* performing this surgery themselves and has more medical training than they, then perhaps *he'd* like to perform the operation?

Other scenes—dealing with other absurd medical practices, para-psychological and paranormal phenomena, and shady business schemes—demonstrate the duo's dazzlingly imaginative game plans and often virtuosic executions of them, as well as their performance skills in plausibly torquing the reality of their audiences. Like "Drug-gist," a number of Coyle & Sharpe scenarios were staged in small businesses, where the team approached someone in his professional role and asked advice. Presenting to a local florist their interest in "florahumanism," or in "abnegat[ing] [sic] part of our humanism in favor of a floral existence—a plant existence—and, if possible, get growth from within our systems." Coyle demands, "Let me ask you this: Would you like to be a flower?" Answers the florist diffidently, "Not particularly." Both jump on him, as if bringing to light a key logical flaw in his objection: "But you haven't *been* a flower." In crafting these ensnaring scenarios, Coyle & Sharpe create a paradox: a space that features the mark's idiosyncratic responses as uniquely interesting while locking him in the scenario's evolving grip.

In their marks' own retail environments, the performance duo openly recorded their interactions with—indeed, it would have been hard to conceal—a bulky reel-to-reel tape recorder. So their marks knew they were engaged in a performance, and responded for the tape and for posterity. By contrast, the premise of Allen Funt's *Candid Microphone* and later *Candid Camera* was that people's spontaneous behavior under extraordinary circumstances was far more interesting than any "performance" they might conjure up knowingly in front of recording equipment.

Funt was enchanted with his ability to conceal his machinery in a briefcase. A reduction in the size of recording technology enabled him to gain access to subjects heretofore unavailable to him, "no longer confined to the tiny radius our earlier nonportable equipment had made necessary, no longer subject to the risks of trailing a heavy cable behind me and thus tipping off my subjects about what I was up to."[3] He contemplated using video as a training device in professional and even quite personal settings:

> One of my pipe dreams is to open a studio which would charge a nominal fee for helping people see themselves as others see them. I think women would spend a small fortune to see how they look when they sit down in a chair, walk down a flight of steps, and get in and out of an automobile. I think men have a right to know how they sound when they're asking the boss for a raise, or dictating a letter, or talking to their wives on the telephone. I wouldn't be surprised if many marriages could be reinforced by secret recordings of the things a man and wife quarrel about. And why shouldn't a doctor be willing to pay a fee to hear exactly how his bedside manner sounds to his patients?

The provocateur felt he provided his public with a vicarious opportunity to imagine themselves as seen by others in unusual situations.

Allen Funt's provocations draw on the traditional vocabulary of the street con. He "finds" a purse filled with $17,000's worth of $100 bills and accosts people with it, trying to see who will claim it as their own. The operator of the Pigeon Drop, his marks' greed becomes a major player in the scenario. However, the center for Funt is not the act of greed itself, but the process by which a given mark comes to the decision that the purse is for him—the combination of moral reasoning, the behavioral idiosyncrasies that appear in the face of crisis, and the desire to outsmart—or at least be as smart as—the situation.

Much as in Coyle & Sharpe's work, Funt's scenes are often morally questionable. He orchestrates a scene in which he chains a secretary to her desk and calls a locksmith to release her at lunchtime because he's misplaced the key. Or he records a conversation with his electrician in which he asks him about rates for building an electric chair. Many of Funt's scenes have pushed people to choose whether to apply their professional skills in extraordinary and frequently problematic circumstances.

Funt shares many scenario settings with Coyle & Sharpe. Whereas the duo tries to convince a fruit seller about the benefits of offering "proven" (that is, used) apples to his customers, Funt bargains with a fruit seller about the price of his nectarines and grapes as he nibbles on samples. Funt's chaining of the secretary to the desk is matched by Coyle & Sharpe's scene sketching out a job for a keen job seeker in a "Living Hell" with bats, snakes, and maniacs. An earnest, mid-twentieth century work ethic undergirds both types of scenes.

Many of both Funt's and Coyle & Sharpe's scenarios deal with the context for public behavior. A Funt scene has the host continually interrupt his neighbors at a baseball game to ask them to explain what is going on, trying their willingness to help a stranger. Likewise, a Coyle & Sharpe scenario involves the pair's asking their mark how he would feel about their erasing the world populace's ability to speak their native languages and teaching them a new language from scratch, one that would serve the pair's unstated political aims.

Like undercovers who think of themselves as straight men or directors of others' performances, Funt designs the scenarios for his dramas and regards himself as "just the straight man." By contrast with law-enforcement and with perpetrators of con games, however, Funt's scenarios are open-ended; they provide a means for the mark to enter into and catapult the scenario into a new direction, which made a perfect fit with the young marks with whom the showman especially liked to work. And of course they were usually tried with multiple marks, in order to get the most broadcast-worthy material. In a scenario at the Henry Street Settlement House in New York, Funt posed as a visiting music consultant who helped children choose the right instrument for them:

> Our first three tries were dismal. ... Then I met a young violinist named David. Up to that day he had had three scheduled violin lessons. On the first, he had come without his violin because his mother hadn't bought it yet; on the second, his teacher had told him about the "E" and "G" strings. His third lesson had been called off because his teacher had a cold. ..

> I painted a picture of the future. I tried to transport him to a scene twenty years ahead. He had mastered his violin. His teachers were bursting with pride in his progress. It was time for his first solo recital. The day of the concert in Carnegie Hall had arrived. "The audience fills the house," I told him. "Their whispering turns to silence as the houselights begin to dim. You, David, are ready to come out on the stage. You walk to the footlights, bow, and, as the enthusiastic applause dies down, you place your violin under your chin. And now," I continued, "I want you to play for me just what you'll play for that audience." Almost transfixed, the boy raised his violin, paused, and looked at me for an eloquent moment. Then he said, "E? ... Or G?"

Although Funt's subject responded beautifully to the scene Funt laid out for him, one could imagine any number of televisable responses. Neither the law-enforcement nor the law-breaking scenarists would be likely to surrender this much control over outcome.

Whereas the more typical con game plays upon people's greed with a particular hope in mind, these art-cons' design quite consciously leads their marks into increasingly ridiculous premises, a technique that depends more heavily on responding in the moment to subjects' responses. As Funt explained, "I apply the stimulus by gradually building up the satirical element of reaction. I progressively make the situation sillier and sillier to see at what point the subject suddenly opens his eyes and sees. "But"—as in Coyle & Sharpe's scenes—"in case after case, that point never arrives."[4] By contrast with the con artist, what Funt searches for is the unexpected in subjects' compliance with his scenarios. All he needs is for them to "buy" the initial scenario; the character of their response is ideally as individual as they can make it, and what makes it broadcastworthy is the range of responses he gets to the same scenario set-up.

A major theme in Funt's scenarios is the underbelly of salesmanship—and, by extension, of con artistry—itself.[5] When a proprietor puts together a special deal and presents it as unavoidably appealing to the customer, how is the customer to evaluate the deal? Or when a proprietor develops generous business practices that appear to yield him no immediate profit, how far can these be pushed before a profit motive will reassert itself? Funt hassles a waitress about the coffee shop's "Blue Plate Special," thereby showing off the con artistry—on both seller's and buyer's parts—involved in ordinary sales promotions. Funt orders the special, then requests one substitution after another for each of the items that comprise it, till there is nothing left of the original "Special." The waitress wants no part of his request, but Funt fails to see any problem: "I want this dinner, but I can't find anything I like on it."[6]

Funt always blows his own cover in the course of a scene—indeed, he regards the "reveal" of the scene as its key part. He is thus intensely interested in the variety of behaviors his marks can display upon learning that the entire scenario is quite literally a set-up. If the showman sizes up his mark as likely to "[break] into a swift run" on hearing the news that he is on television, he at least, at some point during the scenario, gets the mark to hand him something of his own as a kind of insurance policy that he'll stick around long enough to consider signing a release form.[7]

In the scenarios of both Allen Funt and Coyle & Sharpe, human beings are invited to extend their sense of the everyday world, and to contribute their professional expertise to customers off all well-worn paths. In an episode from *Candid Microphone*, Funt visits a tailor to have a zoot suit made for "a boxing kangeroo": Inquires the tailor gingerly, "A kangaroo is inclined to be a little wild, isn't he?" Funt reassures him, "No, this kangaroo is trained to box, but it only boxes other kangaroos." Funt muses about how many fittings he should plan for. Calculates the tailor, as if this were a request he's handled any number of times before: "Well, for a kangaroo, I'd probably need three fittings."[8]

Richard H. Blum talks about deception that is practiced essentially as a status game, "an act which seems to draw its humor from an alteration of status so that one man dominates as another man is made the fool," as being much more common among men than women.[9] By contrast with the con games treated in Chapter 4, in which the mark may well know he's been taken, Font ensures that, in any footage he shows, he's the one playing the role of fall guy, if there is one. Rather than make marks out to be fools, cowards, or inept at their jobs, Allen Funt and fellow art-cons James P. Coyle & Mal Sharpe ensure that they afford their participants the opportunity for their acting and scenic virtuosity to shine—not at the mark's expense, but to his glory.

SOURCES

Abagnale & Associates
1996   Press kit. Collection of author.
Abagnale, Frank W., Jr. and Stan Redding
1980   *Catch Me if You Can*. New York: Pocket Books.
ABC After School Special
1985   *High School Narc*. Television program aired 4 December. Collection of the Museum of TV & Radio, New York City.
Adams, Dennis E. et al.
1992   *National Association of Bunco Investigators' Handbook*. May. Baltimore: National Association of Bunco Investigators. Collection of author.
Adler, Patricia A.
1993   *Wheeling and Dealing: An Ethnography of an Upper-Level Drug Dealing and Smuggling Community*. New York: Columbia University Press.
Alvarez, Tony
1993   *Undercover Operations Survival in Narcotics Investigations*. Springfield, IL: Charles C. Thomas.
Anderson, Kingdon Peter
1988   *Undercover Operations: A Manual for the Private Investigator*. Boulder, CO: Paladin Press.
Bailey, William G., ed.
1989   *The Encyclopedia of Police Science*. New York: Garland Publishing.
Barefoot, J. Kirk
1983   *Undercover Investigations*, 2nd ed. Boston: Butterworth.
Baudrillard, Jean
1984   "The Precession of Simulacra." In *Art After Modernism: Rethinking Representation*. Brian Wallis, ed. New York: The New Museum of Contemporary Art. pp. 253–81.
Baughman, Enest W.
1966   *Type and Motif-Index of the Folktales of England and North America*. New York: Walter De Gruyter.
Beene, Capt. Charles, Ret.
1992   *Decoy Ops: Fighting Street Crime Undercover*. Boulder, CO: Paladin Press.
Bell, Quentin
1989   *Bad Art*. Chicago: University of Chicago Press.

Bell & Howell Close-Up
1963   *Money for Burning*. Collection of the Museum of TV & Radio, New York City.

Bernstein, Judith
1977   "Fakes." In *In the Eye of the Beholder: Fakes, Replicas and Alterations in American Art*. Yale University Art Gallery. pp. 42–43.

Best, Joel and David Luckenbill
1982   *Organizing Deviance*. Englewood Cliffs, NJ: Prentice-Hall.

Blackmore, John
1978   "Deception on the Side of the Law." *Police Magazine*. Vol. 1. No. 4. p. 2. September.

Blum, Richard H.
1972   *Deceivers and Deceived: Observations on Confidence Men and Their Victims, Informants and Their Quarry, Political and Industrial Spies and Ordinary Citizens*. Springfield, IL: Charles C. Thomas.

Bogdan, Robert
1988   *Freak Show: Presenting Human Oddities for Amusement and Profit*. Chicago: University of Chicago.

Bogomolny, Robert L.
1983   "Counterfeiting." In *Encyclopedia of Crime and Justice*. Sanford H. Kadish, ed. Volume 3. New York: The Free Press. pp. 291–92.

Bok, Sissela
1989   *Lying: Moral Choice in Public and Private Life*. New York: Vintage Books.

Boles, Jacqueline and Phillip Davis
1983   "False Pretense and Deviant Exploitation: Fortunetelling as a Con." *Deviant Behavior*. Volume 4. pp. 375–94.

Boston Globe, The
1983   "Bogus Professor Said to Have Many Identities." March 23. p. 7.

Bowyer, J. Barton
1980   *Cheating: Deception in War and Magic, Games and Sports, Sex and Religion, Business and Con Games, Politics and Espionage, Art and Science*. New York: St. Martin's Press.

Breslin, Sgt. John J., Jr.
1979   "Street Crime Unit." *Law and Order*. May.

Breznitz, Schlomo
1984   *Cry Wolf: The Psychology of False Alarms*. Hillsdale, NJ: Lawrence Erlbaum Associates.

Brown, Michael F.
1989   "Criminal Informants." In *The Encyclopedia of Police Science*. William G. Bailey, ed. New York: Garland Publishing. pp. 108–11.

Buckwalter, Art
1983   *Surveillance and Undercover Investigation*. Boston: Butterworth.

Burnett, Andrew
1992   "Coin Faking in the Renaissance." In Mark Jones, ed. (1992). *Why Fakes Matter: Essays on Problems of Authenticity*. Avon, Britain: The British Museum. pp. 15–22.

California Department of Justice
n.d.   "Police Undercover Operations." ca. early 1980s. Collection of Gary T. Marx.

Campbell, Marian and Claude Blair
1992   "'Vive le Vol': Louis Marcy, Anarchist and Faker." In *Why Fakes Matter: Essays on Problems of Authenticity*. Mark Jones, ed. Avon, Britain: The British Museum. pp. 134–50.

Candid Camera
1947   Show aired 5 May. Collection of the Museum of TV & Radio, New York City.

Candid Microphone
1947   Show aired 14 July. Collection of the Museum of TV & Radio, New York City.

Cannell, J. C.
1973   *The Secrets of Houdini*. New York: Dover.

Caplan, Gerald M.
1980   *ABSCAM Ethics: Moral Issues and Deception in Law Enforcement*. Pensacola Bay, FL: Ballinger Publications.

Carroll, John M.
1991   *Confidential Information Sources: Public and Private*. Boston: Butterworth-Heinemann.

Cawley, Janet
n.d.   "Many Names, But Who Is He?" *Chicago Tribune* story, ca. March 1983. Collection of Gary T. Marx.

Chambers, Bruce W.
1990   "J. S. G. Boggs—The Dimensions of Money." In *J. S. G. Boggs: Smart Money (Hard Currency)*. Tampa Museum of Art. pp. 7–16.

Cheek, John Charles and Tony Lesce
1988   *Plainclothes and Off-Duty Officer Survival*. Springfield, IL: Charles C. Thomas.

Clunas, Craig
1992   "Connoisseurs and Aficionados: The Real and the Fake in Ming China (1368-1644)." In *Why Fakes Matter: Essays on Problems of Authenticity*. Mark Jones, ed. Avon, Britain: The British Museum. pp. 151-56.

Cohen, Bernard & Chaiken, Jan
1987   *Investigators Who Perform Well*. National Institute of Justice, United States Department of Justice.

Cole, Sonia
1956   *Counterfeit*. New York: Abelard-Schuman.

Coller, Barbara
1991   *The Realm of the Coin: Money in Contemporary Art.* Hempstead, NY: Hofstra Museum.
Connor, Michael
1988   *Forgive? Forget It!* Boulder: Paladin Press.
Cooke, Edward S., Jr.
1977   *In the Eye of the Beholder: Fakes, Replicas and Alterations in American Art.* New Haven: Yale University Art Gallery. p. 21.
Cooper, John
1994   *The Fugitive, A Complete Episode Guide, 1963–1967.* Ann Arbor, Michigan: Popular Culture, Ink.
Count, E. W.
1994   *Cop Talk: True Detective Stories from the NYPD.* New York: Pocket Books.
Coyle, James and Mal Sharpe
1964a   *The Absurd Impostors.* Warner Brothers. Audio recording.
1964b   *The Insane (But Hilarious) Minds of Coyle & Sharpe.* Warner Brothers. Audio recording.
1995   *Coyle & Sharpe: On the Loose.* Compact disc, 213CD.
Crime Control Digest
1984   "Lexington, KY, Debates Police Policies on Decoys." Vol. 18. No. 37. pp. 5-6. September.
Criminal Law Bulletin
1976   "Forgery—Use of Two 'Real' Names." Selected State Court Decisions. Vol. 12. No. 5. p. 615. September.
Danto, Arthur C.
1990   "Trompe L'Oeil and Transaction: The Art of Boggs." In *J. S. G. Boggs: Smart Money (Hard Currency)* . Tampa, FL: Tampa Museum of Art. pp. 25–31.
D.E.A. [pseudonym]
1981   *DEA Narcotics Investigator's Manual.* Boulder: Paladin Press.
Delattre, Edwin J.
1989   *Character and Cops: Ethics in Policing.* Washington, DC: American Enterprise Institute for Public Policy Research.
DePue, Roger
1995   Telephone interview with author. Berea, KY to Manassas, VA. July 20.
Doherty, Vincent P. and Monte E. Smith
1981   "Ponzi Schemes and Laundering—How Illicit Funds are Acquired and Concealed." *FBI Law Enforcement Bulletin.* November. Vol. 50. No. 11. pp. 5–11.
Douglas, Jack D. and John M. Johnson
1978   *Crime at the Top: Deviance in Business and the Professions.* Philadelphia: J. B. Lippincott.
Dutton, Denis
1983   *The Forger's Art.* Berkeley: University of California Press.

Edelhertz, Herbert, ed.
1987   *Major Issues in Organized Crime Control.* National Institute of Justice, United States Department of Justice. September.

Edgley, C. and R. C. Turner
1975   "Masks and Social Relations: An Essay on the Sources and Assumptions of Dramaturgical Social Psychology." *Humboldt Journal of Social Problems.* 3. (Fall/Winter).

Farace, Theodore and Andrew Camera
1975   "Confidence Games." *The Police Chief.* January. pp. 37–39.

Farber, M. A.
n.d.   "The Con Man." *New York Times Magazine.* post-1985.

Fijnaut, Cyrille and Marx, Gary T.
1995   *Undercover: Police Surveillance in Comparative Perspective.* New York: Springer.

Fitzkee, Dariel
1945*a*   *Showmanship for Magicians.* Pomeroy, OH: Lee Jacobs Productions. Fourth Edition.
1945*b*   *The Trick Brain.* 2nd edition. Oakland, CA: Magic Limited.
1945*c*   *Magic by Misdirection.* Oakland, CA: Magic Limited.

Flannery, Michael
1976   "Ex-Nun Now Decoy Hooker." *Criminal Justice Digest.* September. Volume 4. No. 9. pp. 7–9. Originally published in the *Chicago Sun-Times.*

Flynn, William J.
1976   "Forgery by Phone." *Journal of Police Science and Administration.* Vol. 4. No. 3. pp. 326- 330.

Fox, Deputy Commissioner Harry G.
1978   "Grandpop: The Senior Citizen Decoy." *Law and Order.* June. Vol. 26. No. 6. pp. 20–22.

Freimuth, Kenneth C.
1976   "Confidence Games." *Military Police Law Enforcement Journal.* Vol. 2. No. 2. Summer. pp. 41–44.

Fugitive, The
1963   "Never Wave Goodbye."

Funt, Allen
1952   *Eavesdropper at Large: Adventures in Human Nature with "Candid Mike" and "Candid Camera."* New York: Vanguard Press.

Gay, William G. and Robert G. Bowers
1985   *Targeting Law Enforcement Resources: The Career Criminal Focus.* National Institute of Justice, United States Department of Justice. September.

Gershman, Bennett L.
1982   "Entrapment, Shocked Consciences, and the Staged Arrest." *Minnesota Law Review.* Vol. 66. pp. 567 - 638.

Get Smart
1967   "Cutback at Control." Aired 21 January. Collection of Museum of TV & Radio, New York City.

Ginsberg, Elaine K.
1996   *Passing and the Fictions of Identity.* Durham, NC: Duke University Press.
Girodo, Michel
1984   "Entry and Re-entry Strain in Undercover Agents." In Vernon L. Allen and Evert van de Vliert, eds. *Role Transitions.* Plenum Publishing. pp. 169–79.
1985a   "Health and Legal Issues in Undercover Narcotics Investigation: Misrepresented Evidence." *Behavioral Sciences & the Law.* Vol. 3. No. 3. pp. 299–308.
1985b   "Psychological Factors in Undercover Narcotics Agents." *The Narcotics Officer.* Vol 1. Winter. pp. 59–62.
1991a   "Drug Corruption in Undercover Agents: Measuring the Risk." *Behavioral Sciences and the Law.* Vol. 9. pp. 361–70.
1991b   "Personality, Job Stress, and Mental Health in UC Agents." *Journal of Social Behavior and Personality.* Vol. 6. No. 7. pp. 375–390.
1991c   "Symptomatic   Reactions to Undercover Work." *Journal of Nervous and Mental Disease.* pp. 626–630.
1993   "The Mental Dangers of Undercover Work." *Law Enforcement Quarterly.* August–October. pp. 9–30.
Goddard, Donald
1988   *Undercover: The Secret Lives of a Federal Agent.* New York: Times Books.
Goffman, Erving
1952   "On Cooling the Mark Out: Some Aspects of Adaptation to Failure." *Psychiatry.* November. Volume 15. pp. 451–63.
1959   *The Presentation of Self in Everyday Life.* New York: Doubleday.
1963   *Stigma: Notes on the Management of Spoiled Identity.* New York: Simon & Schuster.
1969   *Strategic Interaction.* Philadelphia: University of Pennsylvania Press.
Goldberger, Peter
1983   "Forgery." In *Encyclopedia of Crime and Justice.* Sanford H. Kadish, ed. New York: The Free Press. pp. 795–97.
Goldblatt, David
1984   "Self-Plagiarism." *Journal of Aesthetics and Art Criticism.* Volume 43. No. 1. pp. 71–77.
Goleman, Daniel
1985   *Vital Lies, Simple Truths: The Psychology of Self-Deception.* New York: Simon and Schuster.
Goodman, Nelson
1968   *Languages of Art: An Approach to a Theory of Symbols.* Indianapolis: Bobbs-Merrill.
Goodrich, David L.
1973   *Art Fakes in America.* New York: Viking Press.
Gopnik, Adam
1997   "Doubting Vincent." *The New Yorker.* July 28. pp. 36–37.

Graham, Fred
1977   *The Alias Program.* Boston: Little, Brown and Company.

Hankiss, Agnes
1980   "Games Con Men Play: The Semiosis of Deceptive Interaction." *Journal of Communication.* Spring. n.p.

Harris, Neil P.
1981   *Humbug, The Art of P. T. Barnum.* Chicago: University of Chicago.

Hayduke, George
1988   *Make My Day! Hayduke's Best Revenge Techniques for the Punks in Your Life.* New York: Carol Publishing Group.
1993   *Righteous Revenge!* New York: Carol Publishing Group.

Heintzman, Ronald J. and Mirau, Stephen J.
1985   "Games of Deceit and Deception: Cracking Down on the Con." *Police Chief.* Vol. 52. No. 6. pp. 40-41.

Henderson, M. Allen
1985   *Flimflam Man: How Con Games Work.* Boulder: Paladin Press.

Hinkle, Douglas P.
1990   *Mug Shots: A Police Artist's Guide to Remembering Faces.* Boulder: Paladin Press.

Holland, Robert C.
1981   "Dramaturgical Scene Manipulation and its Importance for the False Pretender." *International Journal of Comparative and Applied Criminal Justice.* Spring. Vol. 5. No. 1. pp. 81–98.

Howard, Seymour
1992   "Fakes, Intentions, Proofs and Impulsion to Know: The Case for Cavaceppi and Clones." In *Why Fakes Matter: Essays on Problems of Authenticity.* Mark Jones, ed. Avon, Britain: The British Museum. pp. 51–62.

Hughes, William J.
1988   "Confidence Swindling: Crimes Against the Powerless." Bulletin, National Association of Bunco Investigators. Reprint of 1982 article. Bulletin 88-20. December 16. pp. 3–9.

I Was a Communist for the FBI
1953   "Little Boy Blue." Radio program. Collection of the Museum of TV & Radio, New York City.

International Criminal Police Review
1975   "Pyramid or Chain Referral Schemes." No. 288. May. pp. 144–49.

Irving, Clifford
1969   *Fake! The Story of Elmyr de Hory, the Greatest Art Forger of Our Time.* New York: McGraw-Hill.

Jackson, John
1992   *The Black Book of Revenge: The Complete Handbook of Hardcore Dirty Tricks and Schemes.* Fort Lee, NJ: Barricade Books.

Jacobs, Bruce A.
1992   "UC Drug-Use Evasion Tactics: Excuses and Neutralization." *Symbolic Interaction.* Vol. 15. No. 4. pp. 435–453.

1993*a*   "Getting Narced: Neutralization of Undercover Identity Discreditation."
           Deviant Behavior. Vol. 14. pp. 187–208.

1993*b*   "Undercover Deception Clues: A Case of Restrictive Deterrence." *Crimi-
           nology*. Vol. 31. No. 2. pp. 281–99.

1994   Anticipatory Undercover Targeting in High Schools." *Journal of Criminal
           Justice*. Vol. 22. No. 5. pp. 445–57.

1995   Telephone interview with author. Berea, KY to St. Louis, MO. July 13.

Jones, David A.

1986   *History of Criminology: A Philosophical Perspective*. New York: Greenwood
           Press.

Jones, Mark

1990   *Fake? The Art of Deception*. Berkeley: University of California Press.

Jones, Mark (ed.)

1992   *Why Fakes Matter: Essays on Problems of Authenticity*. Avon, Britain: The
           British Museum.

Kadish, Sanford H. (ed.)

1983   *Encyclopedia of Crime and Justice*. New York: The Free Press.

Katz, Jack

1988   *Seductions of Crime: Moral and Sensual Attractions of Doing Evil*. New York:
           Basic Books.

Kaufman, Gary

1996   Telephone interview with author. 8 February. Seattle to Lansing.

Kenny G

1995   "May We Graft Chicken Wings to Your Head in the Interest of Aviation?:
           The Insane But Hilarious Minds of Coyle & Sharpe." *LCD*. June.

Kleinig, John

1995   Telephone interview with author. Berea, KY to New York City. July 24.

Koobatian, James

1987   *Faking It: An International Bibliography of Art and Literary Forgeries, 1949–
           1986*. Washington, DC: Special Libraries Assn.

Krauss, Rosalind

1981   "The Originality of the Avant-Garde and Other Modernist Myths." *Octo-
           ber*. No. 18. pp. 46–66.

Law Officer's Bulletin, The

1988   "Strolling Decoy Officer's Display of Cash Didn't Lead to Entrapment."
           August 18. Vol. 3. No. 2. pp. 7–8.

Leff, Arthur Allen Leff

1976   *Swindling and Selling*. New York: The Free Press.

Lesce, Tony

1991   *Espionage: Down and Dirty*. Port Townsend, WA: Loompanics Unlimited.

Lessing, Alfred

1965   "What is Wrong with a Forgery?" *Journal of Aesthetics and Art Criticism*.
           Volume 23. Number 4. pp. 461–71.

Levine, Michael
1990   *Deep Cover: The Inside Story of How DEA Infighting, Incompetence and Subter-fuge Lost Us the Biggest Battle of the Drug War*. New York: Delacorte Press.

Levinson, Sanford
1983   "Under Cover: The Hidden Costs of Infiltration." In *ABSCAM Ethics: Moral Issues and Deception in Law Enforcement*. Gerald M. Caplan, ed. Hastings-on-Hudson, NY: The Police Foundation.

Lill, Bob
1995   Telephone interview with author. Seattle to Washington, D.C. December 19.
1996   Telephone interview with author. Seattle to Silver Spring, MD. February 12.

Loftus, Rosemary
n.d Interview. Collection of National Association of Bunco Investigators.

Love, Kevin G.
1994   "Transitioning of Law Enforcement Officers Into and Out of Undercover Assignments: Potential Psychological Impact and Recommendations for Program Development." Research Professorship Final Report. May 9.
1996   Telephone interview with author. 8 February. Berea, KY to Mount Pleasant, MI.

Lowenthal, David
1992   "Authenticity? The Dogma of Self-Delusion." In *Why Fakes Matter: Essays on Problems of Authenticity*. Mark Jones, ed. Avon, Britain: The British Museum. pp. 184–92.

McCall, Berdia
n.d.   Interview. Collection of the National Association of Bunco Investigators.

McCaghy, Charles H. and Janet Nogier
1984   "Envelope Stuffing at Home: A Quasi Confidence Game." *Deviant Behavior*. Volume 5. pp. 105–19.

McCampbell, Michael S.
1987   *Field Training for Officers: State of the Art*. National Institute of Justice, United States Department of Justice. April.

McFall (Ret.), S. A. Jim
1995   Telephone interview with author. Berea, KY to Quantico, VA. July 20.

McGovern, Capt. Patrick J. and Lt. Charles P. Connolly
1976   "Decoys, Disguises, Danger—New York City's Nonuniform Street Patrol." *FBI Law Enforcement Bulletin*. Vol. 45. No. 10. pp. 16–26.

MacInaugh, Edmond A.
1984   *Disguise Techniques: Fool All of the People Some of the Time*. Boulder, CO: Paladin Press.

MacKenzie, Ian
1986   "Gadamer's Hermeneutics and the Uses of Forgery." *Journal of Aesthetics and Art Criticism*. Volume 45. Number 1. Fall. pp. 41–48.

McKinnon, Dr. Murlene E.
1982   "A Guide to Nonverbal Deception Indicators." *Law and Order.* Vol. 30. No. 1. pp. 53-58.

McLaughlin, John B.
1980   *Gypsy Lifestyles.* Lexington, Massachusetts: Lexington Books.

Manning, Peter K.
1995   Telephone interview with author. Berea, KY to East Lansing, MI.

Marijnissen, R. H.
1985   *Paintings: Genuine, Fraud, Fake: Modern Methods of Examining Paintings.* Brussels: Elsevier.

Marlock, Dennis M.
1992   "How to Con a Con." *FBI Law Enforcement Bulletin.* July. pp. 1-3.

Marquart, James W. and Julian B. Roebuck
1985   "Prison Guards and 'Snitches': Deviance Within a Total Institution." *British Journal of Criminology.* Vol. 25. No. 3. pp. 217–33.

Martens, Frederick T.
1984   "The Illusion of Success: A Case Study in the Infiltration of Legitimate Business." *Federal Probation.* Vol. 48. No. 1. pp. 40–45.

Martin, James S.
1993   *Scram: Relocating Under a New Identity.* Port Townsend, WA: Loompanics Unlimited.

Martin, Thomas C.
1978   "Seattle Police Department's 'Decoy Squad.'" *FBI Law Enforcement Bulletin.*

Marx, Gary T.
1975   "Of Double Agents and Revolving Doors." *The New Republic.* October 18. pp. 8–13.
1979   "External Efforts to Damage or Facilitate Social Movements: Some Patterns, Explanations, Outcomes, and Complications." In *The Dynamics of Social Movements.* Mayer N. Zald & John D. McCarthy, eds. New York: : Winthrop Publishers. pp. 94–125.
1982   "Who Really Gets Stung? Some Issues Raised by the New Police Undercover Work." *Crime and Delinquency.* Vol. 28. No. 2. April. pp.165–93.
1987   "Restoring Realism and Logic to the Covert Facilitation Debate." *Journal of Social Issues.* Vol. 43. No. 3. pp. 43–55.
1988   *Undercover.* Berkeley: University of California Press.
1990   "Fraudulent Identification and Biography." In D. Altheide et al. *New Directions in the Study of Justice, Law, and Social Control.* New York: Plenum.
1992   "Under-the-Covers UC Investigations: Some Reflections on the State's Use of Sex and Deception in Law Enforcement." *Criminal Justice Ethics.* Winter/Spring. pp. 13–24.

Mathers, Chris
1997   Telephone interview with author, Seattle to Toronto, February 5.

Maurer, David

1940 *The Big Con: The Story of the Confidence Man and the Confidence Game.* Indianapolis: Bobbs-Merrill.

1974 *The American Confidence Man.* Springfield, IL: Charles C. Thomas.

Metzner, Paul R.

1989 *Crescendo of the Virtuoso: Virtuosity in Paris During the Age of Revolution, A Study of Personality and Values.* Unpublished doctoral dissertation, University of Washington.

Miami Vice

1985a "Lombard." Collection of Museum of TV & Radio, New York City.

1985b "Made for Each Other." Collection of Museum of TV & Radio, New York City.

1987 "Definitely Miami." Collection of Museum of TV & Radio, New York City.

1989 "Freefall." Collection of Museum of TV & Radio, New York City.

Michigan Department of State Police

1990 "The Ultimate Role Conflict: Assessing and Managing the Undercover Officer. Part One: Assessment and Management Guidelines." East Lansing, Michigan. Investigative Services Bureau. September 4.

1991 "The Ultimate Role Conflict: Assessing and Managing the Undercover Officer. Part Two: Assessment and Management Guidelines." East Lansing, Michigan. Investigative Services Bureau. December 1.

Miers, David R.

1983 "Compensation and Conceptions of Victims of Crime." *Victimology.* Vol. 8. Nos. 1-2. pp. 204-212.

Miller, Gale

1978 *Odd Jobs: The World of Deviant Work.* Englewood Cliffs, NJ: Prentice-Hall.

Miller, George I.

1987 "Observations on Police Undercover Work." *Criminology.* 25(1): 27–46.

Minneapolis Institute of Arts

1973 *Fakes and Forgeries.* Exhibition catalog. Minneapolis, Minnesota.

Mod Squad

1968 "Teeth of the Barracuda." Collection of Museum of TV & Radio, New York City.

Money Man

1992 Video, directed by Philip Haas. Collection of University of Washington Libraries, Seattle.

Montagu, E.

1964 *The Man Who Never Was.* New York: Bantam Books.

Montanino, Fred

1987 *The Federal Witness Security Program.* Ann Arbor: UMI.

Muehlberger, Robert J.

1990 "Identifying Simulations: Practical Considerations." *Journal of Forensic Sciences.* Volume 35. Number 2. March. pp. 368–74.

Nardi, Peter M.
1983   "Toward a Social Psychology of Entertainment Magic (Conjuring)." Paper
        presented at American Sociological Association meeting. Collection of
        Gary T. Marx.
Nash, Jay Robert
1989   *Encyclopedia of World Crime*. Wilmette, IL: CrimeBooks, Inc.
National Association of Bunco Investigators
1992   *NABI Investigators Handbook*. Collection of National Association of Bunco
        Investigators.
n.d.   Catch/Lame/Partner Script. Collection of National Association of Bunco
        Investigators.
n.d.   Double Play Script. Collection of National Association of Bunco Investi-
        gators.
n.d.   Pigeon Drop Script. Collection of National Association of Bunco Investi-
        gators.
National Gallery of Art
1989   Retaining the Original. Washington, D.C.
Nelson-Atkins Museum of Art
1996   "Discovery & Deceit." Exhibition guide. Kansas City, Missouri.
Ness, James J.
1989   "Reflections Upon Undercover Experiences: Stress, Problems and Con-
        cerns." *Law and Order*. October. pp. 106–11.
Newman, John Q.
1991a   *The Heavy-Duty New Identity*. Port Townsend, WA: Loompanics Unlim-
        ited.
1991b   *Understanding U.S. Identity Documents*. Port Townsend, WA: Loompanics
        Unlimited.
New York City Transit Police Department
ca. 1985 "Task Force Decoy Unit." Collection of FBI Academy.
New York Times
1982   "Judge Drops Indictments in Pornography Case." December 21.
Office of the Attorney General, United States Department of Justice
1981   Undercover Guidelines. Collection of FBI Academy, Quantico, VA.
Olander, William
1987   *Fake*. New York: The New Museum.
Ortiz, Darwin
1984   *Gambling Scams: How They Work, How to Detect Them, How to Protect Your-
        self*. New York: Dodd, Mead & Company.
Paladin Press
1995   *The Revenge Encyclopedia*. Boulder.
Park, Roger
1983   "Entrapment." In *Encyclopedia of Crime and Justice*. Sanford H. Kadish, ed.
        Volume 3. New York: The Free Press. pp. 704–08.
Peoria Police Department
n.d.   "Guidelines on Entrapment." Collection of Gary T. Marx.

n.d.   "Vice/Narcotic Bureau Guidelines." ca. early 1980s. Collection of Gary
            T. Marx.

Phoenix Police Department

1976   Special Investigations Bureau, Undercover Investigations Order No. C-6.
            October 15. Collection of Gary T. Marx.

1983*a*   "Undercover Identification." General Investigations Bureau. Order
            Number A-13. August 20. Collection of Gary T. Marx.

1983*b*   "Undercover Operations." Special Investigations Bureau. Order Number
            C-6. October 15. Collection of Gary T. Marx.

Pinkerton, Robert A. and William A. Pinkerton

1894   *Forgery as a Profession.* Originally published by Pinkerton National Detec-
            tive Agency. Reprint from article in the *North American Review.* Warshaw
            Collection, Smithsonian Institution.

Pistone, Joseph D.

1989   *Donnie Brasco: My Undercover Life in the Mafia.* New York: Signet. With
            Richard Woodley.

Professional Law Enforcement, Inc.

1996   *Undercover Agent's Operation Guide.* Dayton, Ohio.

Puig, Francis J.

1977   *In The Eye of the Beholder: Fakes, Replicas and Alterations in American Art.*
            New Haven: Yale University Art Gallery.

Rapp, Burt

1986   *Undercover Work: A Complete Handbook.* Port Townsend, WA: Loompan-
            ics.

1989   *Deep Cover: Police Intelligence Operations.* Boulder, CO: Paladin Press.

Re/Search

1987   *Pranks!* San Francisco: Re/Search Publications.

Rissler, Larry E.

1975   "The Informer's Identity at Trial." *Federal Law Enforcement Digest.* Febru-
            ary. pp. 21–25.

Robinson, Cyril D.

1978   "The Deradicalization of the Policeman: A Historical Analysis." *Crime and
            Delinquency.* April. Volume 24. Number 2. pp. 129–51.

Rudoe, Judy

1992   "The Faking of Gems in the Eighteenth Century." In Mark Jones, ed.
            Why Fakes Matter: Essays on Problems of Authenticity. Avon, Britain: The
            British Museum. pp. 23–31.

Rule, James B.

n.d.   "The Human Impact of Personal Documentation." Abstract for research
            project. Prob. mid-1970s, certainly post–1974. Collection of Gary T.
            Marx.

Rush

1991   Film, directed by Lili Fini Zanuck.

Sagoff, Mark
1976   "The Aesthetic Status of Forgeries." *Journal of Aesthetics and Art Criticism.* Winter. Volume 35. Number 2.

Sample, John
1991   *The Heavy-Duty New Identity.* Port Townsend, WA: Loompanics Unlimited.
1993   *Methods of Disguise.* Port Townsend, WA: Loompanics Unlimited.

Santoro, Victor and Jordan L. Cooper
1984   *Techniques of Harassment.* Port Townsend, WA: Loompanics Unlimited.

Schechner, Richard
1985   *Between Theater and Anthropology.* Philadelphia: University of Pennsylvania Press.

Secret Squirrel
n.d.   "Five is a Crowd." Collection of the Museum of TV & Radio, New York City.

Semien, John
1985   "Undercover." *Morning Advocate.* Baton Rouge, LA. March 31. p. 25:G13.

Seymour, Richard et al.
1989   *The New Drugs: Look-Alikes, Drugs of Deception, and Designer Drugs.* Hazelden Foundation.

Shannon, M. L.
1993   *The Paper Trail: Personal and Financial Privacy in the Nineties.* San Francisco: Lysias Press.

Shell, Marc
1995   *Art and Money.* Chicago: University of Chicago.

Shoeman, Ferdinand
1986   "Undercover Operations: Some Moral Questions about S.804." *Criminal Justice Ethics.* Vol. 5. No. 2. Pp. 16-22.

Shover, Neal
1996   *Pretenders: Pursuits and Careers of Persistent Thieves.* Boulder, CO: Westview Press.

Sifakis, Carl
1993   *Hoaxes and Scams: A Compendium of Deceptions, Ruses and Swindles.* New York: Facts on File, Inc.

Silence of the Lambs, The
1991   Film, directed by Jonathan Demme.

Sirene, Walt
1994   Interview with author, Quantico, VA. April 1.

Skolnick, Jerome H.
1982   "Deception by Police." *Criminal Justice Ethics.* Vol. 1. No. 2. pp. 40-54.

Slade, E. Roy and James R. Gutzs
1991   *The Pretext Book.* Houston: Cloak & Data Press.

Smith, Alexander B. & Pollack, Harriet
1976   "Deviance as a Method of Coping." *Crime and Delinquency.* Vol. 22. No. 1. pp. 3-16

Smith, John F., James R. Sheridan, and Dennis F. Yurcisin
1991   *How to Set Up and Run a Successful Law Enforcement Sting Operation.* Englewood Cliffs, New Jersey: Prentice Hall.

Smith, Lindsay and Walstad, Bruce A.
1989   *Sting Shift: The Street-Smart Cop's Handbook of Cons and Swindles.* Littleton, CO: Street-Smart Communications.

Solomon-Godeau, Abigail
1993   *Mistaken Identities.* Seattle: University Art Museum.

Stafford, Barbara Maria
1994   *Artful Science: Enlightenment Education and the Eclipse of Visual Education.* Cambridge: MIT Press.

Stein, Gordon
1993   *Encyclopedia of Hoaxes.* Detroit: Gale Research Inc.

Sting, The
1973   Film, directed by George Roy Hill. 129 minutes.

Strazdes, Diana
1977   "Alterations and Adaptations." In *The Eye of the Beholder: Fakes, Replicas and Alterations in American Art.* New Haven: Yale University Art Gallery. pp. 26–27.

Sutherland, E. H.
1967   *The Professional Thief.* Chicago: University of Chicago Press.

Suthers, John W. and Shupp, Gary L.
1982   *Fraud and Deceit: How to Stop Being Ripped Off.* New York: Arco Publishing.

Tafoya, William L.
1990   "The Virtuosos of Policing." *American Journal of Criminal Justice.* Vol. 14. No. 2. Pp. 205-223.

Tampa Museum of Art
1990   *J. S. G. Boggs: Smart Money (Hard Currency).* Exhibition catalog. Tampa, Florida.

Taylor, Bill
1996a   Interview with author. Dayton, Ohio.
1996b   Telephone interview with author. March 13. Seattle to Dayton, Ohio.

Teten, Howard
1995   Telephone interview with author, Seattle to Manassas, VA, September 24.

Thomas Investigative Publications
1994   *P.I. & Security Catalog.* Austin, TX.

Thompson, George J.
1994   *Verbal Judo: Redirecting Behavior with Words.* Jacksonville, FL: Institute of Police Technology and Management.

Time
1982   "Lost Identity: Going Too Far Under Cover." April 26. p. 24.

Trujillo, Nick and George Dionisopouos
1987   "Cop Talk, Police Stories, and the Social Construction of Organizational Drama." (1987). *Central States Speech Journal.* Fall/Winter. Pp. 196 - 209.

Trump, Fred
1965   *Buyer Beware!* New York: Abingdon Press.
United States Department of Justice
1976   "The Criminal Use of False Identification: A Summary Report on the Nature, Scope, and Impact of False ID Use in the United States With Recommendations to Combat the Problem." The Report of the Federal Advisory Committee on False Identification. Washington, D.C.: U.S. Government Printing Office.
United States Department of the Treasury
1978   Federal Law Enforcement Training Center: Undercover Operations. ST-515 (11-78).
United States House of Representatives
1985   "Fraudulent Credentials." Joint Hearing before the Subcommittee on Health and Long-Term Care and the Subcommittee on Housing and Consumer Interests of the Select Committee on Aging. 99th Congress, 1st Session. December 11. Comm. Pub. No. 99-550. Washington, DC: U.S. Government Printing Office.
1986   "Fraudulent Credentials: Federal Employees." Hearing Before the Subcommittee on Health and Long-Term Care of the Select Committee on Aging. 99th Congress, 2nd Session. April 18. Comm. Pub. No. 99-571. Washington, D.C.: U.S. Government Printing Office.
VanCook, Jerry
1996   *Going Undercover: Secrets and Sound Advice for the Undercover Officer.* Boulder, CO: Paladin Press.
Vasquez, I. John and Kelly, Sharon A.
1989   "Management's Commitment to the Undercover Operative." *FBI Law Enforcement Bulletin.* February.
Vaughan, Gerard
1992   "The Restoration of Classical Sculpture in the Eighteenth Century and the Problem of Authenticity." In *Why Fakes Matter: Essays on Problems of Authenticity.* Mark Jones, ed. Avon, Britain: The British Museum. pp. 41–50.
Vaughn, Michael S.
1992   "The Parameters of Trickery as an Acceptable Police Practice." *American Journal of Police.* Vol. 11. No. 4. pp. 71-81.
Vidocq, Eugène-François
1829   *Memoirs of Vidocq.* Four volumes. London: Hunt and Clarke.
Vizzini, Sal, Oscar Fraley, and Marshall Smith
1972   *Vizzini: The Secret Lives of America's Most Successful Undercover Agent.* New York: Arbor House.
Wachtel, Julius
1980   "The Sale of Bait: A Unique Anti-Fencing Strategy." Unpublished master's thesis. Arizona State University.
1982   *Police Undercover Work: Issues and Practices.* Unpublished doctoral dissertation, State University of New York, Albany.

Wade, Gary E.
1990   "Undercover Violence." *FBI Law Enforcement Bulletin.* April. pp. 15–19.

Wainwright, Clive
1992   "The Importance of Provenance: Rehabilitated Fakes." In *Why Fakes Matter: Essays on Problems of Authenticity.* Mark Jones, ed. Avon, Britain: The British Museum.

Wansley, Larry and Carlton Stowers
1989   *FBI Undercover: The True Story of Special Agent "Mandrake."* New York: Pocket Books.

Ward, Gerald W. R.
1977   "Introduction: Fakes, Replicas and Alterations in American Art." In *The Eye of the Beholder: Fakes, Replicas and Alterations in American Art.* New Haven: Yale University Art Gallery. pp. 11–13.

Washington, D.C. Metropolitan Police
1982   "Division Order: Undercover Officers." Series 82, Number 8. August 2.

Watts, K. N.
1992   "Samuel Pratt and Armour Faking." In *Why Fakes Matter: Essays on Problems of Authenticity.* Mark Jones, ed. Avon, Britain: The British Museum. pp. 100–107.

Weschler, Lawrence
1988   "Onward and Upward With the Arts: Value: Part I: A Fool's Questions." *The New Yorker.* January 18. pp. 33–56.

Yale University Art Gallery
1977   *The Eye of the Beholder: Fakes, Replicas and Alterations in American Art.* Exhibition catalog. New Haven.

Zietz, Dorothy
1977   *Women Who Embezzle or Defraud: A Study of Convicted Felons.* New York: Praeger.

ACKNOWLEDGMENTS

Two major kinds of material assistance were key in the completion of this book. First, the Mellon Foundation, through the Appalachian College Association, and the University of Washington's Royalty Research Fund provided critical financial support for the research, including the chance to work with an indefatigable research assistant, Amanda Spears, who has since completed law school and become a law clerk. I am most grateful for John Hennen's interest in and support of the project.

The other form of material support is perhaps less obvious but for a peripatetic writer equally important: the incredible hospitality of the coffee houses of Seattle and Chicago, where staff peered over my shoulder and asked excellent questions during my unconscionably long stays. I should make special mention of Panera Bread of Elmwood Park, Illinois, where I set up residence before they'd even opened.

Many thanks are due to the undercover training organizations that generously, and I hope they will conclude not unwisely, gave me access to their training and students. Two organizations, the private agency Professional Law Enforcement (PLE) Group and a regional training center for state and local law-enforcement officers transitioning to undercover work, allowed me to take part in training sessions and to interview instructors and participants. Bill Taylor, who founded PLE Group in 1981, passed away in 2004; I remember his enthusiasm for his craft with respect and affection. Jon Grow of the National Association of Bunco Investigators shared his organization's meticulously transcribed con game scripts. Sandra Lee Coupe, librarian at the FBI Academy in Quantico, Virginia, was hospitable and helpful. The Washington State Police Academy opened its doors to me for its roleplaying exercises.

I am enormously thankful for the information shared with me by interview by Roger DePue, Chief of the FBI's Behavioral Sciences Unit during the 1980s; Bob Lill; Jim McFall, Director, Society of Former Agents of the FBI; Walt Sirene, ethics professor at the FBI Academy; and Peter K. Manning of Michigan State University. I acknowledge with gratitude and deep affection my conversations and visits with former Royal Canadian Mounted Police undercover partners Chris Mathers and Murray Simms, as well as the anonymous undercover operators who gave of their time and expertise to teach me the easy way what they had learned at high risk. Drs. Gary Kaufman and Kevin Love generously shared their expertise and experience working directing with undercover operators to help me understand their psychology. Drs. Michel Girodo, Bruce A. Jacobs, and Richard A. Leo most invaluably pointed me to printed sources of tremendous utility, and John Kleining, Institute for Criminal Justice Ethics, Jay John College, to live sources. Gary T. Marx, a pioneer in the study of undercover work, openheartedly shared years' worth of documents from his private collection. I benefited from the insight and support of scholars Richard Will and C. B. Davis, and from Dale's heroic data saving, as my Mac crashed and I had to switch for a time to the dark side.

I have always been blessed by the encouragement and support of my family and dear friends. I am especially mindful of the attentive interest and loving support of Mitchell and Nathan Schneider, Charley and Mary Ann Murray, and Antoinette Penney, the only female lawyer working in La Jolla, California in the late 1960s, who took this *Dragnet* fan under her wing to show me firsthand how life in San Diego's courts differs from what a television fiend might think. The 10 members of the "Jane Addams cohort" at National-Louis University—my students and teachers— were a quiet and strong source of inspiration as I readied the book for publication. Finally, I am deeply grateful to Dr. Mary Bast for her crucial contribution to the publication of this work.

ABOUT THE AUTHOR

Sara K. Schneider, Ph.D. received her undergraduate education at Yale and trained at New York University in Performance Studies, the nexus of cross-cultural studies and arts theories and practices. As theatre deviser-director, performance anthropologist, and author of *Vital Mummies: Performance Design for the Show-Window Mannequin* and *Concert Song as Seen: Kinesthetic Aspects of Musical Interpretation,* Schneider has written extensively on the meaning of the body in expressive and material culture. Her current investigative and creative work deals with the relationships among movement, spirituality, and learning cross-culturally (see www.thinkingdr.com), and she conducts professional development workshops for public servants, educators, health-care professionals, and members of the clergy in using kinesthetic, or body-based, methods, to learn across the curriculum and the professions, including building understanding about global cultures using a movement-based perspective. Faculty of the National College of Education at National-Louis University, Schneider has also taught and consulted at the forefront of learning innovation projects at the University of Washington and Andersen Consulting, among others. The author can be reached at sks@thinkingdr.com, and welcomes comments and corrections for future editions of *Art of Darkness.*

ENDNOTES

Notes to Introduction

[1] Indeed, part of what inspires this book is a belief in a brighter, more playful side of fakes, an acceptance that copying, borrowing, and embroidering upon others' work and selves is one way in which people recreate themselves.

[2] Metzner 1989:228; Sifakis 1993:43; Stafford 1994:93.

[3] Stafford 1994:xxvi.

[4] The new medium of photography added a charge to the notion of the authentic. Cole 1956:5; see also Jones 1990:119, 161–62.

[5] In the course of my research, it was of great interest to compare cops' and anthropologists' use of the tools they share. Cops and social scientists both love to capture "evidence" or "raw data," to ask questions, to interview. It's hard for both

of us to be on the receiving end, and hard to adjust to each other's working conditions, as I learned during a course for undercover narcotics work.

I had been trying to schedule an interview with one of the instructors of a course for undercover narcotics work. The instructor had been called away for a day of the course for follow-up work on a real-life assignment. His fellow instructor was in ready touch with him, and relayed messages between us. My conventional expectations for an interview involved setting aside an hour and a half or two hours with an informant and talking in a place relatively free of distractions, knowing how heavily reliant I was on my tape recorder to pick up the verbal and vocal nuances. Cops, however, very often gather their information on the fly, with distractions abounding. So we had a (redeemable) miscommunication when trying to set up an interview. Through our intermediary, the undercover suggested, via a message from his partner, that I meet him late that evening at a men's restaurant and club, a national chain, where, I heard, a number of the male students would also be joining him. Confused, I concluded his choice of site and the preponderance of other students meant he had decided against doing the interview. Meanwhile, he assumed, when I didn't join the men at the restaurant, that I had simply forgotten about it. Thankfully, we were able to recover from the incident and have an excellent discussion the next day, under more favorable conditions— though clearly coming from different cultures of information-gathering.

Notes to Chapter 1: *Craft and Artifice*

[1] See Marx 1975 and 1987:47–49.

[2] Marx 1988:21.

[3] Fijnaut and Marx 1995:2, 10.

[4] Marx 1988:25. Treating undercover work within the context of broader concerns about public surveillance and other forms of social control, Fijnaut and Marx called undercover policing "a risky business involving the invasion of privacy, the exploitation of trust, danger to third parties and the risk of police corruption and a compromised judicial system" (Fijnaut and Marx 1995:1). Bok has written against the use of deception in law enforcement, whether it is performed by undercover agents or by their informants: "Deceit and violence—these are the two forms of deliberate assault on human beings. Both can coerce people into acting against their will. Most harm that can befall victims through violence can come to them also through deceit. But deceit controls more subtly, for it works on belief as well as action" (as quoted in Delattre 1989:168–69). Aware of the irony of relegating ethical issues of a major part of my subject matter to an endnote, I will nonetheless refer the reader to further information on ethical issues in undercover work in such journals as *Criminal Justice Ethics* and throughout Marx's work, and assert my intention to treat the topic from a somewhat more technical perspective. (See Marx 1988 and 1982.)

[5] Delattre 1989:167.

[6] Vizzini, Fraley, and Smith 1972:35.

[7] Fijnaut and Marx 1995:13.

[8] Telephone interview with Bob Lill, 19 December 1995, Seattle to Washington, D.C.; Marx 1988:4–5.

[9] Pistone 1989:23; Wansley and Stowers 1989:8.

[10] Wansley and Stowers 1989:11, 94.

[11] Telephone interview with Bob Lill, 19 December 1995, Seattle to Washington, D.C. See also Pistone 1989:36.

[12] Pistone 1989:35.

[13] Fijnaut and Marx 1995:13.

[14] VanCook 1996:43.

[15] Levine 1990:5.

[16] E. Cookridge (1966), quoted in Goffman 1969:24.

[17] Goffman discusses the aesthetic dimensions of plausibility: in certain situations, a story that feels slightly open-ended in just the right ways will be more believable than one that has all the corners knotted and tied (1969:20).

[18] Fitzkee 1945c:144.

[19] Pistone 1989:41.

[20] VanCook 1996:34, 37.

[21] *Ibid.*, 1996:12.

[22] Nash 1989:2782.

[23] Vizzini, Fraley, and Smith 1972:106.

[24] VanCook 1996:15.

[25] As told by Vizzini, Fraley, and Smith 1972:131, 175ff.

[26] *Ibid.*, 118–19.

[27] Similarly, when Vizzini played a role as Pasquale Lombardi, he made sure that: "when the phone rang in my penthouse suite it also rang on a private extension at Bureau headquarters. If nobody answered after five rings, a sleepy sexy female voice would come on and say, 'Pronto ... No, Pasquale isn't here ... I don't know when he'll be back.' (The voice belonged to Monica Atwill, [a] pretty girl at the Bureau.) I was supposed to be very big with the ladies and she was part of my cover" (Vizzini, Fraley, and Smith 1972:59).

[28] *Ibid.*, 40–41.

[29] Ness 1989:107–08.

[30] Rapp 1986:65.

[31] The preparation of a written character biography is common among actors and has even made its way into the living-history movement as a research and preparation tool in the development of historical characters. Actors hired to work as living-history interpreters at Plimoth Plantation, where seventeenth-century American life is re-enacted for visitors' education and entertainment, are required to combine plausible imaginative work with historical research into the actual lives of the characters whose identities they assume. Developing a notebook with essential aspects

of character is central to the development process. At Plimoth Plantation, the "Personation Biograph" includes an annotated drawing of the costume to be worn, a specimen of the dialect the character will speak, a sample of how his or her signature will look, a list of who else in the relatively limited community of the Plantation comprise the character's friends and associates, a syllabus of what the character has read, and notes detailing the character's moral positions, habits, and bases of knowledge (See Schechner 1985).

[32] VanCook 1996:13–14.

[33] Buckwalter 1983:138.

[34] Department of the Treasury 1978:12.

[35] Vizzini, Fraley, and Smith 1972:32.

[36]A potential problem down the road, however, with this undercover's presentation of the catering business as his own could be that the bad guy might appear out of the blue in some kind of jam and demand that this small business owner front him some money. And it does help the undercover play for time if his cover story can support a line like, "I can't spend that kind of money without checking with my boss. I'll get back to you."

[37] Buckwalter 1983:138.

[38] Fitzkee 1945c:223; Rapp 1986:62-63; VanCook 1996:16.

Notes to Chapter 2: *Being Good at Being Bad*

[1] Goddard 1988:28–29.

[2] Beene 1992:15 45–46.

[3] Goddard 1988:334.

[4] Rapp 1986:66–67.

[5] VanCook 1996:2–6.

[6] Wansley and Stowers 1989:132–33.

[7] Count 1994:225; Ness 1989:109.

[8] Wansley and Stowers 1989:106, 137.

[9] Phoenix Police Department 1976:1.

[10] Buckwalter 1983:140.

[11] A decoy cop who goes too believably into role can raise the spectre of entrapment, as a gifted performance can be construed as a form of inducement. One who "lay on a city sidewalk apparently helpless and unconscious as a result of intoxication, with cash sticking out of his pocket" was regarded as being too tempting to all; he was so believable, he didn't separate out those who would otherwise be "predisposed" to commit a crime and those were normally law-abiding citizens (*The Law Officer's Bulletin* 1988: 7).

Other cases in which the level of involvement on the part of the agent was deemed to be too active (thus dismissing charges against the target) have included situations in which a female undercover agent offered sexual favors to a suspect in return for his selling her marijuana; a male undercover agent offered to pay a suspected heroin user twice the going rate for a day's supply; another male agent provided a sad tale of his girlfriend, suffering from heroin withdrawal symptoms, threatening to leave him unless he could provide her with more heroin (Roger Park 1983: 704–05. See cases *Spencer v. State*, 263 Co. 2d 282 (Fla. App. 1972) and *People v. Turner*, 390 Mich. 7, 210 N.W.2d 336 (1973).

In order to avoid entrapment, the decoy sets up a context in which the bad guy will be tempted to make more damning choices than are ever explicitly proffered. In a world of identity techniques based upon verbal performance, entrapment tends to be predicated more strongly on what is said than on what is suggested by dress, manner, situation, grouping, and other factors. One undercover doing street-level vice work found a good line to open with a potential bad guy was "You want to party? What's it going to cost to party?" With "openers" such as these, he avoided any incriminatingly direct talk of money or sex while providing a strong in for the other guy to act in a definably criminal manner.

Like police officers, informants cannot talk someone back into a crime he has backed out of. However, they can make themselves available to help with an offense that has been initiated by the other guy, as long as the clear intention is to help the police gather evidence for prosecution. Informant guidelines issued by the Peoria Police Department emphasized that "it is absolutely forbidden for you to persuade or encourage any person to commit a crime where the idea of committing the crime was not his to begin with" (Peoria Police Department n.d. "Guidelines on Entrapment").

[12] Vizzini, Fraley, and Smith 1972:297.

[13] In this sense, cops' verbal productions are not unlike those written "authenticating" documents that produce enough believable language in a plausible-enough package to serve as justification for art works. One crooked dealer sold a fake Jackson Pollock with the help of a 38-page document which read, in part: "Condition: In need of deep restoration, relining *à la mercator*, resubstantiation of pigment overlayers, where non-interharmonious media has caused severe flaking, peeling, and crackling. ... Foundation: Irish linen, hand-slubbed but not hand-woven, indicating a type used from 1840 to the present day ... microscopic examination of a filament of the fabric indicates a condition of eremacausis" (In Goodrich 1973:191).

[14] Metzner 1989:137.

[15] Vizzini, Fraley, and Smith 1972:14, 15, 62.

[16] Vidocq 1829 (Vol. 2):212.

[17] Goddard 1988:63–64, 45.

[18] Vizzini, Fraley, and Smith 1972:245; Pistone 1989:113.

[19] Goddard 1988:335.

[20] See Goffman 1969:18.

[21] Goddard 1988:113.

[22] Conceptual artists James P. Coyle and Mal Sharpe found in the "taped terrorizations" they staged with San Francisco passersby during the 1960s that they clinched the artistic element of their outrageous provocations by getting their "marks" to repeat on hidden tape recording, the essence of their proposed action.

Allen Funt's work marked the incursion of "criminological" surveillance equipment into the world of entertainment. The entertainer found ingenious ways to get his radio and television subjects to play for the microphone, and devised scenarios that specifically allowed for the concealment of the recording equipment. In the premiere episode of *Candid Microphone*, he hung a miniscule lapel microphone from a dentist's drill over a patient awaiting work on an impacted wisdom tooth. Funt's ready assumption of the role of dentist—the role into which his subject reasonably, considering the context, cast him—made all the more amusing his simultaneously audio-visual and professional direction to the patient: "Open wide, please" (Funt 1952:16, 17).

[23] VanCook 1996:55.

[24] Goddard 1988:103.

[25] Vizzini, Fraley, and Smith 1972:316.

[26] Pistone 1989:287.

[27] Goddard 1988:108.

[28] Fitzkee 1945c:44.

[29] Pistone 1989:48, 105, 163.

[30] Buckwalter 1983:139-40; Department of the Treasury 1978:6.

[31] Wansley and Stowers 1989:109–110.

[32] Count 1994:223–24.

[33] This comes from police culture more generally. One of the participants in the training, speaking about techniques of interrogation, confirmed how establishing and maintaining the power relationship were key to the success of intelligence-gathering: "You try never to give the other guy any kind of advantage at all. You never want him to think that he has the upper hand, or that he knows more than you. It's like a game of cards: sometimes it's a bluff, but you've gotta have a poker face, you gotta have the voice, you gotta have the eyes, you gotta have the body language that tells him, This is the way it is, this guy's for real. You go in there and you read the person, and you take it from there, and then you act on all the information you had beforehand."

[34] Pistone 1989:156.

[35] Abagnale and Redding 1980:79-80.

[36] Fitzkee 1945c:57, 61.

[37] Pistone 1989:251.

[38] VanCook 1996:28-30.

[39] *Ibid.*, 113-14, 117.

[40] See Goffman 1969:44.

[41] Vizzini, Fraley, and Smith 1972:213.

[42] Fitzkee 1945c:43-44.

[43] Fitzkee 1945c: 112–13, 127.

[44] Rapp 1986:79.

[45] Slade and Gutzs 1991:13, 23.

[46] In building rapport, one must expect to follow the lead of the bad guy's values. When appearing to befriend Lucky Luciano, Vizzini needed to play along with his dalliances. In a bar, Luciano motioned for two women to join them, and brought Vizzini into his romantic plan: "'You like the blonde?' Luciano asked me, indicating, I guessed, that he had already settled on the dark-haired one for himself. I said I did. I decided a dashing Air Force major had better not cop out in an area so dear to the big man's heart" (Vizzini, Fraley, and Smith 1972:83, 90).

[47] *Ibid.*, 107.

[48] Semien 1985:25:G13.

[49] Vizzini, Fraley, and Smith 1972:13, 57.

[50] Of course, no officer is going to look young enough to pass as an elementary or middle school student in schools where drug trafficking now also takes place.

[51] Jacobs 1994:455; Buckwalter 1983:144; Anderson 1988:26–27.

[52] Buckwalter 1983:148–49; Pistone 1989:148.

[53] Rapp 1986:76–77.

[54] Vizzini, Fraley, and Smith 1972:306.

[55] Funt 1952:138.

[56] VanCook 1996:22.

[57] Vizzini, Fraley, and Smith 1972:14, 27.

[58] Nowadays, it is rarer to get involved in simulations at all. To protect the veracity of the cop as a witness, some police departments allow the undercover to enter into such performances "ONLY if the officer feels his life is in danger, he will receive bodily harm, or his cover will be lost." He must always also report any simulation incident immediately to his cover officer, who reports it on up to the sergeant, who in turn reports up to the lieutenant (Peoria Police Department n.d.:2).

[59] Anderson 1988:44–45.

[60] Michigan State Police 1990:12, 14–15.

[61] The film metaphor is not inappropriate: since many buys are covertly videotaped, undercovers have ample opportunity to view themselves as media figures. Chris Mathers has watched his own videotapes critically and harbors no great artistic pretensions: "I just thought it was basically *bad* acting. But who cares, so long as it puts bums in seats? Who cares what I think [of my acting], so long as the crook thinks it's okay?"

[62] Vizzini, Fraley, and Smith 1972:303.

[63] When he has been undercover, he has worn a mustache, a goatee, and a ponytail to the middle of his back, along with a hoop and stud in his ear.

[64] Newman 1991a:43.

[65] In some sense, this may not be unlike the situation of an art forger who found he was much more celebrated in his role as a clandestine famous artist than he ever could be working in his own style. Thomas Chatterton, the celebrated eighteenth-

century literary forger, got little attention when he produced work that reflected his own time and experience, but, as Sifakis remarked, "When Chatterton wrote in fifteenth-century style he was a genius" (Sifakis 1993:53).

[66] This undercover was so affiliated with the renegade role he has developed that he would be hard pressed to play a character of higher social leanings. Several of the other undercovers in the training course took me aside to tell me that they "could tell" this player had gone too far psychologically, in part because he overidentified with the undercover role.

[67] Vizzini, Fraley, and Smith 1972:13, 59.

[68] See Girodo 1984:170.

[69] Ibid., 177. Girodo calls this habit "role generalization" (Girodo 1985a:304); VanCook 1996:65.

[70] Goddard 1988:107.

[71] Pistone 1989:409.

[72] The definition of the workspace can nevertheless be contestable: Is it healthier for the undercover not to have his living space intruded upon by his undercover supervisor, or does such invasion help remind him of his home identity and his responsibilities to it? Whereas some undercover supervisors might find it useful, as a reality-maintaining technique, to hold briefing meetings in the undercover's working apartment, Mathers believes in maintaining undercovers' privacy; he therefore avoids conducting business in an undercover's personal space. He feels that he creates better results when he makes clear to his undercover workers that he sees them as human beings rather than as "tools."

[73] Michigan State Police 1991; Telephone interview with Dr. Gary Kaufman, Michigan State Police, 8 February 1996, Seattle to East Lansing. Kevin Love emphasizes that the undercover supervisor is in at least as much need of a carefully choreographed transition as the undercover himself. Just as the undercover agent is beginning to experience some success as an identity trickster, and can accept more dangerous or challenging assignments, it is time for the supervisor to be helping him to make the transition out of undercover work altogether.

[74] Goddard 1988:168.

[75] Vidocq 1829 (Vol. 2):221.

[76] Count 1994:211.

[77] Carroll 1991:10.

Notes to Chapter 3: *The Artifacts of Identity*

[1] Abagnale and Redding 1980:94.

[2] Marx 1990:146.

[3] Rule n.d.:12, 17.

[4] House of Representatives 1985:23–27.

[5] Sifakis 1993:63, 69–70.

[6] Nash 1989:95, 910, 3056.

[7] Montanino 1987:ii.]

[8] Newman 1991*b*; Nash 1989:3319.

[9] Shannon 1993:131-32; United States House of Representatives 1985:132.

[10] Shannon 1993:186.

[11] United States Department of Justice 1976:xxix, 36; United States House of Representatives 1985:176.

[12] United States House of Representatives 1985:2, 5.

[13] Presented as appendix to United States House of Representatives 1986:63–65.

[14] "Expedited" is the notable descriptor for such mail-order degrees used by Anthony James Geruntino, convicted for his involvement with Vocational Guidance (United States House of Representatives 1985:50, 144).

[15] Newman 1991*b*:5.

[16] *Ibid.*, 34.

[17] Sample 1991:17.

[18] Newman 1991*b*:71, 96.

[19] Rule n.d.:13.

[20] Shannon 1993:10, 120–21.

[21] *Ibid.*, 33, 136, 140, 141.

[22] Irving 1969:115, 169.

[23] Cawley n.d.; *Boston Globe* 1983:7.

[24] However, if one claims to be a member of the American Federation of Atrologers, one has to be ready to demonstrate the specialized knowledge an accuser might demand.

[25] Shannon 1993:24, 135, 126-129; Martin 1993:36, 72; Rapp 1986:63.

[26] Vidocq 1829 (Vol. 1):23; Vizzini, Fraley, and Smith 1972:34.

[27] Thomas Investigative Publications 1994:38; Slade and Gutzs 1991:54.

[28] United States Department of the Treasury 1978:16; see Vizzini, Fraley, and Smith 1972:100.

[29] Washington D. C. Metropolitan Police 1982:2.

[30] See Irving 1969:8, 37, 41, 145, 147; Goodrich 1973:47.

[31] See Metzner 1989:134.

[32] Vidocq 1829 (Vol. 1):142, 156-57.

[33] *The Times.* Monday, 9 June 1845. p. 6. Quoted in Metzner 1989:130-31.

[34] Metzner 1989:141–43, 310–311.

[35] It can be a means of locating a nomadic con artist or a violent criminal. Impostors are also typically nomadic, and the plethora of con games that find their origin in the touring practices of circuses testify to the wandering quality of many con artists. The circus practice of periodic name changes was a safeguard against word of actors' deeds' preceding them (Sifakis 1993:58).

[36] Carroll 1991:129-37.

[37] See Hinkle 1990: 8, 108–111

[38] *Ibid.*, 18-19.

[39] Sample 1993:24, 29, 53, 55, 97, 101, 151.

[40] Hinkle 1990:89–91.

[41] Goffman 1969:22–23.

[42] Martin 1993:51.

[43] Count 1994:210.

[44] Cawley n.d.

[45] Carroll 1991:137.

[46] Fitzkee 1945c:65–66. In parallel with Fitzkee's distinction between dissimulation and simulation, Goffman differentiated between those forms of impression management in which the primary aim is to create "concealment or cover," those in which the result is "accentuated revealment," and misrepresentation (1969:14–16).

[47] Vidocq 1829 (Vol. 1):127, 150–51.

[48] Miller 1978:27.

[49] MacInaugh 1984:5–6.

[50] Montanino 1987:16.

[51] Sample 1993:94, 224; MacInaugh 1984:20.

[52] MacInaugh 1984.

[53] Goffman 1963:79.

[54] The heavy concern in Renaissance drama and baroque opera with female characters passing as male in order to attain particular goals that would otherwise have remained out of reach to them is no simple aesthetic play upon the visceral excitement of giving an audience an opportunity to see members of one gender in the clothes of another in a theatrical system that conventionally had boys play female characters. The excitement is itself predicated upon the transgressive function of drag in a particular political and social milieu in which one gender has powers and functions reserved more or less exclusively to it.

[55] See, for example, the famous essay by Adrian Piper, "Passing for White, Passing for Black" in Elaine K. Ginsberg, ed. 1996. *Passing and the Fictions of Identity.* Durham: Duke University Press.

[56] Her story could be interpreted as one of assumptive power, as much as it could be treated as that of a woman with unbounded sociosexual desire for other women.

[57] S. Alsop and T. Braden (1964). *Sub Rosa: The OSS and American Espionage.* New York: Harcourt, Brace & World. Quoted in Goffman 1969: 25.

[58] MacInaugh 1984:47.

[59] *Ibid.,* 8–10.

[60] Vizzini, Fraley, and Smith 1972:26.

[61] Nash 1989:2186.

[62] New York City Transit Police Department 1985:10; Phoenix Police Department 1982:17.

[63] Beene 1992:21.

[64] See Jacobs 1993b:288.

[65] MacInaugh 1984:79–80.

[66] Beene 1992:35.

[67] Martin 1978:18.

[68] Breslin 1979:43.

Notes to Chapter 4: *The Crafty Expedient*

[1] Cited in House of Representatives 1985: 187.

[2] VanCook 1996: vi.

[3] Hankiss 1980; see also Henderson 1985.

[4] Blum 1972:234.

[5] Levinson 1983:45.

[6] Blum 1972:34.

[7] Leff 1976:19; Blum 1972:26; Ortiz 1984:208.

[8] Adams et al. 1992:8.

[9] Fitzkee 1945c:33.

[10] Jastrow quoted in Nardi 1983:19.

[11] See Nardi 1983:15–16. Bracketing also appears when the magician subtly changes from finishing a trick that's not working to beginning one that has a better chance.

[12] Fitzkee 1945c:59.

[13] *Ibid.*, 58, 94.

[14] Earlier, the term "roping" was used to refer to the ability, when working undercover, to draw a target out conversationally.

[15] Another form of the convincer is the fortuneteller's practice of "demonstrating trouble," in which she creates "signs" that the client is hexed, and therefore needs her help (Boles and Davis 1983:379).

[16] Adams et al. 1992:32.

[17] McLaughlin 1980:76.

[18] See Suthers and Shupp 1982.

[19] Leff 1976:33–34.

[20] Blum 1972:31.

[21] Adams et al. 1992:29.

[22] Typically a con plot involves accomplices who disconnect the overtly criminal act from the act of appearing to befriend an innocent mark; however, a more remarkable story occurs when both of those functions are assumed by a single person: In 1880, Ellen Peck first robbed an old man of $10,000, then volunteered to act as his detective. As a result, she was able to sock him with a generous "expenses" bill as well (Nash 1989:2434).

[23] Freimuth 1976:42; Blum 1972:34.

[24] Pinkerton 1894:5–6.

[25] Adams et al. 1992:3; Hughes 1988:4.

[26] Nash 1989:3115.

[27] Maurer 1974:134–35, quoted in Miller 1978:58–59.

[28] Sifakis 1993: 228.

[29] Abagnale and Redding 1980:170.

[30] One of Abagnale's smartest moves was not to travel across Europe by air, since any one of the young women could have gotten him in trouble by a casual word to a real airline employee. Much as Abagnale ensured his own document forgeries were presented in contexts that didn't support comparisons with the real things, he steered clear of situations in which his young women could be seen side-by-side with real flight attendants (Abagnale and Redding 1980:186–87).

[31] Sutherland 1967:60; Goffman1952:452.

[32] Smith, Sheridan, and Yurcisin 1991:40–41.

[33] Leff 1976:10–12, 16.

[34] Ibid., 15–16. Leff actually treats the con as a parodic though somewhat natural extension of the principles of ordinary selling; thus, the relationship between con artist and mark he likens to that between merchant and buyer.

[35] Sifakis 1993:1.

[36] Doherty and Smith 1981:7. The origin of the pyramid scheme is generally credited to Charles Ponzi, who in 1919 created an extremely lucrative plan to develop false confidence in, and increasing contributions from, his early "investors" (Martens 1984); see also Nash 1989:3312. However, even earlier, in 1876 in Spain, Doña Baldomera Larra performed the first Peter-to-Paul swindle (Nash 1989:3308).

[37] Adams et al. 1992:29.

[38] Maurer 1940, quoted in Holland 1981:95.

[39] Holland 1981:89, 91.

[40] In Blum 1972:33.

[41] Leff calls this the nexus of monopoly and monopsony (a buyer's monopoly).

[42] Henderson 1985:218.

[43] Sifakis 1993:22, 167.

[44] Funt 1952:81.

[45] Beene 1992:6, 23–24.

[46] Blum 1972:16, 24.

[47] Loftus n.d.

[48] Miller 1978:70.

[49] Blum 1972:52.

[50] In Holland 1981:90.

[51] Funt 1952:78.

[52] Paraphrase of Maurer 1974 in Miller 1978:60.

[53] As described in Metzner 1989:470.

[54] Sifakis 1993:221.

[55] Henderson 1985:29–30, 217.

[56] Or, alternatively, on the sense of obligation, fueled by denial, that a parent feels for his child. It's notable that both Abagnale and Vidocq got their starts by swindling their own fathers. In Abagnale's more ingenious early con, he exaggerated aspects of his actual social role, as the dependent, worldly-incompetent, and libidinous teenage son. At the age of 15, having begged a gas station credit card out of

his softhearted father, he carved out a deal with a gas station attendant to periodically "sell" him new tires, placing the purchase on the card while retaining the merchandise and splitting their value with him in cash. Over a three-month period, Abagnale charged $3,400 worth of phony repairs, new parts, and gas that he later—successfully—shrugged off to his father with, "It's the girls, Dad. They do funny things to me" (Abagnale and Redding 1980:15).

[57] *Ibid.,* 217.

[58] In Blum 1972:27.

[59] Nash 1989:2170.

[60] Miller 1978:67–68. See also Boles and Davis 1983:85–87 for discussion of the fortuneteller's methods of keeping a client coming back, or "holding the client down," a process that comprised of acting "to manipulate the client and the setting so that fees are arranged, failure is explained, progress is defined, and the 'work' remains incomplete."

[61] Beene 1992:69.

[62] Fox 1978:22.

[63] McGovern and Connolly 1976:19.

[64] *Ibid.,* 1976:22; see also Beene 1992:29.

[65] Beene 1992:14–15.

[66] Ortiz 1984:206.

[67] Nash 1989:3315.

[68] Irving 1969:49.

[69] Katz 1988:19.

[70] Hughes 1988:3.

[71] Blum 1972:42, quoted in Miller 1978:79.

[72] *Ibid.,* 1972:7.

[73] Funt 1952:189. Funt was a frequent object of viewers' desire to design hoaxes. If the mark is going to be on tape performing embarrassing acts, then so should Funt. In a shoe store scenario, one of the customers suddenly recognized who the salesman really is. A *Candid Camera* crew member recorded the incident in his log:

"Pretending to be a shoe fitter, Allen picks up one of the store's foot-measuring devices. At that point, the customer shouts, "Oh, oh. Wait a minute. I seen you on the television." Before any of the crew can stop him, he turns to the rest of the customers in the store and says loudly, "You know who this is? It's Allen Funk [sic], from that whaddaya-call-it program ... where he hides the cameras and all." Allen manages a smile as the buzz goes through the store, ruining the chances of doing any more sequences until this group of customers clears out. Allen orders our lights put out and takes the crew outside for a breather, until the excitement blows over" (Funt 1952:146).

This customer's engagement of the other store customers in his discovery effectively turned them against Funt with him and made any continued performance impossible.

[74] Sifakis 1993:109–10.

[75] McCaghy and Nogier 1984: 113–14.
[76] *International Criminal Police Review* 1975:148.
[77] Quoted in Irving 1969:173.
[78] *Ibid.*, 222.
[79] Blum 1972:16.
[80] Miller 1978:72.
[81] *Ibid.*, 66.
[82] Sifakis 1993:ix–x.
[83] Blum 1972:26, 242–43.

Notes to Chapter 5: *Muddied Identities*

[1] Metzner 1989:31–32.
[2] Vidocq 1829 (Vol. 2): 204.
[3] Irving 1969:52, 235.
[4] VanCook 1996:95.
[5] Nash 1989:3115, 3311.
[6] *Time* 1982:24; Farber n.d.
[7] VanCook 1996:250–51.
[8] Hicks 1973, in Buckwalter 1983:146.
[9] Girodo 1993:11; 1985a:307.
[10] Count 1994:219.
[11] Slade and Gutzs 1991:7.
[12] Goffman 1963:35.
[13] Girodo 1984:171. The Michigan State Police, which has benefited from extensive studies of its practices for the selection and training of undercovers, emphasizes the bolstering of the support positions as a chief means of ensuring officer safety.
[14] Goffman 1963:137–38.
[15] Abagnale and Redding 1980:149.
[16] According to the academy instructors—only slightly tongue-in-cheek—undercover supervisors have their own construction of the hierarchy, where they protect their own asses first, then the scumbags', who may bring lawsuits. Supervisors, they held, might readily put their cops on the line, and hence keep them as last in the system of those who matter.
[17] Ness 1989:110.
[18] Vidocq 1829 (Vol. 2):211.
[19] Girodo 1985b:61.
[20] Girodo 1985a:304.
[21] Vizzini, Fraley, and Smith 1972:140, 226–27.
[22] Marx 1992:13, 1979:101.
[23] Goffman 1969:66; Lesce 1991:123.

[24] Abagnale and Redding 1980:261–62.

[25] Farber n.d.

[26] Metzner 1989:255, 264.

[27] Goffman 1969:86.

[28] However, after the Chef de Sûreté retired, many of his practices were rapidly outlawed, among them the controversial practice of bringing ex-cons over to the side of law enforcement.

[29] Goddard 1988:189.

[30] Van Cook 1996:vii; Vizzini, Fraley, and Smith 1972:60.

[31] Vizzini, Fraley, and Smith 1972: 36–37, 40. Cook was an informant, used to make the introduction to the high-level target. An undercover with adequate time in the role and rapport with the target could also function in the bridge role. Undercovers who have achieved a high measure of trust from difficult-to-reach bad guys, such as those in organized crime networks, also serve in the usual role assumed by informants, vouching for each other in complicated operations.

[32] Count 1994:217.

[33] Goddard 1988:171.

[34] Sample 1993:4; Montanino 1987:4.

[35] Rapp 1989:36, 38–39.

[36] In some sources, the abbreviation "C.I." is used to stand for "cooperating individuals." (See, for example, Smith, Sheridan, & Yurcisin 1991:231.)

[37] Vidocq 1829 (Vol. 2):202.

[38] Alvarez 1993:57.

[39] See VanCook 1996:85–89.

[40] Alvarez 1993:56.

[41] Vizzini, Fraley, and Smith 1972:255.

[42] Goddard 1988:188; Alvarez 1993:57.

[43] Rapp 1989:33–34; Rissler 1975:22, 24.

[44] Slade and Gutzs 1991:46.

[45] Telephone interview with Bob Lill, Seattle to Washington DC, 19 December 1995. According to James Q. Wilson, Hoover "knew that public confidence in FBI agents was the Bureau's principal investigative resource, and that confidence should not be jeopardized by having agents appear as anything other than well-groomed 'young executive' individuals with an impeccable reputation for integrity" (quoted in Anderson 1988:35).

[46] Goddard 1988:111, 189, 217.

[47] Notably, the power game of the drug-search ritual, like the cop's staying clean, is also essential to maintaining the informant's credibility in court.

[48] It is this same thinking that, at least in part, is responsible for regular beat police officers' keeping their distance from those who have returned from undercover assignments.

[49] Goddard 1988:198.

[50] Brown 1989:109–10.

[51] Alvarez 1993:57.

[52] Vizzini, Fraley, and Smith 1972:101.

[53] Goddard 1988:230, 259-60.

[54] Alvarez 1993:58. Of course, the pipeline can be worked yet another way: a trustworthy informant can be questioned on his knowledge of corrupt police officers, as well as on his impressions of arresting officers (Rapp 1989:46).

[55] Vizzini, Fraley, and Smith 1972:121, 126, 128. Vizzini noticed a sharp rise in his own status during another Turkish operation, based on the quality of information he could provide. While he "had been a pariah for a month," once he'd informed the Chief of Police that he knew who had committed major bank robbery, he became "the honored guest." Like Vidocq, Vizzini alternately suffered and enjoyed grand pendulum swings in the regard he commanded from others as a function of his ability to provide actionable intelligence (1972:203).

[56] Slade and Gutzs 1991:28.

[57] Alvarez 1993:62.

[58] Vidocq 1829 (Vol. 2):230.

[59] Brown 1989:110; Alvarez 1993:56.

[60] A case reported in a Texas prison by Marquart & Roebuck 1985.

Notes to Chapter 6: *Identity Breakdown*

[1] Buckwalter 1983:159-61.

[2] Nash 1989:1382-83.

[3] Goffman 1969:41; Fitzkee 1945c:96.

[4] For an apt warning about the discontinuation of old hobbies and interests, see Newman 1991a:6.

[5] Goffman 1969:30, 70-72.

[6] Vidocq 1829 (Vol. 2):227.

[7] Abagnale and Redding 1980:118.

[8] Martin 1993:5.

[9] Vizzini, Fraley, and Smith 1972: 272-74, 305.

[10] See Goffman 1963:29; Metzner 1989:471.

[11] For this reason, joint identity work rarely flies, since "neither one of you will BELIEVE that you are this new person. In fact when you are together, be it alone at home, or out somewhere, you will probably continue to address each other by your real names" (Martin 1992: 5). For this reason, families relocated under the Federal Witness Protection Program often experience greater difficulty maintaining a consistent cover than relocated individuals.

[12] Vidocq 1829 (Vol. 1):155, 168.

[13] *Ibid.*, 195.

[14] Vizzini, Fraley, and Smith 1972:162.

[15] Jacobs 1994.

[16] *Ibid.*, 448.

[17] Jacobs 1993*b*.

[18] A psychiatrist hired by the FBI advised training new undercovers to take on their job in discrete stages. They should plan for the first meeting, then for the first buy, then for the first introduction to a higher-level dealer. Thinking by plateaus would help, he reasoned, with the psychological fallout of an operation's getting interrupted, for whatever reason, in the middle: the agent could always bank on the fact that the operation had been moving along successfully up to its finish. This kind of strategy was intended to mitigate the kind of all-or-none thinking that caused agents to make stupid decisions, as reflected in Sal Vizzini's sense of the values of undercover workers: "You never worry as much about getting killed as not getting the job done. It's like one of the big race drivers once said, 'You're afraid of losing, not dying.'" (Telephone interview with Bob Lill, 19 December 1995, Seattle to Washington, DC; Vizzini, Fraley, and Smith 1972:15).

[19] Jacobs 1993*a*:192.

[20] Pistone 1989:92. The same principle permits a professional impersonator to slip through the cracks. In the 1985 hearings in the House of Representatives on fraudulent credentials, an assuredly representative case was named of someone passing publicly as a medical doctor on the excellent reputation of his partner, who somehow never questioned his credentials (House of Representatives 1985:40).

[21] Pistone 1989: 46–47, 52, 59–60.

[22] Vizzini, Fraley, and Smith 1972:259.

[23] Jacobs 1993*a*:196.

[24] VanCook 1996:36–37.

[25] Wade 1990:18.

[26] The boredom with it all can be pervasive, as portrayed in the 1989 series finale. When asked where he's headed, now that it's all over, Sonny replies with fatigue, "Somewhere further South, somewhere where the water's warm and the drinks are cold and I don't know the names of the players" (*Miami Vice* 1986 and 1989).

[27] VanCook 1996:23.

[28] See Goffman 1959.

[29] Here, just as in solo plays, it is better to go with the player's actual drug knowledge so as not to make a fool of oneself or get into a dangerous situation; it is possible to present oneself under certain conditions as someone who only deals, but you still have to know quality, prices, etc.

[30] During their preparation session, the two students who were to be in role first hailed the roving instructor, who had established the ground rules of the field exercise. They asked him, "Is he gonna try and separate us?" Returned the instructor, "Wouldn't you?" They answered together sheepishly and certainly, "Yeah." The instructor capped the moment with the lesson: "Think like a bad guy, don't think like a cop."

[31] The recognition of one's old comrade is similarly gratifying. After ten years apart, Vizzini recognized at the American Embassy in Bangkok Bob Manpell, a colleague

from his Treasury academy training. He had gotten even with Manpell once, in a gesture that almost broke Manpell's hand. While Manpell peered at him quizzically, Vizzini "reached for his right hand. Then instead of shaking it I turned it gently and inspected it. 'This hand looks all right now,' I said casually. Recognition. 'Sal Vizzini! Well I'll be damned!'" (*Ibid.*, 254).

[32] See Goffman 1959:222.

[33] Harris 1973:73, 75, quoted in Tampa Museum of Art 1990:14.

[34] Sifakis 1993:47-48, 140.

[35] In the "Never Wave Goodbye" double episode of *The Fugitive*, Dr. Richard Kimble—escaping from imprisonment after a false conviction for the murder of his wife—has posed as a sail maker in a seaside town. Upon seeing Kimble's skill at knot-tying, a fellow sail maker (who, like Kimble, is a fugitive) suspects him of having had surgical training (which he has) and questions him closely. Though Kimble fends Erik off for the time being, it is clear that he is eager to unveil Kimble's true identity. As the show develops, we learn both that Erik has had an egregious history of informing—he informed to the Gestapo first on his cousin, then on his parents—and that he has been a fugitive himself (1963).

[36] The association of the penetration metaphor with disparaging terms for sexual intercourse is obvious in police culture.

[37] Department of the Treasury 1978:4.

[38] Goffman 1969:99.

[39] Vizzini, Fraley, and Smith 1972:283.

[40] Goddard 1988:303-04.

[41] Love 1994; Girodo 1984:172. Goffman (1959:217) also notes the prevalence of teasing as an initiation rite.

[42] Vizzini, Fraley, and Smith 1972:191-92.

[43] Jacobs 1993a:194-195, 204.

[44] Con artists may draw on a similar technique to disarm their marks. If they voice the mark's own most serious doubt before he can, the mark's most likely response is to assume the speaker is an honest person (Hankiss 1980).

[45] Fitzkee 1945c:183.

[46] Perhaps the ultimate tight spot into which the bad guy can thrust the undercover is one in which he is forced to collude in criminal activity in a role that purposely constrains him from endangering the entire operation. Joining a criminal band in an undercover robbery, Vidocq was dismayed to find they had determined that he was to be assigned the part of the lookout, thus making it all but impossible for him to make any discovery of the band by the police appear accidental. Buckwalter 1983:165; California Department of Justice n.d.:57.

[47] Wachtel 1980, paraphrased in Jacobs 1993a:197.

[48] Goddard 1988:92, 160. Joe Pistone used a similar technique to avoid having to accompany the bad guys on hijackings and burglaries, which the FBI forbade because it involved carrying weapons: "I would tell them, 'Hey, packing a gun and all

that stuff, that's too cowboy for me. I'll help you out later on with the unloading'" (Pistone 1989: 66).

[49] *Ibid.*, 94.

[50] Wansley and Stowers 1989:230.

[51] Katz 1988:111.

[52] Abagnale and Redding 1980:65–66.

[53] Pistone 1989:88–90.

[54] As reported in Girodo 1993:11.

[55] Count 1994:226.

[56] Rapp 1989:43.

[57] Marx 1990:159; Fox 1978:22.

[58] Vidocq 1829 (Vol. 2):6–7.

[59] Should an undercover be arrested "by mistake," he of course doesn't pull rank; rather, he tries to notify his control officer but preserves the identity at all costs.

[60] Buckwalter 1983:147.

[61] If an identity artist is not planning to come back, in extreme cases the only way to ensure that others relinquish the search to track one down is to have them believe that one has died, a scenario that necessitates staging one's own death while concealing the "resurrection." In "Never Wave Goodbye," *The Fugitive* Richard Kimble purposely falls behind in a sailing regatta, then capsizes his boat, having it appear that he has been eaten by sharks. Karen, the woman who has fallen in love with him, even goes so far as to cut her wrist, planting the blood on the clothing they discard as evidence (*The Fugitive* 1963).

[62] Abagnale and Redding 1980:88, 99–100.

Notes to Appendix: *Art Cons*

[1] Kenny G 1995.

[2] Coyle & Sharpe 1995.

[3] Funt 1952:200. When it came to counterintelligence, Funt could always be outdone by the government. Having made a recording of a White House guard, Funt recalled a visit he made to the Secret Service in order to get permission to air it. Although 17 mirthless officials attended Funt's playing of the White House recording, permission was denied. At the end of the meeting, Funt lingered in the office of Secret Service chief John J. Maloney, who "turned to me, a little surprised I was still in his office. I hastened to assure him that his decision had merit, and then, trying to end the proceedings with a laugh, I told the chief we had just made a secret record of this whole meeting. 'Would you gentlemen,' I asked, 'like to hear it?' 'No thanks,' was Maloney's direct comment. 'We made one, too.' Then he showed me a microphone under his desk that fed into a recorder in an adjacent room. I realized, with some embarrassment, that I was a rank amateur compared with the federal government's eavesdroppers" (*Ibid.*,169–70).

[4] *Ibid.*, 34ff, 48ff, 52–53, 103, 157.

[5] Arthur Ferguson had been acting the role of an American con victim in a Manchester stage production in the late 1910s, and shortly after made the shift to a different "legitimate" stage, as well as to the role of con artist. Ferguson played tourists off their desire for national landmarks of foreign countries. While working London, he "sold" rights to or accepted down payments from gullible Americans to such property as Big Ben and Buckingham Palace or leaseholds; crossing the Atlantic, he took an advance payment on the Statue of Liberty from a Australian and sold a year's leasehold on the White House to a Brit. Ferguson was one of many con artists working this sort of notable-properties scams in the 1920s (Sifakis 1993:99)

[6] *Candid Microphone* 1947.

[7] Funt 1952:43.

[8] *Candid Microphone* 1947; *Candid Camera* 1947.

[9] Blum 1972:236.

INDEX

Printed in the United States
137940LV00001B/104/P